Jonathan Fisher, 1794

SMALL MISTY MOUNTAIN

The Awanadjo Almanack

ROB McCALL

Nature's Year in a Downeast Village

Rob McCall
Blue Hill

PUSHCART PRESS

WAINSCOTT, NEW YORK & SEDGWICK, MAINE

© 2006 Rob McCall
published by Pushcart Press
PO Box 42, Sedgwick ME 04679
and PO Box 380, Wainscott, NY 11975

Distributed by W. W. Norton & Co.
500 Fifth Ave., New York, NY 10110

ISBN 10: 1-888889-45-4 / ISBN 13: 978-1-888889-45-1
Woodcuts by Jonathan Fisher (1768–1847)
Jacket illustration by Rebecca Haley McCall

Winner of the 20th Editors' Book Award:
Sponsoring Editors: Simon Michael Bessie, James Charlton, Peter
Davison, Jonathan Galassi, David Godine, Daniel Halpern, James
Laughlin, Seymour Lawrence, Starling Lawrence, Robie Macauley,
Joyce Carol Oates, Nan A. Talese, Faith Sale, Ted Solotaroff, Pat
Strachan, Thomas Wallace. Bill Henderson, Publisher.

Contents

Introduction

In A.D. 2000 Blue Hill, a town named after a mountain, had a population of just over 2000 souls. Like many coastal Maine towns, it has a Main Street, a Water Street, a Pleasant Street, a Union Street, and a High Street. The town is situated at the Head of Blue Hill Bay. To the Northeast rises what people around here call "Blue Hill Mountain," just under 1000 feet in elevation. The Mill Brook rushes down over the West shoulder of the mountain, dropping 400 feet in its last half mile through the town, then under Main Street, over the Milldam, and out into the harbor. There are two meeting-houses in the village, the Congregational Church gathered in 1772, and the Baptist Church gathered in 1806.

Halfway between the churches is George Stevens Academy with some 275 students. It serves the town of Blue Hill and several others on the peninsula. Nearby is the Consolidated School which replaced the numerous one-room neighborhood schools sometime after World War I. An alternative elementary school and an alternative high school are on South Street a little farther out of town. There is also the Blue Hill Public Library, truly one of the best libraries anywhere; a temple of books, where no one tells you to hush.

From the top of Blue Hill Mountain the whole village looks like a rough patch in the woods no bigger than its own fairgrounds. The blue water and evergreen forests stretch off to the horizon all around. At every season of the year, the beauty of the place is truly breathtaking in an ancient and archetypal way. Even in the cold dead of winter you can stand on the front steps of Merrill & Hinckley's general store and watch the sun rise over Mt. Cadillac, glowing through the sea smoke. It is a storybook setting and many stories have been written about it. You will find many more in this volume.

According to Maine's late moose-eating anthropologist, Fannie Hardy Eckstorm, "Awanadjo" is an Algonkian word meaning "small, misty mountain," referring to Blue Hill Mountain; but it can just as well refer to your mountain, or any sacred place with the power to transform you and impart the sense of being at home in Nature.

The almanac held a place of honor next to the Bible in the homes of our ancestors for very good reasons. At the parsonage, thanks to gifts from friends and years of collecting, I have a grand shelf of almanacs and books about them. The latest is a tiny inch by inch-and-a-half *Piso's Pocket Almanac* from 1900. This little wonder contains testimonies to Piso's herbal cures, which were apparently effective for everything from colds and croup to consumption. There is a tattered 1815 edition of Robert Thomas's *Farmer's Almanac* showing how little the heart of this publication has changed in 190 years. I also treasure the *Akita Almanac* from the town in Japan where my father was born in 1911. It's written in both

Japanese and delightfully fractured English, with beautiful wood-cuts; and it reads from back to front.

Almanacs fascinate because they are our flawed, finite guidebooks to the infinite workings of the sun, moon, stars, seas and weather. They are the libretto to the Grand Old Opera of the Creation as seen from our cheap seats here on Earth. Like the Bible, almanacs have long showed the mind of the Creator to the best of our poor ability to get it, and showed us how small is our place in the Cosmos. So, we treasure them.

My contribution to this tradition is called The Awanadjo Almanack, and has been appearing hereabouts in the local papers and on the radio for many years. I offer this collection in an attempt to communicate my utter joy in experiencing the power of Nature and Nature's God to inspire, help and heal, and to present the sacredness of places: ours and yours.

Though I sometimes use Latin taxonomic names and other big words and try to be as accurate as possible in my descriptions, I do not claim to be an expert in botany or zoology or geology or anthropology. There are undoubtedly technical errors in this volume. That is why each moon ends with the same dictum: "Don't take it from me; go out and see for yourself." I have only one field of expertise: my own experience of feeling at home in Nature.

Certain places, particularly mountains, make us more vulnerable to the Holy. This vulnerability is a real phenomenon, not some flighty romantic notion. And, it is a spiritual resource fully as valuable as any so-called "natural resource." Some places are sacred places, not poetically or figuratively speaking, but actually, concretely sacred. They are gates to God.

My first born-again experience came when I was 28 and

working in an orchard in Stowe, Massachusetts. There a crow carefully and deliberately showed to me the dance of life and death. The whole story is recounted herein. Since then I have had a huge hunger to break down the wall of hostility between my one soul and the rest of Creation, and to feel at home in Nature. This has led to numerous other born-again adventures, as you will see. As they did for Elijah in the wilderness, the ravens have always brought me "bread in the morning and bread in the evening," and sustained me through time. They can for you, too.

Our Awanadjo is certainly not Mt. Olympus, not Mt. Sinai, not Fujiyama. But it is the center of our world. It is the pillar that holds up our sky. It is our sacred mountain, our Sinai, our Olympus, our Fuji. Through it we are connected to all the world's sacred mountains, and in the mathematics of the holy, our mountain *is* all sacred mountains. Standing on the summit looking down on our village, we are standing on Olympus looking down on Athens, we are standing on Carmel looking down on Jerusalem, we are standing on Fuji looking down on Tokyo, we are standing in the Black Hills looking down at the encampment on the Little Big Horn.

Our mountain is the Mountain of the World. Our village is all villages of the world. Our time is all times. If the Day of Judgment is coming, if Armageddon is around the corner, if this time is the end time, how do we want to be found by the Creator? Anxious and confused? Angry and bitter about far away events? Condemning and judging those around us? Wounding further the wounded? Scrambling for a ticket to heaven? Or do we want to be found binding up wounds in our own villages, comforting our neighbors who mourn, and freeing those who are captives of pain and fear?

This mountain is every mountain, this village is all villages, this time is all time. Every place is a sacred place. What we do in our day in our place with our people is for all time and all places and all people.

The town of Blue Hill is situated in what could be called a "spiritual vortex." It seems to draw numinous energy from the Mountain or from some geomagnetic source deep in the rocky crust of the earth beneath. Nearly everyone around here acknowledges this phenomenon; and nearly everyone describes it differently. This energy pours forth and forms people in amazing ways. You would be hard-put to find a town or village of like size anywhere with so many gifted artists, musicians, craftspeople, seers, prophets, and just plain characters, as you will see.

In the forefront of these is my dear companion of over 40 years, Rebecca Haley McCall, who is also one of my favorite commentators on Nature. "The mountain," she says, "is like a great beast. You can climb up on its back and it will heal you." Her vision has greatly shaped mine over the years; and I have borrowed so many of her insights that it would be impossible to credit each one. She is a co-author of my life and this volume, and has made both far richer and more authentic than they could ever have been without her. One of Becky's many haunting paintings of our small, misty mountain graces the cover.

Jonathan Fisher, the first settled minister of the church of which I am the 40th settled minister, drew upon this same spiritual energy. He built his own house, made his own tools and furniture, raised his own food, made medicines from local plants, carved wood-cuts of every animal named in the Bible, kept a journal of his activities for over 30 years, and painted four portraits of himself, one of which watches over us every Sunday morning. Fisher graduated from Harvard in 1796 and came to Blue Hill that summer. He served this parish for 41 years, as was typical in those days. We are proud to include some of his woodcuts of animals in this volume, by permission of the Farnsworth Museum.

Fisher often walked the 35 miles to Bangor for meetings at the Seminary that he helped to found. He also walked the 160 or more miles to St. Andrews, Canada, and back on missionary tours to start several churches in deepest Washington County. The Fisher house in Blue Hill has been restored and is now the temple of the Fisher Society which reveres his memory. I will not say that there is a Jonathan Fisher cult in Blue Hill, but there is a shrine; there are relics, sacred books.

The Awanadjo Almanack has its headquarters in an old pressed-oak, spindle-backed chair in a front room of the 1800 Theodore Stevens House, the congregational parsonage on Main Street. This calls to mind Abraham Lincoln's comment about one of his Civil War generals who was known for not doing much, and sending back many wordy dispatches detailing the results of his inactivity with the return address, "General McClellan; Headquarters in the Saddle." Lincoln remarked that McClellan "had his headquarters where his hindquarters should be."

I report what I have seen actively on location. In addition to our headquarters [or hindquarters] in Blue Hill, Hancock County, we have two other field stations farther East in Washington County. What I call "Pennamaquan Field Station" is the camp we built 25 years ago in the woods on Cobscook Bay. What I call "Moose Island Field Station" is our small cape in Eastport on Passamaquoddy Bay where we wake up to the sunrise over Campobello. These are the bases for our field studies as we go out to see for ourselves.

Since many of our reports are from that mythical kingdom, some description of Washington County is in order. Our friend Ross Greenlaw is a descendant of an old Down-east family and the man to whom we owe, more than any other, our being here.

Washington County is half the size of Massachusetts but has only three traffic lights of the green-yellow-red variety, all in Calais [pronounced "Callous"]. This does not include the traffic light in front of the fire house in Dennysville [pop. maybe 300] which shows green all of the time, except when the fire engines are pulling out, or when the traffic light is turned off, which is most of the time

The population of Washington County is about 35,000, mainly clustered along US Route 1, the main highway along the coast. Yet, there are plenty of times when you could safely hunker down in the middle of Route 1 and play a couple of hands of poker without being run over by anything more dangerous than a red squirrel. Over half of the county is so under-populated that the maps designate areas as "town-ships" or "plantations" and give them numbers, such as Township 14 or Plantation No. 19. These wild places have no names because the few inhabitants didn't care to hold a town meeting to choose a name. Still, the mapmakers feel they have to call these areas something, so they give them numbers. You can go endless miles on some of the back roads without seeing a human habitation.

All of the roads in this vast territory are two lanes or fewer. You'd have to drive a minimum of three hours South and West to find a four-lane highway, assuming you wanted to. For this reason, many Washington Countians prefer powerful vehicles that allow you to pass that retired couple in their slow-moving sedan in the short distance the up-and-down terrain allows. Thus, big old GM cars from the 80s before gas prices got so high, and huge pick-up trucks with locomotive-sized diesel engines are popular here, as are mechanics who can repair them.

You'll encounter logging trucks lumbering along on these roads with logs piled 15 feet high and lashed by chains onto the rusty truck bed. These tottering loads never look completely secure. Now and then we'll hear that a load of logs broke loose and spread along the road like pick-up sticks, or that someone in a little Japanese car didn't see the faintly flickering, dusty brake light on one of these behemoths and drove right under it. There was a report not long ago of a pregnant woman and her three-year-old son who did just that. All survived after a delicate rescue operation by able local volunteers.

Most of Washington County has been logged in the last 100 years. The ravaging of the forests—whether for pulp, wood-chips, or lumber—provides a major part of available employment. There is no great sympathy for Earth-Firsters or environmentalists here. Yet, from any ridge or hilltop, the forests spread tall, green and clean as far as the eye can see in all directions, except on the blueberry barrens, those vast burned-over expanses of rolling fields watched over here and there by great glacial boulders. There is even a golf course called "Barren View" in Jonesboro.

Economic booms come and go, but the poverty and unemployment rates in Washington County remain right up there with Mississippi. This, combined with a firm Yankee independence and a fierce loathing for taxes and government of any kind, produces a huge black market economy in the form of yard sales, flea markets and the poaching of game.

Yard sales are good. They provide people with social activity and needed merchandise, and keep the money changing hands without the involvement of the government or the banks, which are extending their sinister tentacles farther and farther out into the williwags. It is no coincidence that in the poorest county in New England, the dilapidated old county courthouse in Machias [pronounced "Much-eye'-us"] was bought and refurbished as what? A bank! "The banks are made of marble with a guard at every door, and the vaults are stuffed with silver that we all have sweated for," sings Pete Seeger.

The aboriginal inhabitants of Maine were Algonkian-speaking Abnakis or "Wabanakis." In pre-European times, there were four tribes in Maine, as I understand it. All four are still present. The Penobscot are "the People of the River" centered on Indian Island in the Penobscot River north of Bangor. The Micmac and Maliseet are clustered along the Canadian border.

The Passamaquoddy are "the People of the Dawn." They are centered in Washington County, at Indian Township near Princeton and at Pleasant Point, called "Sipayik," on the coast near Eastport. The Passamaquoddy still have their language and are gathering their history and traditions. There are active and creative traditionalists among them who are presently dreaming new songs and ceremonies, and reviving their healing arts. At this writing the traditionalists are fighting, with every ounce of their considerable courage, the construction of a liquid natural gas depot at Sipayik which would threaten Passamaquoddy Bay and its human and wild inhabitants. Part of any proceeds from this volume will go to support their struggle.

I was born in the Black Hills of South Dakota, raised in Oregon, and have seen natural wonders all over this great country, but I am convinced that there are few places or creatures in this land as mythically and spiritually charged as those here in the real Downeast Maine.

The book you are holding is an invitation to experience these sacred places.

This book is divided into twelve months, covering twelve moons. I have given the moons names borrowed from tradition and old almanacs. Each month is in turn divided into four quarters corresponding to the four phases of the moon: New, First Quarter, Full, and Last Quarter. Since the moon is on a 28 day cycle and calendar months are mostly 31 days, in real time the Full Moon moves earlier through the passing months. In this volume, I have arbitrarily placed the Full Moon around the third week of the month beginning and ending the year deep in January. Entries for most months conclude with "Pericopes." These are selections from sermons I have preached at the Blue Hill Congregational church where I have been the minister for 20 years.

My overflowing gratitude goes to my readers, my neighbors in Blue Hill, and especially to Bill Henderson, seeker, warrior, feral editor, and friend. Bill invited me on this adventure, and has guided me skillfully and wisely past many dangers, toils and snares in the wild world of publishing. He kept us moving along on the right path so as to reach camp by the end of the day without getting lost in the puckerbrush, and with plenty of time left over to lift a glass and laugh.

Finally, here is a riddle. If you read this book and get acquainted with the sacred places described herein, the answer will reveal itself:

We thunder underneath the sky;
Above us both the eagles cry.
The moon will tell us what to do,
And change us twice when day is through.

We're here and there and in between,
But in most places, never seen.
Two gates to God 'tween sea and heaven,
Here in Maine, and Psalm 42:7.
Who are we?

Now, don't take it from me. Go out and see for yourself.

This is the Awanadjo Almanack for the Full *Wolf* or *'Old'* Moon to the Full *Snow* or *'Hunger'* Moon according to the Old Farmer's Almanac. It is the *Stormy* Moon according to Ernest Thompson Seton and *Siqinyasaq or Returning Sun* to the Eskimos of the North Slope. This moon is called *Shebat* in Biblical Hebrew; and January-February in Downeast Maine. It is also called other things in Downeast Maine, including *Hate Month* and others that cannot be printed here.

Almanacking being an inexact science, you will note that in some years these calendar events will not fall between these particular full moons. You'll figure it out, I know.

FULL TO LAST QUARTER *WOLF* MOON

"Here we are, in the homeland. It is winter, and it will be spring again. We have known other winters, and survived them. We have known this year intimately . . . I can report now that grass grows, flowers bloom, birds sing. I can report that the sun rises and sets, the moon keeps its own schedule . . . I know these truths. Lesser truths will take more learning."

From Hal Borland

January 20, the feast day of St. Fabian, the patron of lead founders and potters. He became the 20th pope in 236 AD when a pigeon landed upon his head. Fabian was martyred after a 14-year reign. Legend has it that unmarried women may dream of their future husbands on this day if they eat a hard-boiled egg with salt before retiring, but only if they have fasted for 24 hours first. Young ladies, put down that bagel.

January 21, the feast day of St. Agnes.

January 26, Saints Timothy and Titus Day.

NATURAL EVENTS: Along about midwinter it's easy to forget what summer is like. Maybe we'll happen to look at a snapshot of the garden as it looked last summer—verdant with reds and yellows—then look out of the window and see the same garden brown and gray, with patches of white snow. On a warm day last week I walked out of the house and smelled dirt for the first time since about November. Dirt! A great, sweet wave of yearning came over me; for the taste of grass stems where you pull them apart at the nodes and for wild strawberries; for the smells of wet ground and stones warmed by the sun and even for the smell of low tide; for the crackle of grasshoppers and drone of cicadas; for a plunge in the bay. I am not afraid of the length of winter. I would only be afraid if I thought that I could never smell the dirt again.

FIELD & FOREST REPORT: A recent thaw brought a flurry of activity among birds, squirrels and other non-hibernating creatures. Chickadees' "dee-dee-dee" and Blue Jays' "jay—jay—jay" are a hint that we are nearing the peak of winter and will soon be on the downhill side.

MOUNTAIN REPORT: One day recently I slogged our way up the sides of Awanadjo still covered in snow. The next day I went up on nearly bare ground.

SACRED MOUNTAIN: Adam's Peak which rises over the forests of Sri Lanka and is revered by adherents of more major religions—Buddhism, Hinduism, Islam, Christianity —than any other mountain on earth.

SALTWATER REPORT: It seems likely that the first occupants of the Kollejedjwok seasonal settlement at what is now called the Blue Hill Falls, arrived more than 4,000 years ago and were more interested in fin fish than in shell fish, according to the late Douglas Byers of Blue Hill, about whom more later. Found at the site were plummets for fishing nets and large fish bones including those of deep-sea swordfish. This suggests sea-faring technology and sizable fishing boats or kayak-like craft, perhaps like those of the Northwest Native people.

CRITTER OF THE WEEK: A vote of thanks to Chickadee whose unwavering enthusiasm, even in the bleakest midwinter, and down-right friendliness are an inspiration to us all.

PILGRIM'S JOURNAL: Around here, the towns are Christian, for the most part. But the woods are Algonkian. The boulders, ponds and waterfalls are Shinto. The skies are Taoist. The islands and the bays are Celtic, and the mountains and hills are Buddhist. If you want to survive in the towns, being Christian may be sufficient, but if you choose to survive and thrive beyond the towns, Christianity may not be enough.

SEED PODS TO CARRY AROUND WITH YOU: from Edwin Way Teale, New England's late beloved naturalist: *From cocoon to burr on a winter's day, there is everywhere life, dormant but waiting. Within the earth there are roots and seeds; on the twigs, there are winter buds; buried in soil and mud beneath ice-locked water are the turtles and frogs and dragonfly nymphs; hidden in decaying logs and under snow-covered*

debris are the fertilised queens of the wasps and the bumble-
bees. Everywhere, on all sides of us, as far as winter reigns,
life is suspended temporarily. But it has not succumbed. It is
merely dormant for the time being, merely waiting for the
magic touch of spring.

And from Robert Frost: *Nature is always hinting at us. It*
hints over and over again. And suddenly we take the hint.

LAST QUARTER *WOLF* MOON TO NEW *SNOW* MOON

Across the orchard coyote tracks, fresh in this morning's
snow; the hind feet in the front tracks land. Which way did
Coyote go? From East to West or West to East; how can a
white man know? His frosty muzzle cast in molded snow
with grass beneath; for some poor mouse, today his last,
finds death in coyote's teeth. Old Coyote comes and goes at
will; his belly is his boss. But we must go about our work. It's
Coyote's gain, our loss.   —Old Doggerel

January 28, anniversary of the Blizzard of '77 which para-
lyzed much of the East and Midwest. It's funny how 6 inches
of snow can paralyze some parts of the country and 2 feet
hardly slows down others. Imagine the amount of energy
burned in pushing all that snow off all that pavement. Our
predecessors didn't bother. They'd hitch a team of oxen to a
snow roller and just flatten it down for easy sleighing. Of
course, the roads sometimes stayed icy until June, according
to local lore.

January 31, The anniversary of the first trip both ways
around Cape Horn completed, 1616. First Social Security
check issued, 1940.

February 1, St. Brigid's Day, also the holiday celebrating the Celtic goddess "Bride" or "Bridget."

February 2, Groundhog Day, Candlemas Day, and the Feast of the Purification of Mary. This day marks the halfway point of winter. On this day, according to the ancient wisdom, stalwart country dwellers should still have half their wood and half their hay. You should also be only half-tired of wearing boots and long underwear; half-disgusted with dirty snow and ice, half-annoyed with power-outages, and half-fed-up with that insidious winter virus.

NATURAL EVENTS: Freeze and thaw cycles heave the soil up and down and chip away at the huge boulders and stones along the edges of our fields and the massive ledges on Awanadjo. Tiny grains of sand flake off and fall into the soil. Tiny cracks fill with water and over time can split a mighty boulder the way you and I would cut an apple. Before explosives, holes were drilled in large rocks to fill with water and freeze, cracking them open.

This past week, a large flock of fifty or more cedar waxwings has been cruising the area moving from the apple trees, still hung with mummified fruit that was never picked or fell, and then to the viburnum or high-bush cranberry hung with bunches of red berries. These fruit eaters are smaller than a robin and of a buff brown above with a crest on the head and a yellow border on the tail. They talk in a faint lisping whispering whistle. Edwin Way Teale says that waxwings will snatch snow flakes out of the air for moisture, and unlike many birds, will share their food with each other, passing from beak to beak. They fly closely together from tree top to bush back to tree top and are easily spooked. I saw one mockingbird land in the midst of a score or more

5

waxwings who were feeding on berries and frighten them all off whispering into a nearby elm. The mockingbird does not even eat fruit, but is aggressive and territorial by nature. The waxwings are shy and peaceful by nature.

RANK OPINION: With respect to that phrase, "By Nature:" We say that someone or some creature is shy or aggressive or social or solitary or melancholy or happy "by nature." In former times, we might choose our totem or favorite animal by our similarity to it. These days, the vast bulk of the population is so cut off from the Creation that it is hard to know who or what one is by nature. Instead of comparing ourselves to other creatures of which we know so little, we compare ourselves to other humans like us and thus create a closed feedback loop which greatly magnifies human traits both good and bad. Our models and teachers are all human, so we do not learn from other creatures who have lived here much longer than we and whose habits enhance rather than destroy their surroundings. Losing sight of other creatures, we lose sight of who we are "by nature."

There's another teaching here, too. The so-called "Law of Tooth and Claw" is wrongly attributed to Charles Darwin who was a clergyman for a time and not an atheist. It is also false in suggesting that the most powerful and aggressive will survive. If it were true, there would be no cedar waxwings.

Just as we are finding new medicines from plants in the fields and forests, we might find new solutions to social problems from animals there.

UN-NATURAL EVENTS: Our indoor winter life begins to result in isolated cases of cabin fever in late January and early February, like what is now called Seasonal Affective Disorder. It doesn't become epidemic until March which includes April in these parts. Symptoms include irritability, forgetting to change socks and other items of clothing, an overwhelming urge to hibernate (see Critter of the Week below), and a distaste for cabbage, broccoli, turnips, carrots, squash and other winter vegetables. In most cases, symptoms are completely gone by the end of black-fly season or the Fourth of July, whichever comes first—and it's usually the Fourth of July.

Here's one off the wire: A man who kept a lion, tigers, and a panther in his basement in a town in southern Italy was found dead last week. Neighbors hadn't seen him and called the police, who found his remains in the lion's cage. This is a natural event; it's called natural selection. The un-natural part is that the lion will probably be shot, rather than returned to his native land with apologies.

Here's another one: A while back in "Field and Stream" we read about the present-day hunters coming out of the Tatshenshini-Alsek area near the Alaska/British Columbia border who found a 500-year-old hunter with all of his hunting gear in the receding glacial ice. One of the modern hunters commented on the skill of the ancients. "He was in the same place we were, probably hunting the same game, but his hunting skills were probably 1,000 times better than ours. There we were with our Gore-tex clothes, plastic boots and stainless steel rifles and here he was in a [squirrel] skin cloak carrying tools he probably made himself."

WILD SPECULATION: What would happen if we modeled our hunting after the ancient Tatshenshini-Alsek hunter? Transform hunting and fishing from an exercise in expensive gadgetry into true extreme sports. Simply say that all of a hunter's weapons and gear and all of a fisherman's tackle and watercraft must be self-made out of naturally occurring materials and that all hunting must be within walking distance and all fishing within rowing or paddling distance of home. Then, just watch the elaborate regulations, the laws, the licenses and fines, the bag limits, the wardens, the anti-hunters, and the guns all disappear like a puff of smoke. What could be better? This would also go a long way toward solving the problems of over-hunting and over-fishing, and resolving the controversy over aboriginal hunting and fishing rights. And it might just begin to re-establish the respect and reverence between human and non-human animals. It worked before—for thousands of years.

FIELD & FOREST REPORT: These are pruning days. Across the land in orchard after orchard, pruning crews are at their grim winter work. The trees are now dormant, sound asleep, feeling no pain when the pruners come through, like a patient under anesthesia as the surgeon cuts. With the traditional curved pruning saw that cuts, like Japanese saws, on the pull stroke, pruners are removing the dead or dying wood, the weaker wood, the unfruitful wood. *Every branch that beareth not fruit he taketh away, and every branch that beareth fruit, he purgeth it, that it may bear more fruit*, says John's gospel. The pruner must make a thousand decisions each day that will affect the life of the tree and of the whole orchard in the years to come. Shall I cut this branch or that one? We must judge and carry out the sentence with very little evidence.

Sometimes after several days or weeks of pruning, we used to get the "stymies," a condition of being unable to decide which branch to remove and which to leave. The smallest decision seemed too much to make. Stymied, we might continue to prune blindly for a few hours, but we were soon exhausted in spirit and needed to rest. Then, we would hope for a snow storm or bitter cold to keep us out of the orchard for a day or two, allowing us to sharpen our tools and our minds and let them rest while we stood around the bins of fragrant female apples down at the packing house, chatting and looking out the foggy windows to see if the storm had abated.

All the brush, the pruned-off branches were gathered into a windrow between the trees which we pushed up into a pile at the end of the row by a tractor with a brush fork on the front. In March, around the equinox, we would start burning the brush in great bonfires, tending the fires with pitchforks, celebrating Spring. *If a man abideth not in me he is cast forth as a branch and is withered and men gather them and cast them into the fire and they are burned.*

For apples, for us, January is pruning time.

CRITTER OF THE WEEK: The black bear who sleeps from November or December until March or April. Ernest Thompson Seton suggests that black bears cease nearly all bodily functions except breathing and digesting the stored fat left from their rich Fall and early Winter diet of nuts, berries and small and large animals. Not that different from us, except we watch football.

SEED PODS TO CARRY AROUND WITH YOU: from Jim Bishop: *Winter is fury and white silence. It can freeze a blade of grass at a glance . . . Mercilessly, it strips the orange and russet of autumn and looks defiantly ahead for spring to step onstage.*

From Toni Morrison: *Down came the dry flakes, fat enough and heavy enough to crash like nickels on stone. It always surprised him, how quiet it was. Not like rain, but like a secret.*

And an Old Doggerel: *Old John the Hawk on this cold day wheels on a rising breeze. The wind helps him to make his hunt; the same wind makes us freeze. In deep, cold snows our pruning goes for hour on crystal hour. Old John above,*

he loves the wind, his guide and bitter friend. While far
below, we watch the sun and pray this day will end.

PILGRIM'S JOURNAL: Back around the last quarter *Beaver*
moon, I was at our camp on Cobscook Bay in Washington
County. Waking early, I felt the gale- to storm-force winds of
a dying hurricane barreling along the coast, shaking the
shack, and hooting in the stovepipe. After a nice breakfast of
spuds and eggs, something told me to go to West Quoddy
Head, the Easternmost point in the USA, to experience the
big weather and see if I could stare down the storm god. So I
did.

I'll try to describe the indescribable. Parking my truck outside the closed gates of West Quoddy Head State Park, I
watched the red and white-striped, automated lighthouse
flash and heard the fog horn sounding through the woods.
The high winds were pushing huge combers from the South-
southeast all the way up the Grand Manan channel with
spray and foam being torn off the crests of the waves and
lofted over the tops of the mountainous off-shore ledges.
Gobs of sea-foam were lifted by the wind and flew up into
the empty parking area like white birds. Trees rocked and
bent. At the first cliffs I watched open-mouthed as the wind
took a small waterfall and blew it back in plumes over the
tall, cliff-top spruces, not once, but steadily. Only a small
part of the stream was able to obey the laws of gravity and
fall to the rocky beach far below. I walked through the spray
that was blown like a geyser. The air smelled strongly of salt
and wet fir boughs and the wind forced the odor into my
nose and mouth.

At Gulliver's Hole, salt spray from the tattered waves blew
spiraling all the way up the 150 foot cliffs and over the tops of
the trees. The dark line of Grand Manan was barely visible

six miles across the channel. I chanted Psalm 46 for courage: "Therefore shall I not fear though the mountains shake in the heart of the sea and its waters roar and foam." I stopped now and then to be lifted up and down standing on the roots of heaving trees. At Green Point, spray blew 40 feet above the rocks and rained onto the point. I steadied myself time and again with my hiking stick to keep from being blown off my feet. Wind-blown spray stung my face as I pushed on toward Carrying-place Cove another mile away, excited and spiritually elated by the fury of the great weather. I expected any moment to encounter Jesus/Buddha/Kwan Yin coming toward me along the trail while trees roared like thunder overhead. I bellowed out "How Can I Keep from Singing."

The trail now began to go up and down over ledges leading out to points with roots forming stairways to heaven and back down to earth. Once or twice I held tightly to a swaying tree-trunk to keep from being blown away. Spray and foam flew over the tree-tops as I walked with feet wide apart and hiking stick off to leeward, especially where the trail came out of the woods and to the edge of the cliffs. As I approached Carrying-place, I heard the low sound of surf, like house-sized boulders knocking together in the depths. A crow called. I asked for help. Carrying-place Cove opened up before my eyes with huge breaking surf and ducks riding up and down on the deep swells, calmly facing into the fury of the wind and rain. Looking across the cove I could see crashing waves for another mile West and spray blowing over the tree-tops.

I watched the huge seas roaring into the quarter-mile wide cove for a time, then finally satisfied, turned to go back. A crow feather caught my eye, tucked into the moss and weather-cocking back and forth in the wind. As I pushed the feather into my dripping blue watch-cap, I felt a few large drops of rain. The wind was increasing, the fog moving in, and the rain becoming heavier. By the time I had gone half a mile of my two mile return trip, I was thoroughly soaked; pants, hat and poncho, though my wool shirt underneath was still warm. My pants might as well have blown away for all the warmth they gave me.

The rain was not falling; it was being propelled horizontally by the wind with such force that it felt like bird shot in my face. I began to tire, eager to get back to the shelter of my truck. I clutched trees for stability and sang, "Green trees are bending . . . I ain't got long to stay here." Trees that had been sturdy on the way out were now tugging at their roots and lifting the soil around them on both sides of the trail. I came to a large balsam fir about 18 inches in diameter that had torn its roots asunder and come crashing down since my erstwhile passing. Sap oozed from its ruptured tissues and I could smell the fresh exposed soil now soaking with rain.

Once I stopped before a wind-bucking spruce, afraid to go under it, waiting until between gusts to dash past. I staggered back to Green Point and then toward the lighthouse and its sounding foghorn as rain ran down into my boots. Grand Manan was no longer visible. Soon I ran under the plume of spray from the blown-back waterfall, feeling the anger in the wind and sea.

Tired and relieved to have the wind finally at my back, I was pushed, almost lifted, through the foam-flecked parking area and up the road to the waiting truck, eager to warm it up and dive into the bread, cheese and beer I had brought. Climbing over the locked park gate, I made out the word JEEP on the tailgate, but could tell that something was wrong. Soon I saw that the light camper-back I had so proudly built and firmly bolted onto the sides of my '70 JEEP truck had been ripped off by the wind and lay overturned in the ditch, filling with rain. Once more, my mouth hung open and I was awed by the power which, for no reason I could fathom, had spared me. My short four mile hike had taken over four hours.

This same . . . Ocean will erelong be lashed into sudden fury, and all its caves and cliffs resound with the tumult. It will ruthlessly heave . . . vessels to and fro, break them in pieces in its sandy or stony jaws, and deliver their crews to sea-monsters. It will play with them like sea-weed, distend them like dead frogs, and carry them about, now high, now low, to show to the fishes, giving them a nibble. This . . . ocean will toss and tear the rag of a man's body like the father of mad bulls, and his relatives may be seen seeking the remnants for weeks along the strand. From H. D. Thoreau.

NEW TO FIRST QUARTER *SNOW* MOON

Could it be true we live on earth? On earth forever? Just one brief instant here. Even the finest stones begin to split, even gold is tarnished, even precious bird plumes shrivel like a cough. Just one brief instant here.
—From Nezahualcoyotl, quoted in *Earth Prayers.*

February 3, The anniversary of the plane crash which killed Buddy Holly, Richie Valens and the Big Bopper, 1959.

February 7, Charles Dickens born, 1812. Most of Dead Sea Scrolls discovered, 1947.

February 11, Nelson Mandela released from prison, 1990.

February 12, Abraham Lincoln's birthday, 1809. He said, "The Lord prefers common-looking people, or He would not

13

have created so many of them." Also Charles Darwin's birthday the same day and year.

February 14, St. Valentine's Day. Three different martyred saints named Valentine are remembered on this day. One of these, a doctor and priest beheaded in 269, is invoked against blindness and epilepsy. Eight complete bodies and one head of Valentine are venerated in different European churches. The association of this day with LOVE probably comes from the pagan fertility festival of Lupercalia which fell in midmonth.

NATURAL EVENTS: I am a hunter, of sorts, so here is a hunting story. Just as physical hunting is feeding on the bodies of creatures, spiritual hunting, for me, is feeding on their spirits. Just as physical hunting nourishes the body, spiritual hunting strengthens and nourishes the human spirit by revealing the activity of the divine Spirit in Creation—God the fox and God the snowshoe hare, God the eagle and God the mouse, God the osprey and God the salmon, God the crow and God the Coyote, God the predator and the prey.

So my son Dan and I packed the truck one day in early February and drove downeast to our camp for some spiritual hunting. Dan was in high school and doing an independent study on tracking wild-life. He has been coming to our camp since he was a baby. He was six when we built the cabin. He pounded nails into everything.

We arrived in the clear, cold afternoon, driving down over the snow-covered field as close as we could get to our roadless cabin and carrying our gear the rest of the way through the snow. The stars that first night were brilliant, bright enough to light the trails after dark with no moon. At bedtime, it was

14 degrees and windy outside, but 55 degrees in the cabin with a fire popping in the stove.

Next day was clear, cold, and windy as we walked through the woods. We identified tracks and sign of fox, grouse or "partridge," snowshoe or varying hare, red squirrel, and porcupine. The snow is like the paper upon which a creature writes a very short episode of its own biography. We walked south toward Mahar's Cove, finding many coyote and fox tracks crossing the road as well as snowshoe hare. Coyote tracks are larger and farther apart than fox. Both are "perfect walkers", that is, the hind foot is placed in the track of the front foot, but fox is much more poised, even dainty, than coyote. We saw several places where snowshoe hare had fed on wild cherry twigs. Do they prefer black cherry with its sweet flavor to the bitterness of choke cherry? At the Point we saw much porcupine activity—tracks old and new, scat, and many oak saplings and fir trees whose bark had been gnawed by porky's orange teeth. They must have no taste-buds. The track of a porcupine is a rolling, shuffling, pigeon-toed zigzag, looking like a zipper in the snow. They're not runners—don't need to run away from enemies.

You have perhaps noticed how we tend to give animals personal qualities—the fox is sly, the hare is timid, the red squirrel is nervous and territorial, the coyote is intelligent and tricky. Some would say that this is anthropomorphizing, projection of our own imaginations or fantasies. But I say that 'personal' qualities are inherent in all Nature as surely as in human nature. Nature is personal. I have seen animals grieve, remember, think, play, and perform rituals, and am convinced that personhood is a quality of all creatures, not just humans. Our kind are not alone in our joys and sorrows, our mourning and dancing, our suffering and our playing, not isolated and alone, but members of the family of all Creation.

I wonder what qualities other creatures, if we could understand them, might attribute to humans. They might say that humans have intelligence, craft, language, territoriality, building skills, an ability to propagate the species that makes rabbits look like amateurs, and a terrible gift for killing. Have you ever said to some frightened bird who flies from your presence, "Don't be afraid of me. I won't hurt you"? But surely their fright is not irrational. They know that the ways of our kind have been the death of too many of their kind.

Very early in the morning of our last day—about 3:00 or 4:00 a.m.—while my brave lad, Dan, slept soundly nearby, I woke abruptly from a sound sleep in the loft of our little one-room cabin and looked out the window at the head of our bed over the snow toward the bay. It was by no means pitch dark, though the moon had set. The woods rested in pre-dawn silence. Just then, I heard the rising howl of a coyote close by, long and drawn-out, soon joined by a chorus of yipping barks in accompaniment. My spine tingled in that primitive way at the powerful, eerie sound, a final call not to despise another creature.

Look to the other creatures, like us created, part of the Body of God, and know that you are never alone in your suffering and your joy, your hope and desire, and know that we can be healed.

UN-NATURAL EVENTS: Mickey Mouse. Without turning them into human beings, real mice are miracles enough—to quote Walt Whitman—to stagger sextillions of infidels.

FIELD & FOREST REPORT: *In the bleak midwinter, frosty winds made moan, earth stood hard as iron, water like a stone,* wrote poet Christina Rossetti. That about describes it at this writing. Very cold weather has frozen the earth hard as iron, and cast the water into stone.

SALTWATER REPORT: Stand by the shore in a small bay or inlet and listen to the heaving, squeaking, grinding, gurgling of the ice as the tide flows slowly in and out, like the sounds of a great creature which has a life of its own.

SEED PODS TO CARRY AROUND WITH YOU, from a Hasidic saying: *When you walk across the field with your mind pure and holy, then from all the stones, and all growing things, and all animals, the sparks of their soul come out and cling to you, and then they are purified and become a holy fire in you.*

PILGRIM'S JOURNAL: Coming down the West shoulder of the mountain I flushed a snowshoe hare that bounded silently like a ghost into the woods. Its coat was beginning to show some brown in the white, in magic correspondence to the coloration of the mountain. Continuing down through the blueberry barrens I came to a "deer scratch"—a gentle depression in which a deer had rolled over to scratch its back in the bristly blueberry bushes. Loose gray-brown deer hair had blown a distance down the mountain, here and there catching on blueberry bushes. Looking closer, I saw one tuft of hair attached to a small piece of deer flesh, still red with blood. "The body of Christ," I heard a voice say.

FIRST QUARTER TO FULL *SNOW* MOON

Winter is a dreary season, heavy waters in confusion beat the wide world's strand. Birds of every place are mournful, but the hot and savage ravens, at rough winter's shriek. Crude

and black and dank and smoky; dogs about their bones are
snarling, on the fire cauldron bubbles all the long dark day.
Translated from the Gaelic by Frank O'Connor

February 21, anniversary of the assassination of Malcolm X,
1965.

NATURAL EVENTS: I have always been fascinated with burls,
those odd-shaped growths on trees which protrude from
trunk or limb with swirling rather than straight grain and
bark of a different texture altogether. I have one that I cut
from a big old Cortland apple tree several years ago. It looks
for all the world like an alien brain. Another burl came from
a cedar tree down on Cape Cod. The grain of this one is
packed close; swirling, churning, bulging and rippling like
muscle. These curly burls are the result of a mix-up in the
tree's growth pattern. They are the tree's reaction to an irritation, the answer to a difficult question, the response to a challenge.

The oyster responds to a similar challenge by producing a
pearl, a round growth of concentric layers surrounding the
source of irritation. Oak trees answer a like question by
growing a gall around the sting of an insect.

Because of the beauty of their swirling grain, burls are
prized for woodworking. Likewise, the oyster's pearl is prized
for jewelry. Even the oak gall was treasured for being the
source of a dark brown ink. When John Hancock subscribed
his name to the Declaration of Independence in letters large
enough so that "King George could read it without his
glasses," he used oak gall ink. The pearl, the burl and the gall
are answers to hard questions Nature puts to the oyster, the
apple and the oak—answers which are things of beauty and
useful to other living things.

I'm impressed, and not nearly so graceful. When Nature

puts a difficult question to me, my response is rarely so beautiful, though it could be. An insect sting is likely to elicit a murderous slap or a spray of insecticide, hardly useful to other living things. And my response to man-made toxins might be cancer. In fact, I sometimes wonder if I am a part of the hardest question Nature has ever asked of herself.

But, I comfort myself, we humans are a young species. The oak, the apple and the oyster are immeasurably more ancient. They have learned these beautiful answers to difficult questions. They react harmoniously to challenges. They remain genetically alert to the needs of other lives around them. We can learn that too.

On another subject entirely, a researcher in New Zealand reports in the journal *Nature*, that crows there fashion tools out of twigs and leaves to draw out edible insects from holes and crevices in the bark of trees. Gavin R. Hunt is suggesting a thinking and planning process in this tool-making, and the teaching of this simple technology to the young.

UN-NATURAL EVENTS: Ever since someone wrote that God gave us dominion over the whole world, we have gotten in the habit of thinking of ourselves as better than every other creature and exempt from the laws that govern the rest of Nature: that we can make our own rules. We say that we are the only animal that uses language, until we find that other primates and whales and dolphins do too. We say that we are the only animal that uses tools, until we find that crows in New Zealand do too. Maybe our uniqueness turns out to be that we are the only animal that claims to be better than all the other animals.

RANK OPINION: We can begin anytime to love and respect the creatures and the Creation. We have the ability and the desire and the power. Sure, the earth and the other creatures have great capacity to forgive, but if we do not love them, can we expect them to forgive our hardness of heart forever?

WILD SPECULATION: What would our world be like if we finally loved each animal and bird; each plant, tree, moss, or lichen, the very flesh of the earth, as we loved ourselves, as our Teachers have told us over and over? Then the earth could again love us equally and support us all our life long until we come to our own evening. And then it would take us back ever so lovingly, until it was time to bring us into life again. This is the real everlasting life, and it's right under our noses.

FIELD & FOREST REPORT: Sap beginning to run. Look for little icicles on the broken twigs of maple trees. Sugaring time cannot be far away.

MOUNTAIN REPORT: Awanadjo rests peacefully while the sun warms her Southern flank and life stirs.

CRITTER OF THE WEEK: The crows with their intelligence and their secret muttering plans for the coming Spring.

SEED PODS TO CARRY AROUND WITH YOU: from William J. Long: *If you would know the mind of animals your way is still, as always it has been, the way of an understanding heart.*

And from Henry David Thoreau: *You must love the crust of the earth better than the sweet crust of any bread or cake. You must be able to extract nutriment from a sand heap, else you will have lived in vain.* (Journals, January 25, 1858)

PILGRIM'S JOURNAL: I stepped out of our cabin for a breath of fresh air and was overwhelmed by a sky that seemed to balloon above me into the infinite as soon as I looked up. The moon is finally visible, stars, too. How can anyone live without the sky and the silence? Both are enormous. Perhaps humans are evolving like the bees and wasps. Many people are much more comfortable with the life of the hive with a clear chain of command and clear jobs to do. Yet, some of us remain like the bumblebees and the solitary wasps that have no hive, just bumble from flower to flower and sleep where we land.

PERICOPES

Once a widely-read literary form in this country, the sermon has fallen into disrepute. Though I might say I'm a practicing Christian, I have a lot more practicing to do before I get it right . . . if ever. Still, a little preaching now and then can be good for the soul. To that end, here are some sermon clippings.

In the Gospels, particularly Mark, Jesus is known as a healer and an out-caster of demons. It is not by some magic formula, or subtle psychological tricks that this is done. Jesus the Healer does this by awareness of the power of the Holy to heal, to make the diseased and broken over into the image of the Holy. Health, Heal, Holy, Hallow, Save, Salubrious, Salve, Salvation: they all mean wholeness. It is the wholeness and holiness of God that saves and heals the madness and destruction of our condition.

It is not a question of whether one kind of medicine is better than another. It is not a question of whether Jesus really did these things. It is not a question of whether healing happens. Healing does happen. The healer, be it Jesus or shaman or doctor, may bring it about, but it is the power of the Presence of the Holy that heals. Take away the Sacred and we weaken and fail. Bring forth the Sacred and we heal.

I wish I could communicate something to younger people, something very comforting and reassuring about life as a journey, which I am just beginning to glimpse in later life. So often we set out for one place, but end up somewhere else entirely. Then, we wonder if we have done something wrong, or if we are lost, because we didn't end up where we intended to. But it is not so much where, or even when we have arrived. It is more how well we travel, how well we handle the unexpected, the unplanned, the unwanted, the getting lost; how well we enjoy each place, and how well we treat other creatures along the way. If we keep waiting until we arrive, we will wait out the best part of our lives.

If we choose to follow the leading of the Spirit, we make the road as we go. The journey is our home, as Nelle Morton said it. God does not wait for us at our next stop, or at our final destination, or in heaven. God travels with us, beside us, inside us. God does not enter our lives after we are born, or after we graduate, or after we buy our first home, or after the kids are grown, or after we retire. God was with us from the beginning and will be with us forever.

Back when we used to work in the orchard on a warm day, even in February, we would sometimes see that the pine mice and meadow mice inhabiting the orchard had taken the opportunity to rise and shine and haul out the old and soiled nesting materials that they had been living with for many days or weeks or months under the ground or among the roots of the trees. They would haul them out of their burrows into the light and the air, because if they didn't, the place where they lived would become unhealthy and perhaps poison them. After a time they would begin rebuilding their nest and bring in fresh dried grass bedding to make their lives cleaner and sweeter as they lived through into Winter.

Likewise around here, we're beginning to haul out into the growing light our Christmas trees and other things left from last year. We may wash and hang out the laundry in the sun during the Winter, if the day is warm enough. Or during a thaw, we rise and shine and open the doors and windows a little to let the light and the fresh air in, so that we can be healthy. When we do it, we call it good house-keeping, so when the orchard mice did it, we called it good "mouse-keeping."

To me that is what the ancient practices of confession and forgiveness are all about. We haul our secret, dirty things out into the cleansing light of the Eternal, and let the air and light purge them, clean them and sweeten them. If we don't, they will poison us. The mice know it. So do we.

That's the almanack for this moon, but don't take it from me. Go out and see for yourself.

This is the Awanadjo Almanack for the Full *Snow* or *Hunger* Moon to the Full *Sap* Moon [The *Sap* Moon is also called by some *Crow, Crust, Sugar* or *Worm*]. This moon is called *Paniqsiqsiivik or Bleaching Skins* Moon by the Eskimos. It is *Adar* on the Hebrew Calendar, and February/March in Downeast Maine

FULL TO LAST QUARTER *SNOW* MOON

Where the mountain crosses, on top of the mountain, I do not myself know where, I wandered where my mind and my heart seemed to be lost. I wandered away.

    From a Papago woman, collected by Frances Densmore

February 23, 1868, Birthday of W.E.B. Dubois, one of the foremost spokesmen for African Americans in the late 19th century. He was the first to present a thorough indictment of the pervasive nature of racism in our country and its threat to the whole body.

February 26, 1846, Birthday of Buffalo Bill Cody who turned the slaughter of the buffalo and the attempted extermination of the Plains Tribes into a profitable show business venture. Funny how we can hate other creatures enough to nearly destroy their kind, then when they are almost gone, we get suddenly nostalgic about their nobility. By the way, Cody was actually only 1/16th buffalo.

NATURAL EVENTS: This is the time of the year that seems to move the most slowly. Nothing changes from day to day or even week to week. From here, a month of Winter seems to last as long as the whole Summer. That is why the almanac is such good medicine. Check out the times of sun-up and sun-set and length of daylight and we see that things are changing; the Earth is moving; the sun is returning.

The seed catalogs are good medicine, too, with their hopeful images of prodigious orange pumpkins and tremendous red tomatoes. It's enough to induce olfactory hallucinations of the earthy smells of summer. The longer days, now about the same length as they were back in the second week of October, just over eleven hours in these parts. On warm days the birds are active, singing and attacking the bird feeder. Recently, when the temperature reached about 60 degrees, I detected the unmistakable sign of a surprised or perhaps just exuberant skunk wafting on the air. Skunks sleep but don't hibernate, we understand, always ready for action on a warm day.

UN-NATURAL EVENTS: The creation/evolution debate. Like other debates, the two sides are defined by extremists and we normal people are left with the choice of becoming extremists or staying out of the discussion. The creationists are put in the position of saying that all truth is revealed in a series of religious writings over which even believers argue fiercely. The evolutionists are put in the position of claiming a complete explanation for the origins of life without divine intervention. We common folks are left with the spectacle of grown men claiming loudly to be absolutely certain about uncertainties and absolutely convinced about things for which there is no convincing evidence—not unlike the New Hampshire primaries.

RANK OPINION: We hold the opinion that both creation and evolution can be true at the same time, and will happily try to convince you farther along.

Being as how it is the middle of winter, and Mother Nature herself shows little change of note in these parts, this might be a good time to talk about local human nature. Furthermore, town meeting looms on the horizon as the next notable human event. The month before town meeting has been aptly called "Hate Month," as gossip swarms like blackflies in summer, and old grudges grumble like skunks in the night, turning over trash cans and stinking up the air. To ease this midwinter malaise—and hoping that I do not offend any of the local primate wildlife—let me mention some of the specimens of human nature that make life hereabouts absolutely incomparable. There's the formidable former state trooper and town constable who now and then puts on his leather jacket and bandanna to ride his motorcycle with his buddies, but also tenderly cares for his apple trees because he loves to "smell the beautiful blossoms." There's the burly, toothpick-chewing fire chief who is also an astounding artist and cartoonist, and carves delightful, delicate decoys of local waterfowl. There's the past president of the proper ladies' garden club who trekked the entire Appalachian and Pacific Coast trails, certainly no bed of roses. There's the local dentist who can make you laugh 'til you cry even with a mouthful of cotton wads, and plays the hottest 5-string banjo you've ever heard. There's the ER physician's assistant who can give you a quick tracheotomy with a ball-point pen, if necessary to save your life; and then sing you some rocking gospel with piano or bluegrass bass, if necessary to save your soul. There's the dedicated EMT who is also a Magus of Magic. There's the town meeting moderator who just happens to be a Buddhist and acupuncturist. There's the local elementary school music teacher who has just won a Grammy. There's the artist who can paint pictures and sing songs that will make your hair stand on end, is married to a preacher, and has a dress of Emmy Lou Harris's hanging in her closet. There are countless able carpenters with degrees in philosophy and religion and English and sociology [all of which come in mighty handy on certain jobs]. There are scores of amazing artists who create works of surpassing beauty while their kids are off to school. There are dozens of steel drum players who bring the sweet sounds of the warm West Indies to the cold coast of Maine. Honestly, this is just scratching the surface: these marvels go on and on all around our little towns.

WILD SPECULATION: No matter what small town you live in, I'm guessing that there are wonders of human nature, both native and migratory, on every back road and corner.

RANK OPINION: Before you get too anguished about local or national politics, or where the world is headed in a handbasket, you might do well to take a few deep breaths, take a look around, and marvel at the elegance of your gawky, two-legged, upright, featherless, furless neighbors. Treasure them and the surpassingly peaceful small-town way of life that they—and you—have magically made here. Be thankful, and then, fearlessly uphold this way of life with all your heart and soul forever. It's the soil that will nourish future generations.

FIELD & FOREST REPORT: Leave town and it's easy to see how soil builds. Walk through the woods and see the blanket of twigs, spruce and fir needles, bits of bark and rotten wood, animal droppings, and an occasional feather which lie on top of the shrinking snow cover in surprising amounts. One thin layer of rich organic matter after another, year by year—the leavings of life, the passing of life supporting life. Each spruce peacefully gives its life, its very body, that others may live. The previous generations, by their living and dying, provide for the sustenance and health of generations to come.

MOUNTAIN REPORT: Deer and fox tracks, along with those of squirrel and snowshoe hare, dot the remaining snow. In one clump of staghorn sumac, deer tracks and nibbled twigs show where deer have been feeding on the fuzzy red cone-shaped seed clusters, with bright red particles scattered over the white snow. There is still a good cover of snow in the woods on the north slope of the summit of Awanadjo. The other day there was no snow in town at all, but the mountain appeared white, and sure enough the higher you climbed, the more snow there was. This reminds me of the 100 foot= 100 mile rule suggested by Edwin Way Teale in his *North with the Spring*. He suggests that for every 100 feet of eleva-tion, the climate on the mountain becomes like the climate 100 miles north. That puts the climate on the top of Awanadjo somewhere on the eastern shore of Hudson's Bay.

SACRED MOUNTAIN: Paha Sapa, what we call the Black Hills of South Dakota, where people of the plains tribes go to receive their visions. I was born there, and still remember the twisted red pines and the sparkling flakes of mica underfoot.

SALTWATER REPORT: January's cold has left thick ice in the bays and along the shore heaved into mounds by the tides. If ice did not float, life in the Northern seas would be very dif-ferent or impossible. Think about it.

CRITTER OF THE WEEK: That exuberant skunk. Ernest Thompson Seton supplies this entertaining list of names for the common skunk. French Canadian—*L'Enfant du diable.* Ojibway— *Shee-gawk.* In this we see the origin of the word "Chicago," meaning Skunk Land. Huron—*Scangaresse.* Abenaki—*Seganku.* From these last two, he suggests, we get our word "skunk." That makes scents. The Mexican name is apparently *Zorilla.* Little Zorro?

SEED PODS TO CARRY AROUND WITH YOU: From Rabbi Rami M. Shapiro: *One leaf atop another yet under the next, a vibrant tapestry of arcs and falls all in the act of becoming. Death is the passing of life, and life is the stringing together of so many little passings.*

From Red Hawk, a Passamaquoddy poet: *Snow falls on everyone equally and takes me back to sliding down hills, inviting chills of snow spray on our faces, to days we made long, to homes and their inviting heat. Thoughtful, snow is, as it falls on everyone so equally.*

PILGRIM'S JOURNAL: I climbed the mountain up the Osgood trail in the most difficult conditions in a long time due to ice everywhere. Slipping and sliding, I finally made it to the old stone culvert where a stream runs under the trail beneath flat stones laid over the top of a ditch many years ago. This arrangement works fine for most of the year. In fact, the stream runs only after a rain in July and August, but in a freeze-and-thaw winter like this one, the culvert freezes and the intrepid climber is confronted with a small glacier, a frozen mini-Niagara extending fifty or more feet wide and one hundred or more feet in height encasing huge stones and tree trunks in ice.

This frozen pale blue and opal cascade slopes slightly downward, falling in terraces out of sight downhill. Crossing it without crampons and ice axe, one risks a disastrous slide down a series of slick, slanted steps to land bruised and broken somewhere away down the mountain. In past I have tried to cross this wide and deep ice using trees as hand-holds and even putting my wool shirt down in front of me to give foot-grip. This day I did not even try to cross it, but determined instead to climb up the slope beside the glacier 'til I reached its source or a place where it could be step-stoned across. Climbing carefully up the frozen waterfall, I found tufts of moss, grass, or rocks protruding from the ice for a safe foothold.

An unknown region of the mountain began to open before me, rarely if ever visited by human beings. So many places with no mark of human foot glowed with green of moss, gleam of ice, or glitter of stone, that I might as well have been on the primal tundra. The quiet and peace of the small surface creatures—ferns, moss, lichen in all their innocence—was wildly exhilarating and even intoxicating, big medicine for the soul.

Gradually the sharp ice-filled gully's sides diminished in height, though the steepness remained, and the width of the frozen cascade narrowed until I could, ever so carefully, pick my way across it with much stretching from stone to stone, reaching for branches, and diligent application of the hiking stick for balance. The fog was ever thicker and clouds flew into my face like ghosts on gusts of wind as I found my way out of the declivity and onto some very high, steep, and remote blueberry barrens broken by ledge covered with pale green, fog-soaked lichen and moss. From there it was up through spruce woods, far from any trail, and onto the summit. The remote places on the earth are like the remote places in the soul, and visiting them is restorative. Sweet, wordless mysteries of life.

This is the Winter daring of what we said would die, far on
some winter faring, from names we knew them by . . . Give
them the warmth of your caring, prove that death is a lie.

From David Morton

March 5, the anniversary of the Boston Massacre, 1772, in
which occupying forces fired on colonial guerrillas, killing
five men, including Crispus Attucks, a free black man whose
loyalty was an inspiration to the entire Massachusetts colony.

March 7, the birthday of Luther Burbank (1849–1946), one
of this country's greatest horticulturalists, who developed
new strains of prunes, plums, peaches, blackberries, rasp-
berries, potatoes, potahtoes, tomatoes, tomahtoes, apples,
peaches, corns, squashes, peas and flowers, by cross-
breeding—that is, genetic engineering the way the Creator
does it.

NATURAL EVENTS: March roared in like a lion with high
winds and white drifts. A newly returned mourning dove
called plaintively in the silent snow, bewailing the cruelty of
storm and cold after a long, welcome thaw. Nature luxuriates
in transformation and change. Insects go through metamor-
phosis. Water changes its state from liquid to crystal to solid
to gas to liquid again. Mutation is not always bad, despite the
sci-fi movies. It can create new types and eventually species. A
generation ago, one branch on one MacIntosh tree in the
Marshall Orchards near Fitchburg, Massachusetts began to
yield an apple that was bigger, redder, tastier and a better
keeper than the traditional MacIntosh. Now the "Marshall
Mac" is grown all over the country. Nature does not always
repeat herself and will often do something truly new.

Oh, those sweet icicles hanging from the broken twigs of the maple trees. The sap is running again. The rhythmic drop of sap into buckets provides the percussion to the songs of the returning blackbirds. Long corrugated, rippling, dripping icicles hang from the corners of the eaves; cold, still and glistening all night long. When the morning sun rises higher in the Southern sky, the icicles change shape, dripping rapidly, shrinking down to half their night-time length as the sun warms the roof. Then finally, as night approaches again, they begin growing longer and more crystalline as the dripping slows, and finally stops.

FIELD & FOREST REPORT: Aspen and pussy willow buds have been expanding for some time now and are showing little tufts of soft, gray fur. Buds are swelling with hope during the day, then shrinking with fear during the night in a slow, rhythmic pulse.

MOUNTAIN REPORT: Wintry conditions on Awanadjo. Never mind, though. She has seen millions of Winters and is very patient. She knows Spring will come. Peculiar icicles in peculiar places, emerging from a nearly invisible crack in the cliff as though a frozen Moses had struck it with his icy staff to bring forth a glacial fountain. Many tracks of partridge, squirrel and fox creating a silent movie of absent, invisible creatures going about their business on the head, shoulders and flanks of Awanadjo.

SALTWATER REPORT: Water temperatures barely above freezing with ice floes, icebergs bobbing and sailing in the wind and tide. Our inner bay is still covered with a nearly seamless sheet of ice, broken and crumpled around the edges where it meets the shore or where it is punctured by settling down over a rock or ledge as the tide runs out of the bay, dropping the ice like a clean sheet shaken out and floating down over a newly-made bed. It is mysterious to stand along the shore on a dark night and hear the ice whispering, snapping and creaking in the darkness as the tide pulls out from under it.

CRITTER OF THE WEEK: The sad mourning doves who thought they were coming North with the Spring and flew head-long into Winter.

SEED PODS TO CARRY AROUND WITH YOU: from Kate Barnes: *In February, all of a sudden there is a lot more light, and it's warm light—snow melts off the roof, the first lambs are born in the barn cellar, the hens start laying, the mare comes into season, and I notice that the geraniums at the window have pushed their stalks up eight inches and covered them with brick-pink blossoms. Every day I wake up earlier and my bones crack as I sit up and stretch. When I poke my boot through a drift in the field, I find clover growing green underneath it. Now the sap is running and when I drive my sleigh up to the wood lot, I see three young maple bushes deeply scored with new bear scratches.*

Oh, warm light, couldn't you have waited a little longer? How safe we were in the dead of winter, how gently we dreamed. How beautiful it was to sleep under the snow!

PILGRIM'S JOURNAL: We as a town own only a part of Awanadjo the Mountain in common. A large tract has been given to the town, and the summit has recently been given to a conservation trust. And yet, in another sense, we have held the whole mountain in common for generations. Those who came before us until this day have valued that commonality and with great wisdom have chosen not to limit its use to a few individuals. Since the coming of Europeans here any "owner" of mountain property could have chosen to make an exclusive claim on its use and enjoyment. No one has chosen to do that . . . until recently. This is an admirable demonstration of the holding of an extremely delicate balance for seven generations, though with increasing population no one knows how long this will continue.

It is said that "a man can do whatever he chooses with his own land." This often turns into an excuse to exploit the land for personal gain. Yet, since 1762, our predecessors have chosen to do those things which, for the most part, have been the least detrimental to its beauty, wholeness, ecology, and accessibility to the prudent villager, visitor, or pilgrim who desired to walk upon the mountain and experience its power. They did this for us, whom they would never know. For them, some things were sacred. And for us?

NEW TO FIRST QUARTER *SAP* MOON

For most of us, the knowledge of our world comes largely through sight, yet we look about with such unseeing eyes that we are partially blind. One way to open your eyes is to ask yourself, "What if I had never seen this before? What if I would never see it again?" Rachel Carson

And from Helen Keller: *Hold out your hands and feel the luxury of the sunbeams.*

March 11, the anniversary of the death of Jonathan Chapman—"Johnny Appleseed" 1775–1847. Here is an eyewitness account of his death published 25 years later in Harper's Magazine, November 1871. "After walking 20 miles, he entered the house of a settler family in Allen County Indiana, and was warmly welcomed. He declined to eat with the family but, sitting on the door-step and gazing at the setting sun, accepted some bread and milk. Later he delivered his 'news right fresh from heaven' by reading the Beatitudes. He slept as usual on the floor, and in the morning was found with his features aglow with a supernal light and his body near death. A doctor pronounced him dying, but added that he had never seen a man in so placid a state at the approach of death. At seventy-two years of age, forty-six devoted to his self-imposed mission, he ripened into death as naturally and beautifully as the seeds of his own planting had grown into bud and blossom and fruit."

NATURAL EVENTS: Immigration. The cardinal that has been coming to our birdfeeder off and on and the mockingbird which perches atop the spruce tree are immigrants from away. So are the English sparrows. So are the Eastern coyotes. So am I and my family. So are you and yours. So are most of the trees and shrubs and flowers in our yards. So are most of the crops planted in Maine. Potatoes and tomatoes are from Central America. Apples are from Asia by way of Europe, broccoli from Italy.

Immigration is as natural as the floating seeds of the thistle and dandelion (also immigrants from Europe). There are palm trees in Ireland, possibly sprung from floating seeds. If immigration were un-natural, then why would critters have legs, feet, wings and fins? (Some critters don't even have any of those appendages and *still* find ways to immigrate.)

Humans are among the most mobile of immigrants. Leaving our ancient home in north central Africa 2–300,000 years ago, we humans have spread until we now cover nearly the entire habitable earth—more than any other creature, except perhaps the ant. The first wave of Americans may have come from Asia via the Bering Strait at least 20,000 years ago. The next wave came from Europe and Africa beginning in the 16th century. Now immigrants come here from every country.

UN-NATURAL EVENTS: Laws prohibiting immigration. You might as well try to prohibit osmosis or repeal the law of gravity. Immigrant-bashing used to be called "Nativism." When Abraham Lincoln was running for the Illinois legislature very early in his career, he found out that he was being supported by the Nativists. He rejected their endorsement saying: "Who are the native Americans? Do they not wear the breech clout and carry the tomahawk? We pushed them from their homes, and now turn upon others not fortunate enough to come over so early as we, or our forefathers . . . As a nation we began by declaring that 'All men are created equal.' We now practically read it, 'All men are created equal except negroes and foreigners and Catholics.' When it comes to this I shall prefer emigrating to some country where they make no pretense of loving liberty."

WILD SPECULATION: Suppose we build a big fence along our border to keep the immigrants out? Alas, that won't work. It's been tried. Ever hear of Hadrian's Wall? The Great Wall of China? The Berlin Wall? Bush's Bulwark? The failed dreams of mad emperors.

RANK OPINION: Darwin clearly showed that creatures leave their home territory when life there has become intolerable to find better chances for survival in a new place. The most effective—the only—way to stop immigration is to increase opportunity in a creature's home territory.

MOUNTAIN REPORT: Melting snow from last week's big storm. Water gurgling hidden under the snow and run-off swelling the brooks and freshets that descend the sides of Awanadjo as Spring draws near.

CRITTER OF THE WEEK: Johnny Appleseed, the immigrant.

SEED PODS TO CARRY AROUND WITH YOU: *We are strangers and sojourners, soft dots on the rocks. You have walked along the strand and seen where birds have landed, walked, and flown; their tracks begin in sand, and go, and suddenly end. Our tracks do that; but we go down.* From Annie Dillard

From the Old Testament: *And if a stranger sojourn with thee in thy land, ye shall not vex him, but the stranger shall be unto you as one born among you, and thou shalt love him as thyself for ye were strangers in the land* . . . Leviticus 19:33–34

PILGRIM'S JOURNAL: Very foggy this morning. Fog's light haunting presence is so moving. It makes me ache to recreate the nature of these soft, fluid clouds, to echo it, speak it, paint it, repeat it. Joni Mitchell sings, "I really don't know clouds at all." Clouds are natural to all four elements. Of the element of fire, smoke is a cloud. Of earth, dust. Of water, fog or mist. Of air, wind is a cloud. Doubt is a cloud of unknowing. Faith is a cloud of hope. I want to play a Celtic tune on my fiddle with the fog for my audience as it pours out of the inlets, into the bay. We walk in the fog. We can never see where we are going until we begin to step forward, then the fog recedes. For each step we take, the fog withdraws just as much. If we stand still we are lost.

Climbed the mountain on the third day after the new Sap moon. The wind was gentle from the south, temperature unseasonably warm, about 60 degrees. Saw a wooly-bear caterpillar humping up the trail above the meadow. T. Mason reported seeing a live grasshopper on the mountain last week. These are unseasonable events. The weather has been warm and wet, due, according to some, to the El Nino effect. Today the ice is going out of the bay at high tide. This is very early for such a thing. In past years, ice out has been as late as the second week in April. Working my way up the same trail that the wooly-bear was, I heard a raven call that sounded something like "Hawk." Looking up I saw two large turkey vultures soaring maybe 1000 feet over the mountain.

In *Walden*, Thoreau describes the "distinct trail of a fox" across the snow on a frozen Walden Pond and seeing the tracks as revealing the wisdom of "some mind," and the pond as being a clean slate for that foxy writing. Richard K. Nelson, in his monumental work about deer in America, *Heart and Blood*, talks about painstakingly following the tracks of a deer for hours and then coming upon the deer itself standing at the end of its own tracks "like a pencil at the end of a sentence." I've always felt the same excitement looking at the tracks on the mountain as I have at looking at some archaic alphabet—Runic, Cyrillic, Greek, Chinese— knowing that it contains hidden stories and wisdom which I will never decipher in this life. Not only animals leave such writings in the snow. Last moon, I saw the markings of a linden seed blown by the wind across the snow in the orchard next to our house and marveled at the mysterious script that its tumbling crescent shape had etched in the white, like the brush marks of a Zen calligrapher. Another time, it was the scribing on the snow of a drooping weeping willow branch gently moved by the March wind. All of these are inscriptions. But they are not human writings, and we are at a loss to pronounce the words they spell, or comprehend their meanings, unless we are willing to suspend the rigid categories of the rational mind and let the spirit read in them what it easily can. These are spirit-writings: wind and weather, life and death. "For my thoughts are not your thoughts, neither are your ways my ways," saith the Lord, [according to the prophet Isaiah,] "For as the heavens are higher than the earth, so are my ways higher than your ways, and my thoughts than your thoughts . . . So shall my word be that goeth forth from my mouth; it shall not return unto me empty, but it shall accomplish that which I please, and it shall prosper in the thing whereto I sent it."

Two days after the Full Sap Moon I climbed the mountain in near-freezing temperatures and a high March wind from the SW. The woolly gray sky hung very low over the land as though sky and land were exchanging DNA or in conversation or tender exploratory touching. The heavenly light was muffled and brindled over the land like the coloring of a cowhide. Over there the land was dark, but over there it was light. A ridge jutting out into Woods Pond was dark but illuminated from behind showing its shape very clearly like the silhouettes of family members that hang over our kitchen table. In back-light, features and outlines that are invisible in full light are sharply revealed. Over the village, a cloud trailed long gray streaks which touched the land, like the fine hanging tentacles of a Portugese man o' war; a snow flurry moving towards the mountain. Strangely, the flurry moved much more slowly than, and in a different direction from, the driving wind. I was puzzled that the fierce wind blowing right in my face did not blast the light snow toward me. Instead, the snow seemed to be drawn nearly straight down onto the town as though it had some ponderous gravity or fixity of purpose that was unaffected by the fierce wind. The ground under my feet was dusted with snow as I descended. Then suddenly I stepped onto clear ground and at the same moment, the wind stopped. I was walking through a wind shadow, protected by a stand of trees. Continuing downhill, I felt the sharp wind again, and saw that the ground under my feet was again dusted with snow. Soon, snow flakes salted me, though the flurry was still a half mile away and moving more to the North. By the time I got down to the Mountain Road the pussy willows were burdened with wet snow.

Farther South, the winter is gone, the flowers appear on the earth and the sound of the turtledove is heard in the land; lovers call to each other, "Arise, my love, my fair one, and come away," sings the Song of Solomon. But here, March is more erratic than erotic; warm and cold, loving and hating, clinging and rejecting, sure and unsure, quiet and screaming.

We remember a passionate and devoted defender of Awanadjo. Louise Frederick lived in a very old and impeccable yellow house right below the summit at the foot of the state trail. The Osgoods from whom she was descended had owned for a long time much of the land on the mountain, including the summit. Every day, I am told, she would sit by her window and watch the ever-changing face of the mountain she loved but had not been able to climb for many years. She never discouraged the right use of it, but was so fierce in her protection of it from wrong use that down in the town she was known as "the mountain lion." Years ago she entered into a conservation agreement with the town, declaring that the mountain should remain wild and undeveloped—an absolutely priceless asset to all those who know Awanadjo as a sacred place. On March 14, 1998 after taking care of the mountain's business her whole life, she quietly died in that yellow house in the shadow of Awanadjo. Now the defense of the mountain from the ways of the world falls to the Blue Hill Heritage Trust, and all those who love Awanadjo. May we, like her, be mountain lions. We offer the thanks and blessings of generations to come, Louise. Go to the summit now in peace, and leave us a goodly portion of your ferocity.

All winter long behind every thunder guess what we heard!—behind every thunder the song of a bird, a trumpeting bird. All winter long beneath every snowing, guess what we saw!—beneath every snowing a thaw and a growing, a greening and growing.
              Native American song from *Earth Prayers.*

March 17, St. Patrick's day. Patrick was the patron saint of Ireland, an historical figure who has taken on mythic proportions. We do know that he was born in either Scotland or Wales around the year 387 AD and became a man worthy of his reputation—devout, strong, a lover of Creation. When asked what God he worshipped, Patrick replied:

Our God is the God of all people, the God of Heaven and earth, of sea and river, of sun and moon and stars of the lofty mountain and the lowly valley; above heaven, in heaven, under heaven. God inspires all, quickens all, dominates all, sustains all, lights the light of the sun, furnishes the light of the light; has put springs in the dry land and has set stars to minister to the greater lights . . .

Patrick and the monks of Ireland lived very close to nature, and their brand of Christianity attracted many who had been the bearers of the tradition of the Druids. The Irish Easter celebration was based on the lunar calendar rather than on the solar calendar of the Romans. Here is an account of Patrick's temptation in the wilderness or "vision quest."

Then he went to Croagh Patrick, a mountain in what is now county Mayo, on Saturday of Whitsuntide. An angel came to commune with him and said: "God gives thee not what thou demandest, because it seems excessive and obstinate, for great are the requests."

"Is that God's pleasure?" said Patrick.

"It is," saith the angel.

"Then this is my pleasure," saith Patrick. I will not go from this mountain until I am dead or till the requests are granted to me."

And for forty days and forty nights Patrick fasted in that place, having four stones around him and a stone under him, even as Moses fasted on Mount Sinai.

March 20 or 21, the vernal equinox.

NATURAL EVENTS: The coming of Spring with the vernal equinox marks the most joyful cosmic meteorological calendar event of the year. Marking this day has been the wellspring of ceremonial events in every culture since the most ancient times, as well as the inspiration for architectural marvels like the temple at Karnak, Stonehenge and many Native American structures carefully designed to catch the first ray of the rising sun on that day. Christianity and Judaism have their Spring festivals of Easter and Passover.

With winter winding down it's time for a testimony to the old black iron kitchen range. When we got our Modern Glenwood E, no. 508 made by Weir Stove Co., Taunton, Massachusetts U.S.A. years back, my mother was appalled that we would want "that dirty, dusty old thing" in our house. She was born in 1914 and remembers when her mother was delighted to get rid of a similar stove. Here and there in the New England woods, you may stumble across the rusted remains of stoves just like ours which were banished and dumped out back with great joy when the new gas or electric stove arrived. The old house is gone, but the rusting stove remains.

Having grown up with modern cook stoves, it took Becky and me a while to learn how to use this squat black, six-lidded, bow-legged throw-back to a previous age, which sits like a friendly gargoyle in our kitchen. First, you have to figure out how to control the level of the fire. There is a bottom draft and a top draft. The bottom draft controls how much heat the stove makes. The top draft is still a mystery to me, but it seems to draw the heat under the lids and around the oven, and cool the fire down rather quickly when necessary. Next, you have to learn how to get low, medium or high heat. This is easily accomplished by placing a whistling tea-kettle on each of the six lids one after the other and listening to the tone of the whistle. The higher the whistle, the hotter the lid on which it sits. With six lids, you get six levels of heat. Fine enough.

When we're having a party or a pot-luck, the Modern Glenwood becomes the social center of the household, and indispensible for warming covered dishes, plates, and desserts. It is useful all winter long for disposing of combustibles that can't be recycled, as well as chicken bones and other meat scraps that can't be composted because of neighborhood dogs, raccoons, and the like. Sometimes the smoke from our chimney smells like a summer cook-out even in the dead of winter.

Best of all, during winter and its ice-storms and millennial black-outs, the old black iron kitchen range generously provides warmth for the house, cooking for meals, drying of wet mittens, socks and boots, and hot water for washing. In exchange, all it asks is a couple of cords of stove wood a year. We should all be so useful.

HUMAN NATURE: I heard a story from our church sexton who heard it from her late father who heard it from his parents. When she applied for the church sexton's job, she said, "I think you ought to know that my great-great-grandfather was excommunicated from this church." Since excommunication is a practice of which we are not proud today, this served as more of a recommendation than a detriment to her application. Her work is excellent and her stories are a continuing delight: stories about bears, cougars, a white beaver, and a light of unknown source in the woods. The story her father told concerns the Whistling Snake of Billings Pond. There is a chain of four ponds which runs from what is called "the Kingdom" in West Blue Hill to the Salt Pond in South Blue Hill. The four ponds are strung on Carleton Stream like jewels on a chain. From North to South they are called Fourth or Patten Pond, Third or Woods Pond, Second or Douglass Pond, and First or Billings Pond which finally pours into the Salt Pond through some beaver dams on Carleton Stream. Billings Pond is long and narrow with a deep basin at the North end and long shallows toward the South running between high cliffs around a tiny island with a tall white pine on it where an eagle often roosts. The shallows are full of water lilies and fields of rushes that tangle your paddle when you move through them. The story goes that before the turn of the century, swimmers in Billings Pond would sometimes hear a high sound behind them and turn to see a large snake swimming with its head out of the water and whistling. That is the story. One can only imagine truant children and youths suddenly developing previously unknown swimming abilities as they fled the whistling snake to stand dripping and trembling on the reedy shore, vowing never again to cut school for a dip in Billings Pond. Many a schoolmistress probably recounted the tale for her own reasons.

FIELD & FOREST REPORT: Warm weather has broken the "icy fetters" that have bound many brooks and streams bringing the merry sound of running water to our ears. Snow cover still substantial in the fields and woods, now more often dotted with red squirrel, chipmunk and partridge tracks. Look for an occasional icicle hanging from a broken maple twig. Snap it off. Taste it.

MOUNTAIN REPORT: Last moon, in a fresh snow which had fallen on top of the mantle of ice and under a blue Canadian high, I climbed up Awanadjo under glistening trees to the summit all alone. I was utterly elated, this being my first climb after two weeks recovering from a nasty fall on the ice near our camp which resulted in some cracked ribs, pulled muscles and bruises. Upon saying my usual mountain-top prayers, I was suddenly hailed by Raven the Trickster, the Spirit of the Northern Forest. There is a big difference between a raven and Raven. We often see ravens cavorting in the mountain's updrafts, flying upside down while chuckling and gurgling joyfully. I know the language and voices of the raven. What I heard was the same and yet different. A very loud and clear Raven voice began speaking to me from behind the trees, never appearing to me as a curious raven will usually do, but always hiding as the Trickster does. The sounds were much bigger, louder and clearer and more imag-inative, even creative than those of the raven. Clucks and clacks, sounds like water running over the glacial rocks on the mountainside, rhythms, staccato and percussive, and much closer to the sounds that humans make than the usual raven sound, giving me the distinct impression that this con-versation was directed at me. This had the effect of inviting me to enter into the conversation. I could imitate the sounds with my own vocal apparatus. With a wild and happy heart,

I did so, and was answered many times. Still, the speaker never appeared. But I knew who it was. These things are hard to describe, and easily discounted by the skeptical. Do with this story what you will. It happened. I can only treasure the encounter with Raven, and know that because it has happened before, in the fullness of time it will happen again.

SACRED MOUNTAIN OF THE WEEK: Croagh Patrick, the major holy mountain of modern Ireland, which Patrick reputedly climbed in the 5th century, ringing a bell to banish the snakes and other noxious creatures, then staying for the forty days and nights of Lent.

CRITTER OF THE WEEK: The porcupine who came out from under our cabin on Cobscook Bay around eight o'clock on several sunny mornings this moon appearing to fold his long-clawed front feet piously, sit back on his haunches and give thanks for the warm sun. His deep meditation was undisturbed by the sound of my chainsaw nearby and my dragging piles of brush just a few feet from under his nose.

SEED PODS TO CARRY AROUND WITH YOU: From an Eskimo song, *Life was wonderful in winter, but did winter make me happy? No, I always worried about hides for boot-soles and for boots, and if there'd be enough for all of us. Yes I worried constantly. I'm filled with joy when the day dawns quietly over the roof of the sky.*

From the Book of Psalms: *As the hart longs for flowing streams, so longs my soul for thee, O God. My soul thirsts for God, for the living God.*

And from the Teton Sioux: *A voice I will send. Hear me, the land all over, a voice I am sending. Hear me, I will live!*

PILGRIM'S JOURNAL: Having been hired to do some late pruning, I was sent by the owner of the orchard to prune seven very large and very old apple trees near a pond at the edge of the woods. The ground was frozen but wet due to warming weather. As I approached the first tree, I saw black feathers upon the ground. Feathers always intrigue me, so I followed the trail. Soon I saw some bones and the decayed remains of a crow, with the bones, skull, and rib-cage visible face-down on the ground under the apple tree. Fascinated, I reached down with the tip of my pruning saw and turned over the carcass. As the empty skull turned up to face me, a crow screamed from the woods not 50 feet away, and came crashing down out of a tree into the brush below. The hair on the back of my neck truly stood up. Rudolph Otto calls this the "mysterium tremendum." I was in the presence of the Holy, and I knew it to the marrow of my bones.

For the next several hours, the live crow danced for me, giving me a vision I had never seen before, and forever breaching the wall between one white guy and the rest of Creation. While I watched from the tops of the trees I was pruning, for hours the crow stepped around on the ground in a clock-wise circle, doing the broken-wing dance that many birds do to call attention away from their young. Now and then he/she would go back to the woods only to return some-time later and continue the dance. This happened in 1972, yet I believe to this day that the live crow with its dance was mourning, honoring, and protecting the one that had died many months before. Call me foolish. I do not exaggerate when I tell you that I was changed forever by this chance wit-ness of ritual, liturgy, dance, mourning and grieving, and, yes, love. It was my first born-again experience. I could never again understand other creatures as so different from me, only as so alike. The wall of hostility between me and the rest of Creation was torn down.

Let's answer the little girl who wrote a letter to God asking, "Can a person have two religions? If they do, how do you decide on their fate at the end?" Good question. A humble suggestion: Perhaps it does not matter whether we have two religions or one, or many, or none. Perhaps it does not matter what name we give to the Great Mystery. Perhaps it is of no account whether we pray to the Father or to the Mother, or Allah, or Kali, or the Void. Perhaps in God's house there are so many mansions, and each is filled with those who treat all creatures as they would be treated. Perhaps God's house is not in the sky or in the future or after we die. Perhaps God's house is now . . . here . . . on the earth, and there is room for many more.

The sod must be plowed up in order for the seeds to be planted. Sorrow is the plow, joy is the seed scattered upon the ground which will sprout and grow, we know not how. First the blade, then the ear, then the full grain in the ear. The blueberry fields must be burned before the new growth can spring back green. Sorrow is the flame that scorches the ground. Joy is the new growth in the spring that will bloom and bear fruit in season. Bud, blossom, berry.

Albert Einstein is reported to have said, "The fundamental question is whether the universe is friendly or unfriendly." Perhaps we should answer that question for ourselves. If our behavior is all biologically determined by self-preservation; if survival belongs to the cruelest, the fiercest, the craftiest; if life is a pitched battle of one species against another so that ultimately the most vicious species will destroy all others and be alone in an empty universe; if love, unselfishness, nurturing, compassion and care are all a cruel sham; and if struggle, suffering and death are the only truth; then, my friends, we live in an unfriendly universe.

But if we are a species learning to love just as we learned to walk upright; if we are learning nurturance of our kind and other creatures, and learning caretaking of the earth, just as we have learned to speak and to write; if Jesus Christ and Gautama Buddha are a step in our evolutionary development just as surely as the opposable thumb, agriculture and written language, then the universe is, on balance, a friendly place and getting friendlier. I know which I believe.

Well, that's the almanack for this moon, but don't take it from me.
Go out and see for yourself.

This is the Awanadjo Almanack for the Full *Sap* Moon to the Full *Pink* Moon [the *Pink* Moon is also called *Sprouting Grass, Egg,* or *Fish* Moon], *Agaviksiuvik Tatqiq* or *Whaling Begins* Moon by the Eskimos, *Nisan* on the Hebrew calendar, and March/April in Downeast Maine

FULL TO LAST QUARTER *SAP* MOON

From Nature's chain, whatever link you strike, tenth or ten thousandth, breaks the chain alike.

From Alexander Pope [1668-1744]

March 24, the *Exxon Valdez* goes aground spilling millions of gallons of oil into Prince William Sound, Alaska, 1989.

March 26, Birthday of poet Robert Frost, 1874.

NATURAL EVENTS: Spring began just a couple of days ago around here, according to the calendar. In Winter, the birds seem to be much quieter. The chickadee calls more rarely. The raven bites off each sound and croaks it out parsimoniously. No bird really wants to talk about it. But now, with the sun rising so much earlier, the chorus of avian conversation begins early in the morning and continues to flow during the day like the emancipated streams, brooks and rivers pouring into the bay. The chickadee thrills, and the raven gurgles. So do we.

The last day of Winter brought us the last snow storm of Winter, then with less than a day's hesitation, we got the first snow storm of Spring, thus proving the old Maine adage "If Spring comes, can Winter be far behind?" The town and the mountain received a good blanket of heavy snow and the vernal chants of the redwing blackbirds and the mourning doves were muffled by the soft flakes. The good news was that the tracking was excellent with the signs of fox, snowshoe hare, crow and deer inscribing the clean face of the snow.

Anyone who has followed the tracks of a creature becomes acutely aware of the hundreds of decisions it makes in just a few steps, and the tracks in snow record them for the curious.

Dogs and cats sneak out of the house and lie down on the south side to soak up the warming sun. We do the same if we can. Birds are more active. Nature begins to seem friendly again. Bets are now being made on the date of ice-out on Maine's bays and lakes. More on that as Spring progresses. By now, if the ancient ways still hold, the swallows should have returned to the California mission at San Juan de Capistrano.

HUMAN NATURE: Easter Sunday is the day when we celebrate resurrection, though it happens every day. The word *Easter* comes from the old English word for the name of the goddess variously called *Ishtar, Ashteroth, Asherah,* and *Isis* in the Middle East. It comes from the same root as *estrus* and *estrogen*, making Easter a thinly-disguised pagan fertility festival, and a Christian one.

UN-NATURAL EVENTS: Some events are natural when Nature's Creator does them, and un-natural when we do them. Cloning is one of these, in this poor preacher's opinion. Here's why: It is probably true that we large-brained primates will, sooner or later, use any tool that we invent for any purpose we can imagine. The power of the atom is a good example. Cloning is another. A human will be cloned. The odd thing to me is the thought that it's OK to clone animals and plants, but not humans. What makes us so sacred? I suspect that a small part of the human race will continue in this un-natural direction—playing God. Meanwhile, the vast majority of us will continue to be satisfied with natural agriculture, natural reproduction, natural religion, living close to the earth, being human, and letting God be God. In the long run—if you're betting—bet on the survival of those natural humans and the demise of those who depend on their technology.

RANK OPINION: Here's more on the creationist/evolutionist argument. On one hand, it is odd how certain Christians insist that the creation account in Genesis is a "scientific" explanation of how the universe came into being—by the hand of God in six days—but at the same time would turn pale at the thought of using Biblical cures for diseases (Lev. 11-14), or following dietary laws, or Biblical prohibitions against owning land in perpetuity (Lev. 25:23), or lending at interest (Lev. 25:37). Or how about the Biblical requirement that immigrants be brought into one's own house and cared for as though they were family? (Lev. 19:33) The Bible is not a science book.

On the other hand, it is odd how scientists in general and evolutionists in particular will turn up their noses at the idea of supernatural intervention or any force that does not follow the predictable laws of nature and science. Yet, at the same time they readily acknowledge events that are supernaturally unpredictable, such as singularities like the Big Bang, black holes, mutations on the genetic level, Brownian movement on the molecular level, and Heisenberg's uncertainty principle on the atomic level. If everything is so predictable, how come scientists aren't breaking the bank in Las Vegas? Science cannot explain everything—not yet, not ever. A science book is not the Bible.

FIELD & FOREST REPORT: Mud, mud and more mud. The roads, the walks, your feet, the dog's feet, tracking into the house and all over the nice kitchen floor. But many ancient creation stories tell about a bird diving down below the flood to bring up a bit of mud from which the Creator forms the world and human beings too. In the Genesis story, the first person is called "Adam" which means something like "red dirt" in Hebrew. From mud we come and to mud we return.

A hint of green is appearing in the swelling buds of the wild cherry and birch trees, and fuzzy catkins on poplars and willows. Redwings, starlings, black-birds flocking and cheering for Spring in the tree-tops.

SACRED MOUNTAIN OF THE WEEK is Mount Kailas in Tibet, the most sacred mountain in the world for half a billion people in India, the Himalayas and Tibet.

SALTWATER REPORT: At the Blue Hill Falls, early picnickers are visiting and even some intrepid, death-wish kayakers ride the incoming tide. Flocks of Old Squaw and eiders still gather to chatter where the outflow stirs up fish to feed the ducks from the waters of the bay.

CRITTER OF THE WEEK: The hibernating mama black bear who "adopted" the curious and unwilling beagle that sniffed its way into her den in the Maine woods. The mother bear woke up just enough to embrace the beagle in her great paws, along with her own tiny cubs. She would not let the little dog go until she was fooled by game wardens into releasing it after a day or so. It was in all the papers.

SEED PODS TO CARRY AROUND WITH YOU: from Maine poet William Booth, "*Crocus buds push through the barely thawed soil and who could imagine what they have in mind had we not the memory of former years? All our life we live in the barely thawed soil of an early spring, pushing up buds with glory in our minds, and none can tell what another may accomplish. For memory is all of glory past, and glory yet to come is another thing.*"

PILGRIM'S JOURNAL: Climbed the mountain in the gray damp-before-snow. Coming back down over the blueberry fields off the trail, my eyes roamed over a little valley running down the slope, a shallow groove covered with the red bristles of blueberry bushes and with a glacial boulder nestled in the center of it, looking ready to roll on down the mountain at the first opportunity. Many of the glacial boulders seem to be sliding down the mountain ever so slowly, pushing up a raised berm of soil in front of them and leaving a hollow depression behind. The sight of this nestled boulder produced a comforting physical sensation around my heart. I could feel it stir gently in my chest like a sleeping bear cub. The smooth slope, gentle curves, muted colors, quiescent and yet full of life, moved my inward parts with joy. I prayed for all of those who spend their days walking on flat man-made surfaces surrounded by sharp man-made planes and angles.

Again did the Earth shift, again did the nights grow short, and the days long, and the people of the Earth were glad and celebrated each in their own ways."

From Diane Lee Moomey

April 1, April Fool's Day.

April 5, Booker T. Washington born, 1858. "Let down your bucket where you are."

April 6, Ruins of Pompeii discovered, 1748.

April 7, Billie Holliday's birthday, born 1915. "God bless the child."

NATURAL EVENTS: At our camp on Cobscook Bay last quarter moon the snow was melting fast in the woods and the little brook rushed and sang down to the slate beach where it splashed into the light chop of the bay at high tide, fresh meeting salt. The hairy woodpeckers were courting, chasing each other up and down through the tall hackmatacks chirping and twittering naughtily.

Early Monday morning while the mist was still hanging over the rocky beach I went down to the water. Just as I was about to step from grass to gravel, three deer dashed down onto the beach to the South, and began walking toward me; a doe, with ribs visible under her gray brown coat, and her slightly smaller twin yearlings. They spent more time looking, listening and smelling the air than they did walking. Their noses rose to sample the wind. Their huge ears pivoted in all directions. They were so utterly sensitive that I imagined they could be receiving subtle messages from the Milky Way. Their alertness was profound and all-consuming. Fortunately for me, I was downwind, and they never saw me as they came Northward along the slate beach, finally gently kicking the gravel only a few feet in front of me. Their muscles moving under their soft skins, their translucent ears, their moist black noses and deep dark eyes: beauty in the fog. I stood as still as a stump while they stepped delicately through the water of the brook spilling down the beach.

We were the lucky ones, the four of us—survivors of a brutal Winter enjoying the first days of Spring. Their bellies would soon be full with new green browse, and we would all turn our faces toward the sun with visceral thanks.

UN-NATURAL EVENTS: Fertility is a natural event, of course, but many would agree that rampant human population growth worldwide, straining the limits of earth's resources, is un-natural. The rabbit is a symbol of fertility. That's why you see little Easter bunny icons everywhere at Easter time. But as far as reproduction, we're leaving the rabbits in our dust. And we're running out of carrots! What's up, Doc? Of course, it's the fox and coyote that keep the rabbit population under control. What we humans need is a predator.

RANK OPINIION: Seeing the seasons change I'm reminded how every religion acknowledges these changes with high holy days: Equinox, Easter, Passover, and on and on. Joseph Campbell suggests that all religions stem from the one original religion. Paleontologists suggest that we all come from one race, too. Maybe someday we'll get back to that. I, for one, would be glad. It's amazing how we can be so sure and get so hostile about religion, which deals with the unknown and unseen, and race, which deals with surface appearances.

As the days grow longer, I get to wondering why I dutifully shut off lights around the house while huge skyscrapers, malls, empty parking lots, whole cities, and even our little branch bank next door, are lighted up all night long? Why do we fix dripping faucets and try not to flush any more than necessary while chemical factories, nuclear reactors, and so many other private industries flush untold billions of gallons every day? Why do we try to eat simply, cut down on meat, and compost our food scraps to put back on the garden while large restaurant chains, fast food outlets, and supermarkets put vast amounts of food and recyclables directly into the waste stream? Why do I try to walk whenever possible to save gas at the risk of being run over by a big Ford sport utility vehicle that is 20 feet long, weighs 4 tons, has six doors, and gets 10 miles to the gallon so that suburban moms can go grocery shopping, take Johnny to his soccer game, and Fifi to the vet?

Maybe I'm crazy. Maybe it's because Dad always went around shutting out the lights. Or maybe we just know that as surely as the sun comes up, waste leads to scarcity, and excess wealth causes poverty. Maybe we want to be able to explain ourselves to our grandchildren and great grandchildren. Maybe we remember what our Teachers have always told us. Like the Buddha: *What goes around, comes around.* Or Jesus: *We reap what we sow.* Or Hiawatha and Handsome Lake: *Live for the seventh generation.* Or Immanuel Kant: *Live as you would want everyone to live.* We'll go with them. They've been around longer than Henry Ford. Besides, on Judgment Day, even though he could do it faster, it darn well won't be Henry Ford who's punching our tickets at the Pearly Gates.

FIELD & FOREST REPORT: Sometimes in the Spring when the frost has come out of the ground and before the rains have caused it to settle, there is a time when it is easier than any other time of the year to pull rocks out of the ground. It's a monolithic magic moment. The ground seems to pull away from the rocks and they sit loose. If you can get a bar under them or a chain around them, they can be eased out. And doesn't the neighbor's woodsmoke make a fine incense when one puts ones head out the door to sniff the air these early mornings? Heard any Spring Peepers yet?

Robins and crows and small brown birds seen gathering nesting materials in these parts as courting rituals begin before our eyes. Songs and dances, games and embraces. Watch closely, you'll see. *Wet and muddy* says it all this quarter moon. The Spring chorale of several varieties of blackbirds continues. I can't think of another case of birds of *different* feather flocking together—starlings, grackles, redwings, cowbirds (tenor, bass, soprano, alto)—until their nesting time is fully underway within the next week or so, then they will flock no more until Fall. Their sense of place is strong as they return to their Spring breeding grounds.

MOUNTAIN REPORT: Patches of snow and ice can still be found in the deep woods and run-off water is still freezing in the gullies at night. Some of the streams run underground. Water takes myriad forms, many of which—snow, ice, glaciers, icicles, fog, rain, and sleet—have been seen here on the mountain in the last few days. Winter does not give up easily here on Awanadjo.

CRITTER OF THE WEEK: The chipmunk which lives alternately in our woodshed and, I fear, in our basement, was foraging under the birdfeeder, when it was chased away by a big gray squirrel. It was David and Goliath, and Goliath won the day—this time.

SEED PODS TO CARRY AROUND WITH YOU: from an Aivilik Eskimo chant, *Cold, cold, frost, frost, fling me not aside! You have bent me enough. Away! Away!*

And from John Fire Lame Deer: *A good way to start think-ing about nature, talk about it. Rather, talk to it. Talk to the rivers, to the lakes, to the winds, as to our relatives.*

And from Ecclesiastes: *All streams run to the sea, but the sea is not full; to the place where the streams flow, there they flow again. A generation goes and a generation comes, but the earth remains forever.*

PILGRIM'S JOURNAL: Looking back up at the mountain after coming down, I am shaken by the raw singularity of that lofty, enormous prominence of molten/hardened stone—a huge growth of the bone-matter of the earth. It stands alone in its place, unimaginably heavy and massive against the empty, ethe-real sky; unimaginably old, alive and incomprehensibly patient, busy with its own quiet and large business, not directing or controlling any other creatures; passive yet very active, disturb-ing the wind, reflecting the sun back down on the village, affecting—even causing—the weather by its massive bulk. I felt the same kind of giddy excitement and reverence that I feel in the presence of an alert, craggy, very old person who has many gently and lovingly-polished stories to tell. Multiply that feel-ing by ten thousand and you have the feeling of the mountain's presence. Likewise, being in the presence of the mountain, multiplied by ten million, I suppose, gives a hint of being in the presence of the Creator. For this frail mortal, in the absence of God, the presence of the healing mountain will suffice.

NEW TO FIRST QUARTER *PINK* MOON

This is the one world, bound to itself and exultant. It fizzes up in trees, trees heaving up streams of sugar to their leaves. This is the one air, bitten by grackles: time is alone in and out of mind." From Annie Dillard

April 10, 1866, The American Society for the Prevention of Cruelty to Animals was founded (see Un-natural Events below).

April 12, Feast day of St. Zeno, patron of anglers. Yuri Gargarin became the first man in outer space 1961.

April 13, Captain Cook anchored at Tahiti, 1769.

April 14, Noah Webster copyrighted his dictionary, 1828.

NATURAL EVENTS: The aspens are beginning to bloom out with their long, rich catkin flowers, like huge pussy willows. The red and silver maples are in bloom and the elms are beginning to bloom. These tiny flowers are really quite exquisitely beautiful if you look closely at them. Try a hand lens; it's worth the effort. If these gorgeous blooms were larger, they'd be in Granny's old cut-glass vase on every dining room table, but they are just so small.

It was so terribly poignant, after the great Ice Storm of '98, to see broken branches and tops of poplars and birches, completely severed from the tree by the ice storm and altogether unconnected to the roots which bring life to the branches. Yet the catkins on these broken branches burst open the way they do every Spring, just as though nothing was out of order. Drawing on stored energy, some even put out green leaves, but sooner or later their sap was exhausted and they withered and died on the ground. This happened throughout millions of acres of ice-damaged boreal forest. So very touching, this doomed thrust toward life, this aborted Spring.

April showers, of course, alternating with cool and partly cloudy days. The ice is out of the bays now with only a few big chunks still left on the shore in places, but ponds and lakes are still frozen. For as long as anyone can remember, there has been a lottery held to see who can guess the exact day of ice-out on Moosehead Lake. According to the *Maine Almanac and Book of Lists*, published by the Maine Times, the average date for ice-out on Moosehead is May 8. The earliest recorded was April 14, 1945 and the latest, May 29, 1878. In the nearly 150 years of record-keeping, the trend has been toward ever earlier ice-out.

UN-NATURAL EVENTS: The first daredevils to challenge Niagara Falls were two bears, two foxes, a buffalo, a raccoon, an eagle, a dog and 15 geese: all unwilling passengers on the *Michigan*, a derelict Lake Erie merchant vessel tricked out like a pirate ship in 1827 by hoteliers and tavern-keepers who set the ship adrift over the cataract as thousands of onlookers bought drinks and cheered. The ship broke in half before going over, and one goose survived the plunge, according to *Niagara, A History of the Falls*, by Pierre Berton.

WILD SPECULATION: Imagine the awe and fear of the local Iroquois who watched the spectacle, asking themselves what species of human engineers things like this? Many are still asking the same question.

RANK OPINION: Kind of careless of those hoteliers and tavern-keepers to forget about that little boat they will ride in when grim old Charon ferries them across the River Styx at the end of their days. Some class 10 whitewater on that river, I hear.

FIELD & FOREST REPORT: Red maple buds are swelling and the silver maples in town are beginning to bloom. Pussy willows are nearly out of their bud scales and some aspens are showing the tips of fuzzy catkins. Crocuses are in bloom in warmer corners.

MOUNTAIN REPORT: *Awanadjo* means "small, misty mountain" in Algonkian, and so she has been the last few days—first veiled in mist, then draped with tatters of fog, then completely invisible as if someone had had enough faith to utterly remove her. Fannie Hardy Eckstorm, the Maine historian, taxidermist, linguist, ornithologist and anthropologist, wrote many fine books on Maine life in the early 20th century. Especially to my liking are *Old John Neptune and other Maine Indian Shamans, Penobscot Man*, and *Indian Place Names of the Maine Coast*. It is the latter which gives us the name *Awanadjo* for our mountain and *Kollejedjwok* for our reversing falls. Fannie Hardy Eckstorm was a Maine treasure.

SALTWATER REPORT: The water of the bay in April looks like hammered stainless steel most days reflecting the color of the sky. But every now and then a bright, blue sky and brilliant sun will transform the bay to deep cobalt blue set with millions of glittering diamonds, almost too bright for the naked eye to behold.

CRITTER OF THE WEEK: Cousins of the crows, the Blue Jays whose sharp calls—jay! jay! jay!—alert every other creature when a poor pale boy like me comes walking through the woods. Thoreau says that the jays are responsible for the rapid northward spread of our forests in the barren wake of the retreating glaciers because they plant seeds and nuts far and wide.

SEED PODS TO CARRY AROUND WITH YOU: from Chinese poet Shih T'ao, *Far away in the depths of the mountains, wandering here and there I carry no thought. When Spring comes, I watch the birds. In Summer I bathe in the running stream, in Autumn I climb the highest peaks. During the Winter I am warming up in the sun. Thus I enjoy the real flavor of the seasons.*

And from Red Hawk, an Abnaki woman poet, *A lone tree in the backyard shudders at each big wind. Its scraggly fir has yellowed, moss has taken over its base where there is no bark. Skinny tree like a gnarled hand grabbing upwards for life. Nothing about it speaks of strength, but for the fact that it is still standing.* From Red Hawk "pipikwass"

PILGRIM'S JOURNAL: Last Saturday they came to cut down the big elm tree on the corner of the parsonage lot right on Main Street. It's so poignant that the men who love trees and labor long and hard to save them are the ones called to cut them down. This elm was unusual for its height. In past years, the returning starlings and grackles often chose its highest branches as the perch where they would utter their liquid songs of Spring in March and April before they started their nesting. Taller and straighter than any other big elm in town, its head was in the clouds and its trunk bore no leafy branch less than 60 feet off the ground. We knew last summer, by the untimely yellowing of leaves on the highest branches, that it had the disease that has doomed the American elm all over town and throughout our country. Several summers before it had dropped a huge limb onto the street blocking traffic, taking with it a big limb from the neighboring oak at the same time. I cut these up myself and saw the dark brown rings in the elm wood—*phloem necrosis.*

Saturday morning early, the tree crew came with their machinery: a crane truck, a bucket truck, and some smaller trucks. They spent more than an hour milling around under the huge column of its trunk, with much looking up, talking, making of hand gestures, checking of gear, saws and belts and ropes. Finally, one young man tossed the last drop from his coffee cup onto the ground, climbed into the bucket, and was hoisted as high up the trunk as the cherry-picker could reach. From there he climbed, roped, to the first crotch using a line that had been left swinging from a previous climb like a tattered old harpoon tether trailing from Moby Dick.

Now the chain saws roared high in the air and the dismembering of the great tree began in earnest. Each enormous limb was first snubbed up by the crane, then amputated, and then lowered to the ground very carefully where other men waited to cut it into pieces to be lifted by hand onto waiting trucks. This went on, limb by limb, for several hours until the truncated column of elm-wood stood still 40 feet above the street. One long rope was affixed high on this remaining pillar. The other end was made fast around another sturdy elm about 100 feet away. Then the big saw with the 40 inch bar was started for the final cuts, and the air filled with roaring and oily smoke. First a huge wedge was carved out of the North side of the trunk and kicked out onto the ground looking like a half-moon. Then the back-cut was started on the South side of the tree. Soon the huge trunk moved in a way it had never moved before—never in a fierce wind, never even in an earthquake. Its perfectly straight trunk jerked slightly out of plumb toward the North. As soon as it gave way, the men on the rope took up the slack, tilting it a bit more as the saws continued to roar and other men began to drive wedges into the back-cut to widen it. The great trunk tottered more toward the men pulling on its tether, then it began to fall of its own weight, very slowly at first, then faster, pushing the air away as it plunged toward the frozen ground. In order to minimize damage to the ground the tree men had placed several cut limbs where they expected the enormous trunk to fall. Now the huge trunk crashed precisely onto these waiting logs. Several of them exploded sending shingle-sized fragments of wood and bark flying thirty feet or more. The ground shook under our feet, the seismic reverberations of the impact passing through the frozen layer of soil like a great drum being struck hard once.

A shout went up from the men who watched. Then, as the sawdust settled, we all moved close to inspect this lofty creature of the air brought to the ground for the first time at the end of its life. We walked along its length touching its rough bark, marveling at its size as if it were a beached whale: And it was—a whale not out of the sea, but out of the air. A huge mass of several tons filled a space where only seconds ago there was nothing. More spectators approached to examine the trunk and the surface of the cool, sweet-smelling stump so many years in the making, now seeing the light for the first time. The sawyers went to work again cutting the trunk into four lengths that could be lifted onto a logging truck. Each length was massive as an elephant.

Several days later when Kendall Hodgdon's big, battered truck came with its huge hydraulic claw, I was drawn out of the house to witness the solemn removal of the body. I was also concerned about a little apple tree which I had planted a bare eight feet from the giant elm several years ago and which had so far avoided any damage. But now the huge pieces of trunk had to be dragged through the space between the stump and the little apple tree before they could be hoisted onto the truck. A choke chain was wrapped around the first section and its leading end hooked to the hydraulic claw. With remarkable precision, Kendall skidded the great log safely past the tiny apple tree, then grasped it with the huge claw and as the truck's engine raced and smoke filled the air, began to lift. The greasy log truck heeled over dangerously, threatening to roll on its side—the clash of the titans. Setting the truck's outriggers to widen its stance, Kendall heaved the first piece onto the back of the truck as the engine roared. I asked how much the piece weighed. "Maybe 3 or 4 ton," answered the logger, "about the same as a Cadillac." (Between hauling logs, they haul old cars.) Aware of my concern for the little apple tree, they skillfully loaded the next three pieces onto the groaning truck, then released all their hydraulics, hopped into the cab, and with smiles and waves roared off to the dump, leaving me relieved and sad looking at the piece of empty sky above.

All that remains of one magnificent living creature are a stump with more than 175 rings of varying width, some ashes at the dump, and this account. The stump will sprout in the spring, but the diseased sprouts will be cut off. The ashes will blow away on the wind. And this story is yours to do with as you will.

FIRST QUARTER TO FULL *PINK* MOON

Soul of Earth, sanctify me. Body of Earth, save me. Blood of Earth, fill me with love. Water from Earth's side, wash me. Passion of Earth, strengthen me. Resurrection of Earth, empower me. Good Earth, hear me. Never let me be separated from you.

—Adapted from "Anima Christi" by Jane Pellowski

April 15, Income taxes come due, making liars out of more Americans than even golf or fishing.

April 17, birthday of J.P. Morgan 1837, who never had to pay income taxes.

April 19, anniversary of the tax-related Battles of Concord and Lexington in 1775, celebrated as "Patriot's Day" in New England.

NATURAL EVENTS: In New England, the term "unusual" weather is used to describe the usual weather. Here's a handy generic forecast that you can use at any time or place in Maine and be reasonably sure of total inaccuracy: Northeast to Southwest winds, backing and veering to the Southward, Westward, or Eastward and points in between. High and low temperatures swapping around from place to place. Partly cloudy to partly sunny. Probable areas of rain, drizzle, fog, snow, sleet, hail and precipitation, followed or preceded by earthquakes, tornadoes, hurricanes, and a possibility of drought, flood, famine and war. Probability of unpredictable weather: 100%.

Long, cone-shaped eel nets are set up at the mouths of local brooks and rivers now to catch the young eels or "elvers" as they move upstream in the dark of night. Once caught, elvers bring a high price on the Japanese market where they are raised to full size and eaten as a delicacy. I suppose eels might be good if you could get past the way they look. Jonathan Fisher records his observations of the Passamaquoddy catching eels on the Pennamaquan River c. 1810 not far from our camp in Pembroke, Maine: *They had chosen a shoal place, the water about two feet deep, running over pebbles; obliquely across the stream they had driven down thin lathes, each about two inches wide woven together at the top with strings of cedar bark, and so near together that an eel of moderate size could not go between them. Near one side of the river the line of laths formed an obtuse angle at the point of which was a small aperture, opening into an enclosure made to receive the eels as they descend the river . . .*

UN-NAUTRAL EVENTS: Shipping perfectly good eels half-way around the world seems un-natural to me, but then, so does eating an eel. Also un-natural is the sad decline of both the Atlantic and Pacific salmon fisheries due in part to habitat changes—dams, agricultural run-off, silt from logging and other causes.

WILD SPECULATION: The salmon may be failing for now, but the once-diminished buffalo, beaver, osprey, moose, eiders, black ducks, and the bald eagle are increasing. And what about the wolves recently seen in Northern Maine? I talked to a man of singular integrity who affirmed that he had watched a cougar in his field in Central Maine not long ago, and a woman in Blue Hill who saw one along the Millbrook. "I don't mention this to many people," each of them said, "because no one would believe it." Remember the Ghost Dance prophecies of Wovoka that the buffalo would return and the prairies grow up in grass again? So it shall be.

RANK OPINION: On Patriot's Day 1995, the federal building in Oklahoma City was bombed with great loss of life by those claiming some connection to the patriots in Concord and Lexington. There is no comparison between the defending of one's home-town from invasion by armed soldiers of a foreign power and the bombing of a building full of defenseless men, women and children going about their daily business. "Patriotism is the last refuge of scoundrels" quoth Samuel Johnson.

FIELD & FOREST REPORT: The wild cherries with their bright red bark are beginning to show green, and the aspens, red maples and elms are in riotous bloom. Clover is turning bright green and the lupine leaves are the size of a baby's hand. Springtails, known as "Snow-fleas" in Winter, dust the water in the ditches like a black powder.

MOUNTAIN REPORT: Tiny white buds are beginning to swell on the blueberry bushes as the sun continues to drive the cold out of the glacial stones on the South side of Awanadjo. Water still trickles underground and seeps out along the tops of the ledges, seeming to come from nowhere, varnishing the rock shiny and dark and greening the mosses and lichens. These patches of moss and lichen look like a God's-eye view of New England forests from above. Mourning cloak butterflies, with their maroon wings edged in ivory, spring up from the path. Halfway up the mountain, tucked amid the blueberry bushes, the tiny bleached-white shell of a crab. In the low meadow a small square piece of charred wood, a cedar shingle that had ridden about a mile on the wind from the barn fire just North of the village last Saturday. Several turkey vultures were circling then swooping beneath me as I ate lunch on the East cliffs looking down on their tawny backs and out over the bay. Earth, air, fire, and water. All things needful. And a good sandwich.

SACRED MOUNTAIN of the week is Glastonbury Tor, in southern England; a hill associated with the Druids and later with Joseph of Arimethea who provided his own tomb for the burial of Jesus and who, one tradition says, brought the Holy Grail to that sacred mountain. Later the site was associated with Avalon, home of Arthur and Guinevere.

SALTWATER REPORT: The loons are back, commuting from fresh to saltwater in the morning and from salt to fresh at night. Eagles have returned; ospreys any day now. Have they knowledge of the depletion of several of the world's major fisheries, according to the UN Food and Agriculture Organization, and the serious decline of several more due to over-fishing with high technology nets, boats, and communication gear? Our boundless appetites are ravaging other creatures on land and sea.

CRITTER OF THE WEEK: The brave and hardy Atlantic fisher-critters: eagles, ospreys, loons, seals, whales, gulls, ducks and men. What will become of them when the Atlantic fisheries collapse?

SEED PODS TO CARRY AROUND WITH YOU: from Annie Dillard again: *We have drained the light from the boughs in the sacred grove and snuffed it in the high places and along the banks of sacred streams. We . . . have moved from pantheism to pan-atheism.*

And from Wovoka, the prophet of the Ghost Dance: *You must not fight. Do no harm to anyone. Do right always.*

PERICOPES

Who is responsible for everything bad, from genocide to war to a stubbed toe? Many Christian interpreters, usually male, have authoritatively announced that Eve was responsible. Others were quick to blame the snake, which fits in well with our fear of these legless slithering creatures. Others blamed the man. "In Adam's fall, we sinned all," said the Puritan children's books.

We might also question God's innocence in all this. After all, was not God the omnipotent Creator of all, including the snake, the apple and the couple with the fig-leaf aprons?

That is why we can imagine God questioning the serpent, the man, the woman, not in a loud, angry and scolding voice, but in a hesitant, anxious voice. We can hear deep disappointment, not condemnation, when God tells them all what will happen to them: pain, hard work, and a return to the dust. I see even a tear in God's eye while fashioning clothing for them out of skins and helping them get dressed before they leave the beautiful garden, just as we send our beloved children off to somewhere with prayers and care packages, and aware of their flaws.

God could have chosen to create a perfect world, I suppose, a world without change and decay, without growth and pain and progress. But God chose to create an imperfect, evolving world of life. Why? For the same reason we choose to have children, or pets, or raise a garden—not for perfection . . . for love.

God loved that garden, that serpent, that apple tree, Eve, Adam. And God chose to give them a choice. When they chose to eat the apple, I can imagine God was sad and wept a little, but did not desert them, continued to love and care for them from a distance, as God continues to love and care for us; joyful for our joy, sorrowful for our sorrow, in the place we live now, East of Eden.

By pushing the sacred out of Nature, we have endangered many species, but just as disastrous for us, we have endangered the human soul and pushed it to the edge of extinction. Jeopardizing Creation, we jeopardize our own health, our own wholeness, our own salvation. This we are beginning to understand as the third millennium begins. There is a power in Nature, in the Earth, in the Universe that is far beyond the measurement of our finest instruments, far beyond what the eye can see, far beyond the abilities of physics, biology, chemistry to know. Yet, it can be known by the soul, with which we are all equipped, or nearly all. This power will not continue to be challenged or contravened or ignored. It is the power that makes all Nature—from lilies to ravens to the human soul—holy: dangerously holy. It is God.

———

Let's look around to see what we have. We have small towns that still preserve, to some extent, local culture. We do not fear our neighbors, nor fear walking about at night. We are not strangers to each other. Many of us still make a part of our living from the land and the water. But the battle is on for the land. Already our economy is dependent on interests hostile to those of the small town. Can we begin to think—as members of a town and church that have survived for more than 235 years—about being shepherds together of all we have? There will be no better time than now, no better place than where we are.

It may very well be that when our last judgment comes, it will not be in some far away heaven. It may be right here on earth, in our seed, our children and grand-children that we will be judged by coming generations; by their peace or war, their plenty or want, their joy or sorrow. It may be that our final judgment will be, not at the pearly gates, but on the earth as it is in one hundred years, or in one hundred generations.

That's the almanack for this moon, but don't
take it from me.
Go out and see for yourself.

This is the Awanadjo Almanack for the Full *Pink* Moon to the Full *Flower* Moon [The *Flower* Moon is also called *Corn-planting* or *Milk* Moon], *Suvluravik* or *Rivers Flow* Moon to the Eskimos, *Iyyar* or *Ziv* on the Hebrew calendar or April/May in Downeast Maine.

FULL TO LAST QUARTER *PINK* MOON

April 26, 1865, John Wilkes Booth was killed, leading to still unresolved speculation about conspiracies in the death of Abraham Lincoln. So it is always when renowned people die an un-natural death. Today is also the birthday of John James Audubon in 1780, perhaps this country's greatest painter of birds. Ironically, he shot many of his subjects so that he could paint them.

April 28 marks the anniversary of the mutiny on the HMS Bounty, an event which still inspires those who love the sea and who seek a higher justice. If only tyranny always wore as manifest a face as Captain Bligh's.

April 30, Arbor Day, a forgotten holiday.

May 3 is Pete Seeger's birthday. Pete inspired a generation, maybe two, to play the banjo, sing in harmony, clean up the earth and the water, and resist oppression. Not bad for one lifetime. Happy Birthday, Pete.

NATURAL EVENTS: We're still here, waiting out April, a seductive month which can give us Spring or Summer one day and Winter the next, burying us in snow. This is not easily borne by those who have felt the darkness and cold bite of Winter for four or five months and crave the warmth of sun on skin. Still, the songbirds have returned and are enduring April with us, giving us great encouragement, and sending us out to the bird feeder to reward them for their comforting company with sunflower seed in these last days before the greening of the earth.

Of course, then we have blackfly season. To the question, "Why the blackfly?" the late Leon Sylvester of Blue Hill Falls would answer, "To feed the birds." Leon was the sort of man who repaired and maintained his own machinery, house and grounds. The kind of man who bathed and put on his Sunday suit to go into town for a doctor's appointment. After his wife of 50-some years died, he kept their house exactly as she'd left it, that is, spotlessly clean right down to the chrome on the black iron range in the kitchen. He was what we used to call a "Christian man," before that had any overtones of smugness. I once complimented Leon a little too profusely, saying that he was one of the truest gentlemen I had ever met, to which he shyly replied, "Wait 'til you get to know me a little better."

Mourning cloak butterflies flutter in the updrafts rising from the sun-warmed earth. As mentioned before, they are the first butterflies to appear in the Spring, since, unlike others, they winter over as adults. Also watch for the hatch of tent caterpillar and webs appearing in wild cherry and apple trees as the days get warmer.

FIELD & FOREST REPORT: Apple buds at silver tip to green tip. Elm trees in bloom here in town. Some violets in bloom in the grass here and there. Recent rain and warm weather turning the grass emerald green. Blackbirds nesting, their treetop chorus nearly at an end as they get down to housekeeping. The wild cherries with their bright red bark are beginning to show green, and the aspens, red maples are in riotous rufous bloom. Clover is turning bright green and the lupine leaves are the size of a new baby's hand. Springtails dust the water in the ditches with a slate gray.

MOUNTAIN REPORT: The other day it was foggy in town, in the lee of the mountain, but no where else. The next day I saw a hawk, crows and ravens surfing on the invisible wave of the wind breaking over the mountain. She creates her own weather. Nowadays, looking out from the summit of Awanadjo over the woods stretching in all directions one can see the cloudy white patches of poplars here and there plumed with their tassels of catkins catching the sunlight. A garter snake rests in the sun here. Over there a bright topaz green tiger beetle jumps out of the path in front of our feet. Last year at this time there was still a foot or more of snow in hidden places on the north side of the summit, and little rivulets of snow-melt still trickled down the mountain.

SACRED MOUNTAIN OF THE WEEK is Mount Kilimanjaro near the border of Kenya and Tanzania, with three peaks, the highest of which, Kibo, rises over 19,000 feet above sea level. The Chagga people call the lower slopes "kari ko ruwa" or

"God's back yard." They use the name of the mountain as a blessing for long life; "May you endure like Kibo. As Kibo ages not, so may you never be old."

SALTWATER REPORT: With the ice out of the bay early this year, boats have been going in and out for a month. All the talk is about new regulations that would require time-consuming re-rigging of lobster pots designed to save whales from entanglement.

CRITTER OF THE WEEK: The little olive-backed thrush that somehow died on our front porch, with speckled breast and gray-green back. Here is a prayer I offer for a dead animal, or when disposing of a roadkill:

All our Kindred, All Living things, See this one who has
fallen,
See this one who lately walked the earth (or flew through
the air)
And busied itself with (food, song, love, play, plants,
trees, water.)
All our Family, take this one to the earth. Hold this one in
the family.
Do not let it be out of life long.
All our Kindred, hold this one.

SEED PODS TO CARRY AROUND WITH YOU: from Luther Standing Bear: *The old people came to love the soil and sat or reclined on the ground with a feeling of being close to a mothering power. It was good to touch the earth and the old people liked to remove their moccasins and walk with bare feet on the sacred earth. That is why the old Indian still sits upon the earth to come closer in kinship to other lives around.*

And from Genesis 8:22—*While the earth remains, seedtime and harvest, cold and heat, summer and winter, day and night, shall not cease.*

LAST QUARTER *PINK* TO NEW *FLOWER* MOON

Be a gardener. Dig a ditch, toil and sweat, and turn the earth upside down and seek the deepness and water the plants in time. Continue this labor and make sweet floods to run and noble and abundant fruits to spring. Take this food and drink and carry it to God as your true worship.

From Julian of Norwich

May 4, 1886, Haymarket Square riots in Chicago in which 11 people were killed and 100 others wounded at a rally promoting an 8-hour work day.

May 6, 1961, a minimum wage was finally set. How much? A dollar and a quarter an hour.

May 10 is the anniversary of the inauguration of Nelson Mandela as president of South Africa; also the feast day of St. Job, one of several Old Testament figures who were declared saints retroactively. Job is invoked against depression and ulcers, for reasons apparent to anyone who remembers what Job purportedly endured.

May 11 is the anniversary of Bob Marley's death in 1981.

May 12 is Yogi Berra's birthday. "If he were alive today, he'd be rolling over in his grave."

NAUTRAL EVENTS: The heart of earth is beginning to beat faster as the ground warms up and the buds begin to swell. The sun draws up the sap from the deep wet roots into the buds as the days get longer and green tissue begins to swell into birth. The grass begins to push up green and rich.

One of the unpleasantries of preparing the garden for planting is the turning up, and often injuring, of so many earthworms, "the intestines of the earth," as Aristotle called them. Their ceaseless digging and burrowing and their hardy digestive system make the soil what it is. What we call topsoil is made up primarily of worm castings. They alternately fascinate and repel. The fascination is in their smooth shape and energetic motion and their subterranean existence. The repulsion is in their function as composters of all life, including ourselves eventually.

The earthworm's natural enemies are mice, moles, voles, fishermen and birds like the grackle, crow and robin often seen with head cocked to the side watching and listening for their motion. Perhaps robins love the rain so much—even sing a particularly pretty song in the rain—because it drives the worms up out of the ground.

Charles Darwin studied earthworms all his life, and his last book was devoted to them. He wrote, "The plough is one on the most ancient and valuable of man's inventions; but long before it existed the land was in fact regularly ploughed, and still continues to be thus ploughed by earthworms. It may be doubted whether there are many other animals which have played so important a part in the history of the world, as have these lowly . . . creatures."

UN-NATURAL EVENTS: Spreading petroleum-based fertilizer on the grass so it will grow faster so we can cut it more often with a petroleum-powered mower. The voice of the lawn-mower is heard in the land. Why is this an un-natural event? Ask any grazing animal how they feel about a gas-guzzling, smoke-blowing machine devouring the new, sweet, tender

Spring grass. If you've ever seen the cows let out to pasture for the first time in the Spring, you know what I mean.

Also, designer garden tools, like that silver trowel for $125.00.

WILD SPECULATION: Think of all the fresh local vegetables you could buy for $125 and still have enough left over for a new trowel.

RANK OPINION: New England tradition says plant your peas by Patriot's Day, April 19, but it doesn't necessarily help to get your peas in all that early. If it's warm and dry they slow down for lack of moisture. If it's warm and wet they get moldy. If it's cold and dry they die. If it's cold and wet they freeze.

FIELD & FOREST REPORT: Some green tip on early apple buds, not too late to do your dormant oil spray unless you see a half-inch green. It is a hard truth of Mom Nature that as soon as the leaves of the fruit trees, wild and domestic, begin to unfurl she hatches out the Eastern tent caterpillar to emerge with a big appetite! Fiddleheads are up and the Canada Mayflower leaves are up but still curled.

MOUNTAIN REPORT: Last Friday on the mountain we were swept up in snow flurries, but this week we startled three snakes sunning themselves in different places. Or should I say they startled us? Two looked like garter snakes, though differently marked. One was very smooth, small and brown. A brown snake. From the summit we could see the clumps of aspen showing a pale green. The lupine leaves are emerging rapidly, many with a crystal drop of water in their center. The jewel in the lotus.

SALTWATER REPORT: Fishing boats leaving the harbor before dawn. Some pleasure boats are being returned to their moorings in the Bay and canoes and kayaks are venturing out. Cormorants—sometimes called "shags" or "fish crows"—are fishing in the Blue Hill Falls. Maybe cormorants are crows that took to the water just as seals are dogs that took to the water eons ago, or maybe crows are land shags and dogs are land seals.

CRITTERS OF THE WEEK: The mockingbirds and cardinals, both were originally southern birds but they've found a niche in our northern climate. They are hardy and opportunistic. Of course, our kind did the same, originating in warm climates, moving into some of the coldest. The mockingbirds are still summer visitors, but the cardinals are now year 'round.

SEED PODS TO CARRY AROUND WITH YOU: from Susan Griffin, *We know ourselves to be made from this earth. We know this earth is made from our bodies. For we see ourselves. We are nature. We are nature seeing nature. We are nature with a concept of nature. Nature weeping. Nature speaking of nature to nature.*

And from Annie Dillard: *It is the best joke there is, that we are here, and fools—that we are sown into time like so much corn, that we are souls sprinkled at random like salt into time and dissolved here, spread into matter, connected by cells right down to our feet, and those feet likely to fell us over a root or jam us on a stone. The joke part is that we forget it. Give the mind two seconds alone and it thinks it's Pythagoras.*

*Believe not half you hear; and how to believe of what you
read in the newspaper is not in my power to tell or imagine in
these wild party times.* Old Farmer's Almanac 1806

May 14, 1923, Flogging was abolished in Florida labor
camps.

May 16, birthday of Liberace. After someone accused Liberace of being gay, the pianist said, "I cried all the way to the
bank." Also the birthday of Studs Terkel, social commenta-
tor, leftist and bon vivant.

NATURAL EVENTS: These days the good orchardist is repeating a familiar litany describing the delicate dance of apple
buds unfurling, as follows:

Silver tip, green tip,
Quarter- to half-inch green,
Mouse's ear, tight cluster,
Early pink, pink, late pink,
Bloom, late bloom, and petal-fall.

'Silver tip' is the first swelling of the buds as the sap rises
and the tight brown bud scales relax. 'Green tip' is the first
emergence of that pale vernal leaf tissue. 'Quarter- and half-
inch green' are the first pushing out of embryonic leaves.
'Mouse's ear' is when two tiny leaves about the size of a
mouse's ear peel away from the buds and spread themselves
to the sun. 'Tight cluster' is the time when the immature
flower buds, still clumped together like tiny hatchlings in the
nest, appear from under the unfolding new leaves. 'Early
pink' is the time when the pointed flower buds have separated

from each other and are beginning to open and show a bit of color. At 'late pink,' the buds are round, with the pink petals still closed over their delicate inner parts. At 'bloom,' the petals have opened widely into a perfumed bowl and turned white, revealing their hidden inner parts: pistils and stamens, and releasing their haunting fragrance, calling the bees to begin their work. At 'late bloom,' the bees have gone, the petals relax and begin to bend away from the center where the fertilized ovary begins to swell; a tiny green apple. Then, the petals fall away in the breeze to the ground in a snowy shower of fullness.

As a lover knows each tiny change in the countenance of the beloved—each expression of the face, each flush of the cheeks or flash of the eye—so the lover of apple trees watches in rapture each change in its buds and blossoms.

Lilacs are showing some color. Shad bloom is beginning in some warmer locations. If you find the web nests of the Eastern Tent Caterpillar in your fruit trees, I'd prune them out and burn them, harsh as it sounds. Toxic sprays won't penetrate the webs anyway. Most birds have settled down to nesting.

UN-NATURAL EVENTS: Sign on the lawn of a local business next door. "Keep children and pets off. Lawn pesticides in use."

RANK OPINION: Lawns are of little enough use anyway, but if children and pets can't play on them, what earthly good are they? What's wrong with some dandelions in the grass anyhow? Dandelion greens are good to eat and children can enjoy playing the "do-you-like-butter?" game, making chains with the stems and blowing the seeds around. Poison lawns, heaven help us.

WILD SPECULATION: Just as bacteria quickly become resistant to antibiotics, insects quickly become resistant to pesticides. We will either put more and more billions into antibiotics and pesticides in an escalating war against so-called undesirable species, making medicine and agriculture ever more expensive, or we will learn natural controls and natural medicine. This knowledge is available at a fraction of the cost.

FIELD & FOREST REPORT: Now we can watch the procession of hardwood trees bringing forth their leaves like the banners of the bands and scout troops in the Memorial Day parade— only the trees move much more slowly. Our Memorial Day parade is so short they turn it around and march it back through town. At the head of the tree troops are the willows and poplars. The poplars are beginning to display their small heart-shaped translucent green leaves at this writing. The red maples and elms are just losing their flowers now and their leaf buds are beginning to open. The Norway maples are just coming into bloom, and the sugar maples are right behind. Bringing up the end of the march are the oaks whose buds are just beginning to expand and have not opened yet. Last of all are the white and brown ash which show hardly any sign of life yet. Now, this is here in Blue Hill by the water. Inland the trees may have progressed farther in their march through Spring.

MOUNTAIN REPORT: There is so much to report from the mountain, after so little to report for the past several months. We could say that the largest living creature around here has come alive in the last few days. Like a gigantic bear coming out of hibernation, Awanadjo is stirring herself as the heat of the sun begins to warm her flanks. See the tiny Bluets (or "Quaker Ladies", as my mother used to call them) and blue violets in bloom. Canada mayflowers are up and the green blossom stalk is visible. Fiddleheads are up. The buds are swelling on blueberry bushes and insects (yup, including blackflies) are active when the sun is warm, yet there is still a pocket of dull gray winter ice in the cavity left by a blown-down spruce on the north side of the summit. In the little pool in the Wisdom Woods, only a stone's throw from the summit, soft clouds of salamander eggs like tapioca with dark spots float in the cool water. Awanadjo is reborn.

SACRED MOUNTAIN is Mount Taylor near Albuquerque, the sacred mountain of the south for the Navajo. This mountain has suffered a horrible desecration. It has been poisoned by uranium mining, a prison has been built on its slopes, and a ski resort is planned near its summit. As we do to our sacred places, so we do to our selves.

CRITTER OF THE WEEK: The blackfly. Along with winter, the blackfly is a test of the extreme hardiness and tough condition of Mainers. We shall not be moved. I imagine that if the Earth is depopulated by cold or heat or epidemic or other disasters, natural or un-natural, our globe will eventually be repopulated from pole to pole by Mainers, bean suppers, rubber boots and all. Think of it!

SEED PODS TO CARRY AROUND WITH YOU: from Crowfoot, orator of the Blackfoot nation, born 1821. *What is life? It is the flash of a firefly in the night. It is the breath of a buffalo in the winter time. It is the little shadow that runs across the grass and loses itself in the sunset.*
And from a Northern Cheyenne Ghost Dance Song. *The earth has come, the earth has come. It is rising, it is rising. It is humming, it is humming.*

*Just being in the woods at night, in the cabin, is something
too excellent to be justified or explained.*
From Thomas Merton

May 17, 1873, the first Kentucky Derby was run.

May 20, 1932, Amelia Earhart first woman to fly solo across
the Atlantic.

NATURAL EVENTS: *"Birds make their nests in circles,"* says
Black Elk, *"for theirs is the same religion as ours."* Much
nesting is going on these days. The bird's nest may be the
most remarkable creation of any animal, with the possible
exception of the electric kitty litter box. The oriole's nest is
like a hanging basket. The robin's is like a clay pot. I keep a
robin's nest on my mantle to admire its craft and beauty.
Once I found a nest that had a long fish-line, complete with
hook, woven in. I remember a kill-deer who built her nest on
the ground not ten feet from the road into a big construction
project in West Concord, Massachusetts. Kind workmen
built a fence around it with a DO NOT DISTURB sign on it.
Day after day the brooding kill-deer sat while huge dusty
dump-trucks thundered past. She steadfastly hatched and
raised her young 'til they could fly. Then she left . . . probably
for a long quiet vacation.

The other day while sitting on the kitchen stoop in the
warm and welcome afternoon sun, the plaintive cooing of a
mourning dove [*Zenaidura macroura*] came to my ear and
the thought came to me, "How wonderful—this beautiful
creature—utterly meek, yet utterly self-sufficient—whose
purpose in the world is all its own." Its purpose is not to be a
hawk or an eagle or a chicken. Its purpose is not even to feed

the hawks, though a hawk may drop upon it from the sky at any moment and the dove may explode into a cloud of feathers and become food for the hawk. The purpose of the mourning dove is not to provide Biblical writers with a paradigm for peace or innocence or the Holy Spirit, even though doves may appear peaceful, innocent and spiritual. Nor is the purpose of the dove to provide an example of love, though doves do display spousal affection as they waddle in pairs in the dust or sit billing and cooing in the sheltering branches. Nor is the dove's purpose to serve the human race, as we once thought was the purpose of all creatures; though strangely we chose to exempt ourselves from that purpose by doing things that served neither the human race nor any other creatures. Remember what we did to the Passenger Pigeon, lost cousin to the mourning dove? Nor, apparently, is the purpose of the mourning dove to determine what its purpose in the world is, as so many of our species are inclined in anguish to ponder endlessly. No, the purpose of the mourning dove is *all and entirely its own* and will forever be a mystery to us, and to our children's children. At least, that is what I hope.

These were my thoughts. Was I in the sun too long?

RANK OPINION: Each creature has reasons to be here as good and sufficient as our reasons. No more proof is needed than that they are here—and we—all brought into being by a Higher Cause.

WILD SPECULATION: If, as we try to do with them, the doves should try to determine the purpose of humans on the earth, it would doubtless be that we should be more like them: peaceful, innocent, spiritual, and loving—and, by the way, that we should put a little more sunflower seed out on the grass, please.

ANOTHER RANK OPINION: Perhaps you heard a comment by Maine's governor. *"So much of our economy,"* he said, *"is dependent on the environment."* Right you are, Governor. I'm still waiting for someone to discover something, anything, anywhere that is *not* dependent on the environment.

FIELD & FOREST REPORT: Violets, bluets, trailing arbutus, dandelions are in bloom. Lupine leaves are the size of a four-year-old's hand. Leaves are emerging on birches, red maples, wild cherries and early apples. Some white-crowned sparrows gathered at our bird feeder. To me they look like any other small brown bird, but wearing a cheerful black and white striped cap. According to Peterson's field guide, they're probably headed North to the edge of the tundra where the trees grow stunted and then disappear.

Robins love these rainy days, and stalk about in the grass while most other birds seek shelter. Water is central to their religion, which is the same as Black Elk's. Come to think of it, water is important to all religions and their practioners. Just watch the robins baptize in a puddle. They even sing a "rain hymn" when the sky gets dark and a shower begins to roll in.

MOUNTAIN REPORT: Often the summit of Awanadjo is draped in fog these mornings. A couple of days ago the whole mountain was smothered in fog so thick one couldn't see even a hundred yards. The trail led up into invisibility. But with each step ahead, more of the trail was revealed, just enough so that we could know our general direction and enjoy our immediate surroundings. Thick fog was dripping off the trees, so that in the woods it seemed to be raining, while out in the open it was not. Half of a white egg-shell about the size of a thimble lay in the trail filling with water. Raggedy ravens floated on the wind with feathers missing and beaks full of straw.

There's fire on the mountain this week as one of humankind's oldest agricultural practices is repeated hereabouts with the burning of the blueberry fields. The blueberry is a very hardy little bush, surviving the intense cold of sub-arctic to arctic regions and seeming to flourish in burned-over areas. It is easy to imagine how our ancient forebears in these parts noticed an increase in the yield of blueberries after a natural wild-fire swept through, and so decided to undertake their Spring burning of the barrens some thousands of years ago. The fires incinerate competing grasses and shrubs, exterminate insects that may damage the blueberries, and add minerals to the soil. The old way was to gather all available manpower to spread combustible straw or other materials over the barrens and wait for the right wind and weather conditions before setting the fire. Even still, the fires sometimes went out of control and the occasional house or barn added its ashes to the soil. Nowadays, a huge flame-spouting dragon-machine burning hundreds of gallons of fuel oil is pulled behind a tractor over the barrens, scorching everything. Yet the hardy blueberry bushes, with their tender buds already swelling, somehow survive the conflagration. Field studies indicate that burning surpasses mowing for increasing yield, and often equals or surpasses the use of pesticides for controlling weeds and insect pests. From the top of Awanadjo these days, many such fires can be seen in all directions and the spicy smell of burning leaves fills the air.

CRITTERS OF THE WEEK: The amphibians. Frog, toad and salamander eggs floating in still vernal pools. Spring peepers sounding their cheerful whistles in the cool evening.

SEED PODS TO CARRY AROUND WITH YOU: A hymn of mine for late April in Maine to any 8.7.8.7. meter like *Stuttgart* in the old hymnals:

Though the icy mist of winter, lingers on, will not forgive,
Though the chilly days may hinder; like the eagle, we will
live.
Though the shades of old still haunt us, day and night
without relief,
Though the fleeting sun may taunt us, like the raven, we
will live.
Though our fears and doubts assail us, in our struggle to
believe,
Though our vision sometimes fails us, like the coyote, we
will live.
Though the cruel world displease us; war, disease, no
comfort give,
Though I'm crucified like Jesus, I may die, but we will
live.
Eagle, raven, coyote, Jesus; timeless resurrection give.
Sing your song that it may seize us. We, beloved; we will
live.

PERICOPES

An intimate connection exists between ourselves, our lives, and our environment, the bay, the brooks, the rocks, the mountain, the soil. We are highly privileged to live in a place where we can feel this connection so deeply, in our blood and our lungs, and the very marrow of our bones.

Wendell Berry, poet, farmer, and professor at the University of Kentucky says, "Our land passes in and out of our bodies, just as our bodies pass in and out of our land." The power and the glory of the bit of earth upon which we live is not simply to be taken and used as a resource, but preserved. The congregation of the faithful is called to the preservation of a just, righteous relationship with each other and the land. This is health, this is wholeness, this is salvation—not some pie in the sky when we die.

One of the things that so many of us like about small-town life is that it is rooted in agricultural values. At one time, our village derived its income and its sustenance from the land and water around. Now, the economy of our town is dependent less on local resources and more on money from far away. It is often easier to get grapes or potatoes or apples or milk from another county or another state or even another country, than it is to get food grown in our own town. The best practices of agriculture which were evolved over thousands of generations of farmers, approximate as closely as humans are able to do, the values inherent in life within the Creation. These values are not dependent on time or place, but hold true on Earth in all times and places. Agricultural truth is a reflection—not perfect, but a reflection—of Divine Truth.

Whatever our view of the causes of the present environmental crisis, it is clear that we have reached the limits of the Old Testament Dominion/Stewardship covenant with the earth by which we humans decide how the earth is to be used. It's past time to move to a new model of covenant with the earth. Ecology teaches that in living systems, we cannot do just one thing. What is done to one part of the biota—no matter how seemingly insignificant—affects the whole. Surprisingly, a New Testament "Eucharistic" model teaches the same truth. Every drop of water is the blood of Christ. Every clump of dirt is the body of Christ. Whatever we do to the least of these [Matthew 25:31ff] in Creation we do to God, and to ourselves. Every creature, every thing is sacred. Ecology and faith here join hands.

What does it mean to serve the Creation as the Body of

God? It means that we do not tell the Creation what to do, anymore than we tell God what to do. The Creation tells *us* what to do. The Creation becomes the teacher and prophet and apostle. "The Word of God is the Creation we behold," wrote Tom Paine in *The Age of Reason*. The continuing revelation comes, not from Scripture alone, but from Scripture *and Nature*, John Scotus Erigena's "Two Shoes of Christ." In this view, science and religion become partners instead of adversaries in the search for the whole, the healthy, the holy.

We and all creatures are members of one body—God's. We are never alone. Never apart. Never lost. Never forgotten. Never wasted. Never thrown away. We are being invited into the life of the whole Creation. Not to dominate it, but to love it. Some may say this is too mystical and abstract, too far out to experience. *It is not.* Walk around in wood or field. Lie down on the ground and look at the sky. Plant something and watch it grow. Buy locally-grown food: we are so fortunate to have plenty of productive small farms on our peninsula. Keep learning the names of plants, birds, animals and call them by their names. See how quickly they are brought back into the greater life when they die. Understand how they die so others might live. Come to the old burying ground and see how the oak trees have thrust their roots deep into the graves of our forebears, drawn the dead up into leaves and nuts and wood and water vapor and returned them to the world of life. Resurrected, they are. Just like Christ. And us. That is all. Amen.

[The following is from the service for young Andrew Collier who died in a canoe accident Memorial Day weekend, 2000.]

When the young die, as two have in our towns recently, we may feel a kind of cold dread; that the world is out of balance, the center is not holding. Or worse, we may feel that the spirit of the universe is a cruel and perverse spirit who brings us into a cold world of pain only to hurt us over and over again. Or, we may conclude that we live in a world without feeling, passion or desire—a soul-less, mechanistic world governed by mathematics and physics; and that our deepest feelings of pain and sorrow, or joy and hope are simply meaningless neuro-chemical reactions crossing our synapses.

Or, I suppose, we might conclude that tragedies are simply the mysterious will of God and not to be questioned, but simply passively accepted.

But, none of these explanations will do. They will not do, because the very grief that cries out from our bodies emphatically refutes and denies them. These tears are real, not imaginary. The pain belongs to us, just as we belong to the universe. They are all real. We are fashioned by the universe out of love for the purpose of loving. And that is why we cry. If we did not feel love, then we would not feel loss, then we would not feel pain. This is real.

You could say that we live at the meeting of love and physics. God cannot miraculously repeal the laws of physics to save humans from pain, no matter how good those humans might be. But that does not mean there are no miracles. Light, gravity, water, life, love and music are miracles.

In the face of tragedy we are staggered and shaken by what seems like the terrible absence of meaning. For a time, everyone stumbles along as if by rote. This has to be done; that has to be done. Some have strong religious beliefs. Others have none. But comforting words are exchanged, hands are held, tears spilled, doors opened, plans made, food and flowers brought.

As we watch, the absence of meaning begins to fill. Not with answers, but with love: the one sure remedy for pain and suffering in a world of many different answers. And that love is poured forth in abundance. You can feel the healing going on as shattered souls begin the long process of knitting themselves back together. Death doesn't come to an end, but it doesn't win, either. Today, death has again lost the attempt to dominate Life, as it always will in the presence of Love. That is the miracle: the patient application of love counteracts death, and makes even death itself surrender and give over to love.

As time passes, we will begin to notice that Andrew left us some things—a memory, an object, some words, an image of him—things that we might not have seen for what they were until now: gifts that we might not have even known he gave us. For his parents and his brother he left so much that they already know he will never cease being a part of their family. For the rest of us, he left many or a few things that will glow brightly in us through time.

Transformed by his passing, the commonplace things Andrew left with us now become treasures. They become touchstones, talismans that we can carry around with us. They gain a power to change us and heal us as we re-collect them and review them day after day. These simple treasures that he gave us will continue to capture and hold the love we have for him and he for us. In time, if we hold onto it, this love will transform these mementos and memories into concrete evidence, actual proofs, that love overcomes death. In this universe where love meets physics, death is an ending. But love is patient. And love, like the universe, never ends.

That's the almanack for this moon, but don't
take my word for it.
Go out and see for yourself.

This is the Awanadjo Almanack for the Full *Flower* Moon to the Full *Rose* Moon [also called *Strawberry* or *Hot* Moon], *Irnivik* or *Animals Give Birth* Moon to the Eskimos, *Sivan* in Biblical Hebrew, and May/June in Downeast Maine

FULL TO LAST QUARTER *FLOWER* MOON

Look you out northeastwards, over mighty ocean, teeming with sea life; home of seals, sporting splendid, its tide has reached fullness.

Translated from the Gaelic by James Carney

May 22, Birthday of painter Mary Cassatt, 1845. Anniversary of the Great Train Robbery in Canada, 1868.

May 24, Birthday of Bob Dylan.

May 27, Birthday of Isadora Duncan.

May 29, Birthday of Patrick Henry, John F. Kennedy and Bob Hope.

May 30, Memorial Day. Around here we visit the cemeteries and commune with the departed for a while. Also the birthday of our daughter Sarah Morgan McCall Wass, 1968

NATURAL EVENTS: We are constantly amazed at the striking events which play out before our eyes when we wander the mountain, woods and fields with open heart and no expectations. The Creation seems to utter truth in these moments without speech or language. The creatures are the words, the symbols, the characters of each statement. But not everyone will learn to read it.

My father was born in 1913 in Akita, Japan in the Northwest snow country of the island of Honshu. I have an almanac from that town. Here are some natural events from the *Akita Almanac* by Nobutaro Aiba. *Flowers on plums cherries, peaches and pears begin to blossom at a time. Next young buds shoot forth on every tree and they gradually turn green. Hills are crowded with those picking mountain vegetables. Farmers worship "Otaue-no-kami" praying for the good harvest. It may be fairly said that for the people who live in snow for nearly half a year, so-called a visit of spring means just as if they were revived and re-born, and this refreshing idea proceeds to a hope that fills their hearts with bright spirits and their bodies with activities.*

Our neighbor reports that he and his children were watching a pair of mourning doves doing the sarabande of Spring on the roof when suddenly a middling-sized hawk plummeted from the sky striking one of the doves in an explosion of feathers. Predator and prey rolled down the roof to the ground. The hawk flew away with the dove in its talons. The next morning the family noticed only one dove on the roof, mourning. The next time they looked, however, there were two doves again, and the dance had resumed.

UN-NATURAL EVENTS: Wild animal rehabilitators report that 75-80% of injured animals brought for help at this time of the year are the young of wild animals—birds, raccoons, squirrels—injured by domestic cats. There is no law requiring that cats be under control of owner as with dogs. Personal responsibility is crucial here. If you find an injured wild animal, call a vet who can refer you to a rehabilitator. If you discover a nest with young but no adult, do not disturb it. Do you know where your cat is? If you let your cat roam, be aware that it may be doing dire damage.

FIELD & FOREST REPORT: Blueberries are in bloom and the bees are in the blueberry fields. The Shadbush or Juneberry, sometimes called highbush blueberry or even Serviceberry, is in bloom with fine white blossoms tinged with copper. Pears are in bloom with apples coming on soon. Hummingbirds and catbirds are in residence. Other birds are busy nesting. Cherry, including wild cherry, are also in full bloom. Lilac buds are deep purple and beginning to bloom in warmer places in time for Memorial Day. Four-lobed flowers of bunchberry, the dogwood of the boreal forest, are appearing on the borders of the woods. Wild strawberries are in bloom nestling close to the ground. Now is the time to note the location of wild strawberry patches for later picking of these perfect tiny fruit that pack ten times the ambrosiac sweetness of those huge, pulpy supermarket mutants. They will be much harder to find when the blossoms are gone. Wild strawberry patches are often closely guarded family secrets. Lupine leaves are nearly full-sized and some blossom stalks beginning to emerge like an upright bunch of green grapes. The leaves of the lupine, like the blossoms, vary in color.

MOUNTAIN REPORT: Rain and fog one day, bees and black-flies the next. Look for the *Rhodora* wild azalea in bloom in secret places soon. Canada Mayflower in bloom, Star flower fallen from the sky onto green mats of moss, Blue-eyed grass peeping out in a few places, buds swelling on spruces under ruddy, translucent bud scales still intact. We did a wedding on the mountain this season a few years back. Just before the ceremony began, a rooster crowed in the woods. Searching, we found it perched in a spruce tree. Seems a good omen, crowing a new day.

SACRED MOUNTAIN of the Week is Hlidskjalf, the mythical mountain home of Odin, chairman and CEO of the Norse gods.

SALTWATER REPORT: Harbor seal pups may be found on the shore at this time of the year, appearing to be in trouble when they are not. They should be left in place, according to those experienced with marine mammals. Once someone picks them up they really are in trouble. Kayakers should avoid passing closer than 100 yards of ledges where seals may be raising young. Such disturbance can disrupt the mother/young bond. If you find a seal pup on the beach, let it be.

On Memorial Day, as well as going to the local cemetery one might do well to go to Kollejedjwok, the Blue Hill Falls, and pay respects to the Red Paint People who were buried there before the time of Moses, and some of whose bones remain. This site is still a cemetery and deserves the same respect as any other holy ground.

CRITTER OF THE WEEK: The curious harbor seal. These friendly creatures will steal up behind us when we paddle our kayak on the bay and startle us with a loud splash. Sometimes they rise out of the water with whiskers dripping and stare curiously with enormous dark eyes, so silently that we can hear their breathing.

PILGRIM'S JOURNAL: Sitting on the small glacial rock on the very summit of the mountain, I spotted some bones in the grass, apparently a deer pelvis and femur. Thinking to take them home, I tucked them into my wool shirt, then felt an eerie shiver from head to toe telling me they were not mine and should remain where they are. I placed them carefully back on the ground. Then dog and I scrambled down over the cliffs past the porcupine's cave.

As we neared the base of the cliffs, a bright, bushy red fox dashed down the mountain about a hundred yards ahead of us. Quoddy did not see her, for which I was greatly relieved, but before long we got down to the Abnaki path and soon we crossed Sis Fox's trail. Instantly, Quoddy picked up the scent and bounded off nose to ground. I did not worry about the fox, knowing she would easily bewilder a domestic dog, but wondered when I would ever see Quoddy again. While I wondered, I glanced up the mountain to my left and saw another creature watching me. It looked like a small cat. "Whose kitty would have come all the way up here, and especially so young?" I asked myself. Then another identical creature popped up its little head, then two more, and I realized I was being watched by a den of attentive fox kits—all buff-colored with black tips, and quite young. Now I knew why the fox had raced so visibly across the trail in front of us. I retreated slowly and quietly to a safe distance to watch the kits roll and wrestle in the sun.

After a while I heard the joyful bark of Ol' Sis Fox in the woods to the West along the state trail and knew Quoddy was being led on a merry chase. After what seemed like hours, he came dragging and panting down the mountain nearly tripping over his own tongue. He flopped himself down panting in some standing water to cool off while his sides heaved. Sis Fox had led Mr. Quoddy way down the mountain, around to the West, then up over the summit, then, after a couple of miles or more, back down to the trail again within a short distance of the den. She out-foxed him. He never even saw the kits. As Quoddy and I proceeded down the mountain I glimpsed them a few more times over my shoulder and was overwhelmed with a vision of Spring as a time of birth—fox kits, seal pups, lambs, everything. Then, I had a vision of the whole mountainside wriggling with kit foxes in exuberant infant fertilitude.

SEED PODS TO CARRY AROUND WITH YOU: From Psalm 104, King James Bible: O Lord, how manifold are thy works! In wisdom hast thou made them all: the earth is full of thy creatures. So is this great and wide sea, wherein are things creeping innumerable, both small and great beasts . . . There is that Leviathan whom thou hast made to play therein.

From Chief Seattle to Governor Isaac Stevens, 1855—To us the ashes of our ancestors are sacred and their resting place is hallowed ground. You wander far from the graves of your ancestors and seemingly without regret. Your religion was written on tables of stone by the iron finger of your God so that you could not forget. Our religion is the traditions of our ancestors—the dreams of our old men, given them in the solemn hours of night by the Great Spirit, and the visions of our old ones is written in the hearts of our people. When the last Red Man shall have perished, these shores will swarm with the invisible dead of my tribe, and when your children's children think themselves alone in the field, the store, or in the silence of the pathless woods, they will not be alone.

LAST QUARTER FLOWER MOON

"Worlds can be found by a child and an adult bending down and looking together under the grass stems or at the skittering crabs in a tidal pool."   From Mary Catherine Bateson.

June 1, Birthday of Brigham Young, 1801.

June 2, Birthday of our son Daniel Sequoyah McCall, 1975. P.T. Barnum & Co. begin first tour, 1835.

June 4, founding of the Sierra Club, San Francisco, 1892.

June 5, Robert Kennedy assassinated, 1968; anniversary of the Big Blackout which left 40 million people in and around New York City in the dark for 10 hours. Methinks many still are.

Henry David Thoreau, the naturalist of Concord, wrote in his journal for this week in 1849: *Somewhat warmer at last, after several very cold, as well as windy and rainy days. Was soothed and cheered by I knew not what at first, but soon detected the now more general creak of crickets.* Jonathan Fisher wrote in his journal this week in 1797: *Worked on log fence . . . Finished fence. Wrote sermon. Mr. H. planted potatoes.*

NATURAL EVENTS: The bees are hard at work in the blueberry fields and orchards whenever the sun shines. The hives are rented from beekeepers for a period of time. Many of these hives travel "North with the Spring" from Florida to Maine, pollinating oranges, peaches and apples as they go. This practice unwittingly led to the destruction of most of Maine's—and the nation's—wild honey bees, as two forms of mite, first found in Florida in 1987 and deadly to bees, were spread throughout the country. Mites are not insects, but more closely related to spiders, and are resistant to most pesticides.

Twenty years ago when I was foreman in a large commercial orchard the bees arrived in a hundred decrepit hives patched together with tarpaper, wire and flattened tin cans by an old beekeeper named Louie who had an unpronounceable last name. He told us "it rhymes with 'unconscious'" so we called him "Louie Unconscious." We waited for a cool gray early May morning so that the bees would be inactive when we brought them in. Nowadays, the hives are strapped to pallets and moved by fork-lift, but in those days we put on heavy gloves and bee-nets over our heads and handled each hive by hand. Invariably one of those old hives would disintegrate while being lifted from Louie's decrepit truck; and the sleepy bees would switch immediately to attack mode, punishing us for our rudeness among the blissful, blooming apple trees.

I've often thought that the honeybee could be a model for creating world peace. Every soldier gets a gun that fires only once, and in both directions, so that to hurt another, the soldier must sacrifice his own life as the bees do.

When the hives were taken out of the orchard a couple of weeks later, a few orphans would always remain behind. They would return to the exact place where the hive had been and huddle there forlornly for days until they died, while I watched them helplessly. Honeybees need the hive, and cannot survive alone as can their cousins the hardy, self-sufficient bumblebees who make their peaceful and solitary way from flower to flower during the day and sleep under any convenient blossom at night. Unlike the honeybees, the bumblebees rarely sting, having no laid-up treasures to defend.

The native tent caterpillar has emerged from its egg case—a shiny dark brown dime-sized piece of hardened foam deposited in the Fall on the branches of fruit trees, especially wild cherries and apples. Upon hatching, the larvae are so tiny as to be almost invisible. During the first warm days, the newly-hatched caterpillars begin spinning a protective shelter of silk, coming out of their tent on warm days to begin feeding on the new leaves and returning to shelter at night and on cool days. The caterpillars from one nest can defoliate several branches of a tree as they grow to their full size of nearly three inches over the course of several weeks.

UN-NATURAL EVENTS: The gypsy moth caterpillar, sometimes mistakenly called "browntail" by the old timers, is a non-native insect from Europe which escaped into the wild from the entomology lab at Tufts University a century ago where it was being studied as a commercial producer of silk. The gypsy moth does not make a nest, but floats many miles from its hatching site on a long silk thread that catches the wind. Since its escape, it has spread to most Eastern states and into the Midwest and annually defoliates millions of acres of oak and other hardwoods. I can remember an infestation in the late 70s. Walking in the woods, the droppings of the gypsy moth were so abundant they sounded like rain falling through the trees. I was quite thankful for my hat at that time.

RANK OPINION: Using broad spectrum insecticides on caterpillars (and many other insects) is shooting yourself in the foot. The natural enemies of the marauding larvae are killed too, not to mention all the beloved butterflies and moths. Entomologists know that caterpillar populations rise, fall, and then crash naturally in cycles of 8-12 years. Spraying may delay or prevent the crash and so increase the damage they do. Also, these defoliators seem to attack the weaker trees, thus practicing a type of natural culling, improving the whole stand.

FIELD & FOREST REPORT: I don't know what got me started on lepidopterans (moths and butterflies), but the familiar yellow-and-black-striped Tiger Swallowtail butterfly emerges about this time and can be seen floating and feeding peacefully on nectar on warm days. They are harmless, as are most caterpillars, moths and butterflies, though the Tiger Swallowtail may now and then be found on carrion, including its own dead, showing that blood is as good as nectar to them.

Crickets are chirping in the fields when the sun shines. Like Thoreau, we are soothed and cheered by the sound. Lupine is just beginning to come into bloom in some places. Its rich varied color and peppery smell are a delight, and a trademark of downeast Maine. Lupine seems at the same time both wild and domestic. Also Blue-eyed grass winks in the meadows and along sunny footpaths.

MOUNTAIN REPORT: To be honest, the black flies have kept us off the mountain. They are tougher than we are. Of course, much of the torment they administer is psychological. They fly into your eyes, nose, mouth ears, and burrow into the back of your neck at the hairline. If you don't tuck your pants into your socks, you may later find a row of red dots around your leg where the little devils hid under the edge of your sock while they exacted their measure of your blood.

SALTWATER REPORT: Warmer winds over the water from the South bear the fragrance of lilacs in bloom. Seals, exuberant and protective of their young, follow our quiet wake curiously. Loons fly over the village very early in the morning, commuting from the fresh water ponds where they nest to the bay where they feed, calling from the air just as they do from the water. They are not graceful fliers, appearing to hurtle through the air as if flung from a catapult, yodeling all the while their wild calls.

CRITTER OF THE WEEK: The loon, voice of the Northern forests and shores, the great Northern diver, with a primitive fiery red eye and great fishing equipment, able to swim a quarter mile or more under water. Loons have strong family bonds with both male and female staying close to the one, two or three young all summer. The hatchlings scoot up onto the parent's back when an eagle or an osprey or a hungry seal threatens. Later in the season the family fishes at some distance from each other, hooting gently back and forth as a warning of danger or just to be reassured where each one is.

SEED PODS TO CARRY AROUND WITH YOU: from Robert Ingersoll, the great 19th century atheist: *In Nature there are neither rewards nor punishments—only consequences.*

NEW TO FIRST QUARTER *ROSE* MOON

June 6, Nathan Hale born, 1755.

June 9, Twenty-five pirates hanged in Boston 1704. And speaking of pirates, the IRS began withholding income taxes from paychecks on this day in 1943.

June 11, birthday of Jacques Cousteau. Mount Pinatubo erupted in the Philippines, 1991.

June 12, *Anne Frank: The Diary of a Young Girl,* published 1952. Medgar Evers assassinated, 1963.

NATURAL EVENTS: Bunchberry, our Northern dogwood, is spreading its beautiful ivory cruciform blossom to the sun. Along the roadsides Horsetail, sometimes called "pot rush" because its high silica content makes it good for scrubbing pots, is spreading its primitive fringed stalks as did its larger relatives in the age of the dinosaurs, long before any seed-bearing plants. Ferns, also seedless, uncurl their fronds.

Last week we heard from an early-rising neighbor that she

had seen a moose in the village. It came out from behind Weymouth Howard's house, crossed Union Street in front of her "as big as a horse", then walked over the brook and into the old cemetery where the town's founding mothers and fathers quietly rest. Our friend was alarmed at the sight of a moose only 100 yards from the town hall. The town founders, however, seemed to be quite unmoved by the experience.

The last few warm nights we have heard the portentous sound of something bumping against the window screens. This marks the arrival of the blood-curdling "Night of the June-bug" striking terror into the heart of my dear Rebecca and heroism into mine. These large beetles belong to the family of scarab beetles which include such charming creatures as Dung beetles, Tumblebugs, Skin beetles, Chafers, and the Rhinoceras, Hercules and Elephant Beetles. There are over 100 species of June bug in North America. They spend the winter as large white grubs underground and emerge in Spring. No more walking outside at night to enjoy the fragrance of lilacs lest one of these bugs be crunched underfoot. No more peace at night if even one of these creatures finds its way into the bedchamber, droning through the air and bumping into walls. Then, she disappears under the bed covers and then I must rise from rest and endeavor to capture the offending creature and dispose of it outside, even if it takes all night, or there will be no rest for anyone. In Becky's defense, let it be known far and wide that she has dauntlessly liberated many another bug and spider trapped in the house.

The peculiar anatomy of the June bug presents another dilemma to the tenderhearted. It seems to be grossly top-heavy and is often found on its back with its six legs waving helplessly in the air. If a Friend of Nature and part-time treehugger like myself comes upon a June bug in this condition, a serious ethical problem presents itself. Though I had nothing to do with this creature's unfortunate design which causes it to end up on its back, must I then upright it so that it may walk away today and tonight find its way into my bedroom to terrorize my beloved and ruin my repose? I leave this problem for greater ethical minds to resolve.

UN-NATURAL EVENTS: Plastic surveyor's tape, particularly in bright day-glo colors. Marking and measuring the land lead to division and defense of it as "private property." The land belongs to itself. There is nothing more jarring than bright glaring tape around an old tree. I have quite a tape collection at home. Perhaps you do too.

FIELD & FOREST REPORTS: Like his tiny charges, the beekeeper is busy. The beekeeper and the grower both hope for some warm sunny days in the 70s during the bloom so that the bees will get out and work the blueberry blossoms. If they do not, then there will be few blueberries for the grower and little honey for the beekeeper. Another fear of the beekeeper is that Bruin will be overcome by his raging sweet tooth and attack the hives. I've seen the sturdy wooden hives smashed to smithereens like matchboxes. One black bear was more delicate, neatly slipping the cover off one hive and partly removing one of the frames loaded with honey. Bruin comes in the cool of night so that the bees are nearly helpless to defend their treasure.

One June day I saw two men at the bottom of the blueberry fields on the South slope of Awanadjo, dressed in heavy clothes, gloves and bee-nets over their heads, repairing the hives and the electric fence the bear had breached. They were hanging strips of bacon over the electric fence hoping that, before raiding the hives, Bruin would first try to steal the bacon and get a poke in the nose not soon to be forgotten.

MOUNTAIN REPORT: Lupine bloom is underway on the South slopes of Awanadjo. Each year there seems to be more of it along the hillside above the meadow. The flowers are multicolored—from purple to blue to salmon to pink to ivory to white as well as bi-colored— showing great genetic variation, like Mendel's sweet peas, and like them, legumes which fix nitrogen, enriching the soil. Watching the bees work the lupine, we see something fascinating. The pollen-bearing anthers are quite hidden from sight, but the bee knows how to land on the lower lobe of the blossom so that its weight opens the flower and exposes the pollen. Try it yourself. Just push down on the lower lobe of the blossom, and watch the flower stick out its tongue.

SALTWATER REPORT: See the jelly fish floating in the water. We have two kinds around here. One is deep red-brown and as big as a dinner plate. The other is *Aurelia,* the moon jelly, clear with an etched four-part white outline within like the shape of a Celtic Cross. These are the ovaries. It is a wonder that this soft creature can survive the raging rigors of the sea. The jelly fish moves by opening and closing its body like an umbrella. They do sting. The word is that meat-tenderizer sprinkled on the sting will ease the pain.

CRITTER OF THE WEEK: The jellyfish.

SEED PODS TO CARRY AROUND WITH YOU: From the Old Farmer's Almanac, 1858: *June is the month of roses—and this reminds me of thorns; and, if we don't want thorns in our sides, we must make head and hands work well this month. Fishing may be fun, but the hoe handle must take the place of the fishing pole, if we want to sing merry tunes in harvest time.*

First Quarter to Full ROSE MOON

The rain falls upon the earth and grass and flowers come perfectly into form from its liquid.

From William Carlos Williams.

June 14, St. Basil's day in the Anglican church. (Could be pronounced Bazzil, Bayzil, or, as around here: Base-ul.) Basil the Great was born in 329 in Caesarea in what is now Turkey. He was a staunch opponent of the Arian "heresy" which held that Christ was not God. Basil is patron saint of Russia. In the Roman Church, however, it is St. Dogmael's day. It is also Flag Day, which is not a religious holiday (except for members of the flag cult).

June 17, Battle of Bunker Hill (fought on Breed's Hill), 1775.

June 20, the opening of the trans-Alaska pipeline. The 1798 Old Farmer's Almanac reports that "a wag advertised a carriage to perform without horses, with only one wheel, and invited the curious to see it. Many of the members of the society of the arts attended, and, in ardor of expectation, were shown—a wheelbarrow." Jonathan Fisher reports in his journal this week: "Spent most of the week planting potatoes. Had my barn raised."

Natural Events: Ample rain is a boon to the slugs that are native to our clime. They are mollusks, related to snails, clams, mussels, scallops and other shelled aquatic creatures, like the multi-colored sea-slug. I saw a big one on the mountain recently that reminded me of the legendary "banana slugs" of the Pacific Northwest which the natives of that region celebrate on T-shirts and baseball hats. I've seen the so-called "banana slugs" and the name is a gross exaggeration. They are definitely not as big as a full-grown banana. Maybe as big as a middle-sized banana, and they are yellow with black patches.

Our Maine slugs are smaller and brown, but no less fascinating. Legless, wingless, finless, they ooze along on their own road of slime at a snail's pace, their bodies rippling like water, their eyestalks shortening, lengthening, and waving in different directions with their eyes like glittering glass beads at the ends. Their silence is absolute. Their internal shell or carapace rests on the back where their shoulders would be if they had shoulders and looks slightly like a saddle or even a small pair of wings. They eat green leaves, as any gardener will tell you, but they also have one habit that I find repellent. They eat their own dead. If you step on one in the path, its remains will soon attract numerous others. Theological question: Is this wrong? But enough of slugs.

FIELD & FOREST REPORT: We are seeing more poison ivy in fields and on roadsides. Watch for three shiny, reddish leaves coming from the same point on the stem, also reddish. The widely accepted herbal remedy for the rash of poison ivy is Jewelweed which grows in wet shady places and is related to the *Impatiens*. Huckleberry bushes are in bloom now like tiny apple blossoms. The magenta Sheep Laurel is coming into bloom on slopes, field-edges and road-sides.

MOUNTAIN REPORT: Fog on Awanadjo this week. Fog is a cloud of water; as smoke is a cloud of fire, dust is a cloud of earth, and wind is a cloud of air. Doubt is a cloud of unknowing and faith is a cloud of hope.

SACRED MOUNTAIN of the Week is called "Denali" by the Koyukon people who live near it. Denali means the "High One." It is Alaska's and North America's highest mountain. On maps it is Mt. McKinley, but the native name has more power and gains wide acceptance.

SALTWATER REPORT: Floating on the bay in evening, total calm and cool air, loons echoing for miles on all sides, seals belching loudly and splashing around the ledges, minnows flashing, and deep indigo sea worms with soft pink spots floating, levitating gently a few inches below the surface. Everything seems to be aware of everything else and in silent communication. A mysterious, solitary, and yet very companionable time.

CRITTER OF THE WEEK: The hairy woodpecker found stunned in the street just inches from speeding cars. I put on heavy gloves for protection from its powerful, sharp beak and brought it home and wrapped a towel around it. After about two hours in the sun on the front porch, it raised its head, looked around and flew gladly into the nearest tree.

SEED PODS TO CARRY AROUND WITH YOU: From Red Hawk or "pipikwass," Abnaki woman poet: *Rabbit fur tufts, down feathers, a bird's ruff, dandelion's ghost, baby's hair, cat o' nine tails, floating on air.*

And from Walt Whitman: *I believe a leaf of grass is no less than the journey-work of the stars.*

PERICOPES

Soon the sun will reach its northernmost point in the sky; or more properly; the earth's axis will be tilted so that the

Northern hemisphere is closest to the sun—the Summer solstice. Now our nights are very short and our days very long. The robins start singing around 3:30 in the morning, and it is twilight until 9:00 at night. We move about in the light of the sun and let it drive the cold and dark of the winter out of our bones, letting the light soak into their marrow. Green plants rise toward the light and the daisies and sunflowers turn their faces following the sun's journey across the sky. Our hearts rejoice. Meanwhile, in the Southern hemisphere it is getting darker, winter is on its way, and the nights are at their longest.

The scripture passage from Genesis reads, "In the beginning God created the heavens and the earth. The earth was without form and void, and darkness was upon the face of the deep . . . And God said, 'Let there be light,' and there was light. And God saw that the light was good; and God separated the light from the darkness." God created both the darkness and the light. This echoes Isaiah 45:7: "I form light and create darkness, I make weal and create woe, I am the Lord, who do all these things." Here light is compared to wellness and dark is compared to woe. And in Genesis, God declared the light "good," giving the feeling that the darkness, even though God created it too, is not so good as the light.

The scripture from John echoes the creation account from Genesis and reads, "The light shines in the darkness and the darkness has not overcome it." There is a subtle implication here too that the light is good and the darkness is not so good, since it threatens to overcome the light.

The gospels talk about sinners being "cast into the outer darkness." Paul writes about the "works of darkness and the dominion of darkness," and asks, "What fellowship has light with darkness?" The author of I John writes, "God is light, and in him is no darkness." Christian mystics talk about "the dark night of the soul." The great English poet, John Milton, describes hell as a place of "no light, but darkness visible," a phrase that William Styron uses in his autobiographical account of his battle with depression.

This might suggest a legitimate question: "Are Christians afraid of the dark?" After thousands of years of hearing about the evil darkness, are we conditioned to see the darkness of night as worse than the light of day? Do we see dark-skinned people as worse than light-skinned people? Has our treatment of the darker races in the name of Jesus, the Light of the World, returned to haunt us in the night causing us to fear the dark? Do we fear what we will do to others as much as we fear what they will do to us?

Is light good and darkness evil? There are surely times when light can be evil. At the detonation of the first atomic bomb at Alamogordo on July 16, 1945, Robert Oppenheimer quoted the Bhagavad Gita, thus: "If the radiance of a thousand suns were to burst forth at once in the sky, that would be like the splendor of the Mighty One." When that diabolical radiance burst forth in the sky over Hiroshima it was the last light to be seen by more than 100,000 Japanese men, women and children instantly killed or blinded by the light. Each year in Hiroshima on the anniversary of that day, Buddhist, Shinto, and Christian priests read prayers, schoolchildren read poems, and survivors retell their stories. Near the epicenter, people fall to the ground in reenactment of that manmade cataclysm. As night falls, thousands of paper lanterns are lighted and set adrift on the Motoyasu River to be received into the gathering darkness.

And can the darkness be good? Surely, the darkness of the earth gives birth to the seed. The darkness of the womb gives birth to the creature. The dark night of the soul gives birth to the light of redemption. The night gives us our dreams. Before there was light, there was darkness. Darkness is the mother of light.

Is darkness good and light evil? No. Neither is darkness evil and light good. Day unto day uttereth speech, and night unto night shows forth knowledge. There is no speech nor are there words, but God's voice is heard. Darkness and light are mysteries.

To the artist, white light can be broken into all the colors of the rainbow, yet those same colors if applied together on canvas, create darkness. In the West, black is the color of death. In the East, the color of death is white.

To the scientist, light is the mystery of an energy form that travels faster than anything else in the universe, and behaves sometimes like a wave and sometimes like a particle: a motion or a thing, unlike any other event in the cosmos.

To the poet, light is the mystery of illumination both within and without—the light of the soul as well as the light of the sun. Light and darkness are external, physical phenomena, measurable by instruments. Light and darkness are also internal phenomena; invisible to the eye, but visible to the heart.

Yes, we are afraid of the dark. We fear that the darkness will overcome the light. So we try to dominate the darkness with light. We leave so many lights on at night that they blot out the stars because we fear darkness—the time and place where others will do unto us as we have done unto them. Yes, we need the light, but we need to overcome—not the darkness, but our fears of the darkness. We need the darkness, that quiet and still and protective place where the light can be conceived and the seed can grow in secret. We need the darkness. The light shall not overcome it.

After the Creation, God looked upon everything that had

been created and saw that it was good, both darkness and light, night and day; God created them all. Are we to take God's light only and refuse God's darkness? Are we take only joy, and refuse sorrow?

To God, darkness and light are all the same. "Whither shall I go from Your Spirit," says the psalmist, "or whither shall I flee from Your presence? If I say, 'Let only darkness cover me, and the light around me be night, even the darkness is not dark to You, the night is bright as the day and darkness is as light to You." [Psalm 139]

That's the almanack for this moon, but don't take it from me.
Go out and see for yourself.

This is the Awanadjo Almanack for the Full *Rose or Strawberry* Moon to the first Full Moon of Summer or *Buck* Moon [The *Buck* Moon is also called *Thunder* or *Hay* Moon], called *Inyukuksaivik* or *Birds Raise Their Young* Moon by the Eskimos, *Tammuz* in the Bible, and June/July in Downeast Maine.

FULL TO LAST QUARTER *ROSE* MOON

I wish all to know that I do not propose to sell any part of my country, nor will I have you cutting our timber along the rivers, more especially the oak . . . I love to look at them, because they endure the wintry storm and the summer's heat, and—not unlike ourselves—seem to flourish by them.

From Tatanka Yotanka or Sitting Bull.

June 24, the traditional Midsummer's Day. Why this name when summer is only beginning? Apparently the word "summer" is related through Indo-European ancestry to the Sanskrit "sama" which means "year or half-year" because it is halfway between planting and harvest. If it rains on this day, tradition says, the harvest will be wet. The church calls this day the Nativity of John the Baptist who, according to tradition was just half a year older than his cousin Jesus, born on December 25th.

June 25, 1876, the crushing defeat of General George "Armstrong" Custer and troops at the Little Big Horn or "Greasy Grass" by warriors under Sitting Bull and Crazy Horse. The news of this event reached the Eastern press at the same time the country was gearing up to celebrate its centennial on July 4, 1876, resulting in a furious outpouring of racial hatred and military might being unleashed against the Plains tribes, culminating in the massacre at Wounded Knee, South Dakota just after Christmas of 1890.

June 26, Abner Doubleday, father of baseball, born 1819.

NATURAL EVENTS: A world of lush green spotted by every living color and projected against a cloudless blue June sky creates a shudder of hope from head to toe. I've heard that the Arctic tundra blazes forth with an amazing array of flowers during its short growing season. Our growing season lasts a little longer; last frost in the Spring, maybe second week in May, first frost in the Fall, maybe late September. But we have an amazing array of flowers here today in the boreal fields and forests nearly half-way to the North Pole. Short life; blaze of glory; live fast, die hard.

Here's my census of current wildflowers, and I know I'm missing a lot—added three to my list just today. In the fields: White and red clover, yellow hockweed and its cousin Indian paintbrush, buttercup, yellow rattle, phlox, lupine, daisy, eyebright, blue flag or wild iris, yellow cinquefoil, raspberry and blackberry, dame's rocket, purple vetch, shepherd's purse, bluets still hanging on, meadow rue, chickweed, and sheep laurel; as well as the so-called "heliotrope" which does not appear in the books as such, but every Mainer knows it. It is wildly profuse around here with a hollow, fluted stalk up to 6 feet tall, and a heavy, sweet scent so strong that many people dislike it. In the forest: Bunchberry, several viburnums, nannyberry, lady's slipper, dogwoods, black locust [this is a blooming tree], meadow rue, columbine, and Jack-in-the-pulpit along streams and marshes. On the mountain: Three-toothed cinquefoil, pale corydalis, bird's-foot trefoil, still some Canada mayflower, and many of those mentioned above.

I'm telling you, it is luxuriant. The pale corydalis on the mountain is among the most amazing. Small, pale and unbearably spindly with a pink flower edged in yellow and less than an inch long; and with feathery leaves more gray than green; it looks like a tropical rainforest refugee which has chosen the thin, acid soil in the cracks of rocky ledges of Awanadjo at nearly 1000 feet above the bay for its home. It has to endure some of the wildest weather in these parts, yet comes back. I am baffled and humbled by its hardy strength.

FIELD & FOREST REPORT: Flamboyant and exotic columbine is in bloom in shady places, one of the most beautiful woodland flowers of Spring. The oak leaves are full-sized but still light green and translucent, and even the ash, last to leaf-out, is full-fledged. The apple trees are going through their annual "June drop" in which the smallest apples of each cluster are forced off the tree to lie tiny and yellow upon the ground. We needn't draw any needless conclusions about human society from this phenomenon. The apple trees know no other way. We do.

MOUNTAIN REPORT: Climbing the mountain the other day, I stopped to snap up my raincoat as a heavy shower started. A slate gray junco landed and hopped under a blueberry bush to get out of the rain, staying put as I walked very close by. Farther up the trail as I pushed a wet branch out of the way with my walking stick, a large moon-milk-raspberry-tinted moth fell to the ground in front of my feet from its dry perch under the leaves. Its pale luminescence stood out dramatically in the gray rain. Gently picking it up, I put it in the shelter of a log and placed a little roof of bark over it.

The lupine is in full bloom turning several acres of the south face of Awanadjo into a profusion of purple-to-pink-to-white, bee-buzzing, peppery-smelling wonder: a waist-high jungle. Climbing the mountain these days is like climbing from first heaven, through all the succeeding heavens, until reaching the seventh.

SACRED MOUNTAIN OF THE WEEK is Bear Butte, just east of the Black Hills in South Dakota. Sacred to both the Sioux and the Cheyenne. Crazy Horse is said to have received vision there.

SALTWATER REPORT: Just below the low-tide line the five-pointed star fish inches along to find a mussel it can pry open with its powerful arms. Deeper in the water lies the sea-urchin with its sharp green spines disguising its five point-designed shell.

CRITTERS OF THE WEEK: All five-pointed creatures, from apples (just slice through horizontally to see the five-pointed star) to urchins to star-fish to stars and beyond.

SEED PODS TO CARRY AROUND WITH YOU: From Crazy Horse— *Now you tell us to work for a living, but the Great Spirit did not make us to work, but to live by hunting. You . . . can work if you want to. You say, 'Why do you not become civilized?' We do not want your civilization!*

Consider the lilies of the field, how they grow. They neither toil nor spin, yet even Solomon in all his glory was not arrayed like one of these.

—From the Sermon on the Mount.

June 30, 1859, Emile Blondin crossed Niagara Falls on a tight-rope

July 1, Canada Day, Prince Edward Island became a province, 1873.

July 2, Birthday of Thurgood Marshall, 1908. Amelia Earhart disappeared, 1937.

July 3, Dog Days begin. Birthday of George M. Cohan, 1878.

NATURAL EVENTS: A love letter to Lupine, which is now going by all too soon:

Dear Lupine,
The keen anticipation of watching your first leaves grow from the size of a newborn's hand to their full dimensions, the fascination of watching the small, pale green flower spikes appear then get larger, open, and turn color to pink, red, white, cream, but mostly purple conical stalks of nearly a foot in length, and the pleasure of smelling your heavy peppery scent is fading now. You are one of the first glories of approaching summer, Lupine. But more, you are a benefit to the earth as well as a boon to our winter-worn hearts. Your tough perennial roots fix nitrogen in the soil just as do your cousins Vetch and Alfalfa. You flourish in places where the soil is poor or has been disturbed or neglected, turning it into

a garden. Your flowers are multi-colored like your cousin Sweet Pea. All shapes and sizes of bees—honey, bumble, wild and domestic—flock to your blossoms landing on the purse-like lower lobe of your flower, their weight pushing it down and bringing forth the stamen laden with pollen, which they gather hungrily to feed their kind. Now, Lupine, gray, furry seed pods are forming near the bottom of your stalks, working their way up until the whole spike is covered with pea-like fruit. By next month, the pods will have dried, curled, and cracked open, flinging your seeds to the four directions where they will root if the ground is bare enough, bringing an even richer crop next Spring. Yes, we know you are perhaps from away—escaped from some flatland garden long ago to range over our fields and hills. But we love you still, if only for a season. And now you are leaving and our hearts are sad. We will wait for your return

Sincerely,
Your friends in Northern Maine.

During the enlightenment or "Age of Reason," as historians confidently called it, the fashion became measuring and explaining everything using the scientific method and at the same time, denying the mystery or the sacredness of Nature because it couldn't be measured. Reverence was replaced by scrutiny. Animals have no souls and feel no pain, Descartes told us. We went, as Annie Dillard says, from pantheism to pan-atheism. That worked fine for several generations, and we did a remarkable amount of measuring, listing, describing and explaining of Nature, much of which has been of great value. Unfortunately, this desecration [which simply means to deny the sacredness of something] also gave implicit permission for us to treat the Creation as though we had made it, it was ours, and we could do whatever we wanted to do with it. Then, one day we began to notice that species were disappearing. Rachel Carson was one of the first prophets in the wilderness. Soon, a surge in reverence for Nature began which continues to this day. Now, animals such as whales, wolves and dolphins have entered the popular culture as revered environmental totems. They show up on mass-marketed T-shirts and collector plates. Our young children love them. I say this is good. We are beginning again to view Nature as sacred.

This may sound silly to some, but saying grace or just a silent moment of thanks before eating is an act of deep ecology. The destruction of the environment comes from taking it all for granted instead of being deeply thankful for everything Nature gives us. If we are thankful for something, we try to preserve it.

UN-NATURAL EVENTS: Apropos of nothing in particular, it's perplexing how the most important work—raising and teaching children, growing and preparing food, making clothing, caring for the infirm—seems to pay the least; while the manipulation of money—moving little black marks around on paper or video screen—seems to pay the most. That's un-natural.

RANK OPINION: Many peoples have survived and flourished for millennia without computers, insurance, automobiles, skyscrapers, credit cards, and televisions, but none could survive for long without food and care for children.

FIELD & FOREST REPORT: Crickets and grasshoppers hopping about when the weather is warm enough. Buttercup, daisies, yellow hockweed, Indian paintbrush, blue-eyed grass, all in bloom.

MOUNTAIN REPORT: Blueberries beginning to turn blue. Bunchberries beginning to bunch. Huckleberries beginning to huckle.

SALTWATER REPORT: Harbor porpoises rolling through the waves in pods of six or eight or more, blowing quickly as they arch above the water, then slipping just as quickly and quietly back into the water. Seals curiously bobbing, then pointing nose up and slipping back under the waves.

CRITTER OF THE WEEK: Lovely lupine.

SEED PODS TO CARRY AROUND WITH YOU: from the gospel of Luke: *The kings of the Gentiles exercise lordship over them and those in authority are called benefactors, but it shall not be so with you. Let the greatest among you become as the youngest and the leader as one who serves.*

NEW TO FIRST QUARTER *BUCK* MOON

The song of the hermit thrush suggests a serene and religious beatitude as no other sound in nature . . . He seems to say, "O holy, holy! O clear away, clear away! O clear up, clear up!" It is not a proud, gorgeous strain . . . but seems to be the voice of that calm, sweet solemnity one attains in his best moments.   From John Burroughs.

July 4, Independence Day. T. Jefferson and J. Adams both died, 1826.

July 5, P.T. Barnum born, 1810.

July 7, Birthday of legendary "Negro" pitcher Satchel Paige who joined the majors in his 40s and pitched until he was in his 60s. Year of birth unknown. His folk wisdom is still widely quoted. One Satch quote, "Don't look back, something might be gaining on you."

July 8, 1835, The Liberty Bell cracked. 1910, Nan Jane Aspinwall becomes the first woman to cross the continent on horseback, in 301 days.

July 9, William Jennings Bryan's "Cross of Gold" speech at the 1900 Democratic convention. Bryan was not the backward, anti-intellectual he was made out to be by his critics during the Scopes trial. At the unprecedented age of 36, he was nominated for President by the Democrats; he urged the direct election of senators, supported women' suffrage, and public knowledge of newspaper ownership. He held crowds of 10,000 spellbound without notes or microphone. He was defeated by corporate steel interests.

NATURAL EVENTS: In mid-July we were at our Awanadjo Almanack Cobscook Field Station overlooking Cobscook Bay in beautiful Washington County where the hermit thrush sings. It's the camp we built there twenty-five years ago with a frame of logs cut on the property, boards from Hallowell's sawmill in Dennysville, and shingles from Alton Curtis's shingle mill there in Pembroke. The cabin is neither plumb nor square, but we love it. It sits on a clearing of a couple of acres more or less which was carved out of second growth woods. Most of the clearing was done with horses by Irving Mahar of Lubec in '82. Since that time we have kept it clear by hand mowing each June with a scythe. Over the years we've learned that June is the best time for hand mowing because the weather is usually cooler and the grass and brush are softer, and for other reasons which I don't always remember until it is too late. This year, due to circumstances beyond our control, we didn't get to the mowing until mid-July. Everyday I'd mow for a little while in the early hours and then again later in the day when it was cooler. We made pretty good progress.

On the third day of mowing I got up early singing, "I like to rise when the sun she rises, earlye in the mornin' . . . and go ramblin' in the new-mown hay," and went to work with the scythe. As I swung to and fro, I began to think of the Alcotts—you've got to love those wacky Transcendentalists—harnessing themselves to the plow at their short-lived Fruit-lands utopia because they didn't believe in enslaving animals, and Henry David Thoreau being thrown out of jail because he just wouldn't leave after his bail was paid. As my own quiet and self-righteous transcendentalist scythe cut the grass and my thoughts floated thus, I was suddenly startled back to the present by a sharp stabbing pain like a hot needle in the back of my arm, then a hot stab in my cheek. In a second, I was screaming through the new-mown hay with the sharp scythe bouncing over my shoulder and an angry line of yellow-jackets trailing off behind me. It's a wonder I didn't butcher myself to death. That is when I remembered another reason not to leave the scything until July, when the little hor-nets are nesting in holes in the ground. They have no rever-ence whatsoever for self-righteousness or Transcendentalism.

Wild strawberries are now ripe in secret places. You may have to get down upon your knees to find them, if that won't hurt too much. Their fruit is small but the flavor is concen-trated and delicate. The small jar of wild strawberry jam is more valuable than King Solomon's riches. The fruit is bright red, attracting birds to spread the seeds around. The bird helps the berry and the berry helps the bird.

UN-NATURAL EVENTS: The recent glossy fold-out advertise-ment for Jeep vehicles which states that they have "improved on Nature." Not quite. Off-road recreational vehicles have done a lot on Nature, but they have not improved on it. Not yet. Not ever.

FIELD & FOREST REPORT: Crickets chirping away merrily. They share the glossy, deep black color of the crows and ravens—so black that rainbow colors flash from their backs. Black-eyed Susan, more properly, Yellow Cone-flower, coming into bloom.

MOUNTAIN REPORT: Mountain pilgrims multiply during the summer months. Some days we'll see a dozen vehicles or more at the trail-head with license plates from a half-dozen states and Canadian provinces. It is marvelous exercise to climb Awanadjo: for the soul as well as the body. At the top we get the sense of how the world and our little town look to the eagle and the osprey: trees, land, and water with here and there a tiny white human settlement.

SALTWATER REPORT: Sharp silvery mackerel with their muted rainbow markings are stippling the surface of the bay, first here, then over there. If mackerel are here can bluefish be far behind? The seals are in heaven.

CRITTER OF THE WEEK: The harbor seal, seen in all our bays. Curious and yet timid, clumsy on land, but fast and agile in the water, jumping and splashing even leaping out of the water like a porpoise, and swimming as fast. They growl and bark like dogs. And belch like humans.

SEED PODS TO CARRY AROUND WITH YOU: from the Old Farmer's Almanac 1839: *The fee for pasturing long-tailed horses is more than that for short-tailed ones. The long-tailed ones can whisk off the flies and eat at their leisure while the short-tails are running around from morning to night and not eating much.*

*Weather was once a matter of life and death. The sailor,
the hunter, and the herdsman had to read the skies aright or
perish. Flood, drought, hurricane, and blizzard were not simply things that happened to somebody else's bank account.
They were personal and deadly.*   From T.M. Longstreth

July 10, 1877, the cork life preserver patented.

July 12, Wild Bill Hickock and McCaules Gang shoot-out at
Rock Creek Station, Nebraska, 1861. Hickock survived, but
was later killed by a cross-eyed bandit named Jack McCall
[possibly no relation to your author].

July 13, 1985, first "Live Aid" famine relief concerts held.
Draft riots begin in New York, 1863

July 14, 1789, Bastille Day, the beginning of the French Revolution. On this day in 1806, Lewis and Clark become the first
whites to enter Washington from the East under the guidance
of "the Bird Woman," Sacajawea, their Native American
guide.

July 18, 1964, Harlem riots. *Mein Kampf* published, 1925.
Nero fiddled while Rome burned, 64.

NATURAL EVENTS: The Dog Days—so-called because of the
rising of Sirius, the Dog Star— are here. These hottest days
of summer turn the tall timothy and orchard grass brown.
The crickets chirp drowsily, grasshoppers clatter dryly as they
fly away at our approach, showing dark yellow-banded wings
that look like a butterfly's. The blueberries and apples begin
to show their true colors, and the fruit grower hopes for rain
to fill the fruit with juice. When the South wind comes up
later in the day, we breathe the air of Boston and points

South and West—not the sweetest breath. The elm trees hang limply. The fire department, too, hopes for rain, and memory goes back to the drought summers of '46 and '68 and the big fires, as the younger and older firefighters meet for coffee at the firehouse.

UN-NATURAL EVENTS: We find *styrofoam* floating in the waters of the bay, washed up on the beach, in our beach coolers, and even mixed in with the soil of potted plants. Whatever happened to cork, a natural substance with all the same uses, made from the bark of a tree?

RANK OPINION: Throughout the 20th century there was a movement afoot to replace all natural products with refined and processed petroleum products. Some day the oil will run out and we will have forgotten how to make so many things out of the bounty that Nature provides—all renewable, all bio-degradable. Then where will we be? Helpless as a hog on ice, that's where, and at the mercy of "primitive" cultures and so-called "developing" countries who still remember how to survive with only what Nature provides.

FIELD & FOREST REPORT: The fields are often mowed this time of year, even if they yield no hay. There is a deep reluctance or even abhorrence, in the descendants of those who first cleared these fields of trees and stones by dint of unimaginable effort 200 and more years ago, to let them become overgrown by the quickly seeding aspens, birches and alders. Even when no crop is taken from the mown fields, the children of this tenth generation perhaps imagine the day when these hard-won acres will be re-cultivated, and we will provide our own food again, as we once did in these parts.

MOUNTAIN REPORT: More Pilgrims climb our Awanadjo these days. The lichen covering the rocks crunches crisply under foot. The rock tripe, a large round, flat lichen which clings to vertical rock surfaces, turns black and dry in the South wind, but bring a piece home and put it in water and it turns green instantly. Not dead, only sleeping. It's edible too. The ill-fated Franklin expedition reportedly subsisted on it, but not for long.

SALTWATER REPORT: At the Blue Hill Falls, perfect days to lie on the rocks, play in the water, or just watch the tide come in and out over the barnacles and the rich mussel beds. Look for the slow-walking starfish or sea-stars creeping over the mussels, embracing one, prying it open inexorably. The starfish extrudes its stomach through its mouth, then engulfs the mussel with it, digesting the mussel as it draws its stomach back in. Digested mussel, raw Nature—stark, grim, beautiful. Not Disneyland.

CRITTER OF THE WEEK: The familiar barnacle with its round white shell attached to the rocks looking like a tiny volcano. Try this to amuse yourself: Touch the barnacle lightly to watch it pull its neck back in and close tight, then open again after you leave. Or watch them when the tide just covers them, stretching their necks and waving their fine, feathery tentacles. Here's a question for you: Do the barnacles' shells grow as they do, or do they cast them off and run around naked waiting for a bigger shell to grow?

SEED PODS TO CARRY AROUND WITH YOU: From Rabindrinath Tagore, the great poet of India: *Today the summer has come to my window, with its sighs and murmurs; and the bees are plying their minstrelsy at the court of the flowering grove. Now it is time to sit quiet face to face with Thee and to sing dedication of life in this silent and overflowing leisure.*

PILGRIM'S JOURNAL: This is a story of how we try to make the circle unbroken. Among other things, this story is about a sacred place, and some bones. Those whose names are mentioned have given prior permission for their use.

Mardi Byers Gay made me aware years ago that there was an ancient Red Paint burial ground at the Blue Hill Falls. "I think you might be interested in this," she said, and handed me a small blue book called "The Nevin Shell Heap: Burials and Observations." Mardi's father was the author of the book and had been the director of the museum of archaeology at Phillips Academy in Andover, Massachusetts. After his retirement, he lived in Blue Hill until his death in the late 70's. During the 30's, as had been the practice for generations, many of the bones and other objects were removed from the site and taken to the museum for study and display. The blue book is full of evocative drawings of bones and daggers and tools and skulls, and maps of the area. The current consensus is that these burials may be 4,000 years old, or as old as Abraham.

For someone who has not seen the Falls, it may be described as a narrow channel of about 50–60 feet wide at low tide, between Blue Hill Bay and the large Salt Pond which stretches miles into the heart of the peninsula and is fed by fresh water streams. Through this narrow channel, with a magnificent slow tidal pulse, an enormous volume of water roars into the pond and then out twice a day like the blood rushing in and out of a great heart beating. In summer, human beings play on the rocks and in the water, harbor seals play and fish in the turbulent waves, and cormorants, great blue herons, ospreys and bald eagles glide above. Great strands of kelp are pulled furiously by the running water, first in toward the Salt Pond, then out toward the bay in a primal dance, pausing only four times a day for a short rest.

There is a sacred geometry to the place. Rising above the mussel beds on the bay side is the largest ice-borne boulder among many which are partially submerged at high tide. Resting on this great accommodating stone, one is in the center of a holy place. Above is the sky with its sea and land birds. Below is the stone and the earth. Toward the East is the saltwater of the bay and open ocean beyond and the sunrise. Toward the West is the Salt Pond, freshwater, the land, and the whole continent. To the South is the rushing water of life, the Falls. And to the North is the burial ground and the Mountain. The very design of the place, as well as the presence of the ancient cemetery, confirm that it has been a sacred place for our kind for thousands of years. The memories of ancient people living, laughing, praying and dying here inform the religious practices of the present, including memorial services, the scattering of ashes, burials, baptisms, sunrise services, worship and prayer, confirming this as a sacred place today.

Still, a wistful apprehension lingers there. Some recognize the place as sacred, but most do not. The bones of children, youths, men and women once buried here with devotion and bright gifts, now lie nearly forgotten in drawers and boxes somewhere far away. People toss trash on the site. The ancient shell heap erodes. It is not safe from development. There is a broken-ness about it that wants healing.

At our camp on Cobscook Bay in Washington County reading the Bangor paper one July morning in the roaring silence, I came upon an article about the Native American Grave Protection and Repatriation Act of 1990 which requires that artifacts, sacred objects and human remains now being held in museums be returned to appropriate Native American claimants. An old dream began to stir: to see the bones brought back from the museum and placed in the holy ground, and to see the Falls rededicated as a sacred place. I clipped the article from the paper. A little while later, I went to Pleasant Point, the Passamaquoddy reserve just across the bay, to talk to someone about this old dream.

The smiling, white-haired director of the Waponahki Museum & Resource Center was sitting alone in the museum of his own making for the purpose of educating the people about their past. He began recovering the old dances in the '60's and the Passamaquoddy language in the '80's. "I've tried to retire three times, but they wouldn't let me," he said in a gentle voice. Old photos, old baskets, birchbark canoes, old tools lined the walls. I told him about the bones and the Blue Hill Falls and the Repatriation Act. He listened intently, like a doctor hearing my symptoms. He gave me a tour of the museum and a short lecture on the language. It is of the Algonquin group and has a grammar which discriminates between animate and inanimate objects. An apple is animate, an orange inanimate because it is foreign. A fork is inanimate but a spoon is animate because it holds something. He was especially proud of the military service of the Passamaquoddy who fought in our wars even though they did not get the right to vote in national elections until 1960.

Later in the day, at the tribal governor's office, I met the Lieutenant Governor, a bright, energetic man in his 40's in a button-down shirt. He was very attentive while I told him the dream. He had read the newspaper story about repatriation. He felt that the tribal council would be supportive and suggested that I contact the Peabody Museum at Phillips Academy and keep him posted. After our business talk, he said, "Did you come in that truck with the kayak on top?" "I did," I said. "Do you want to see it?" He did, so we trooped out to the parking lot with another man, a woodcarver, and there the Lt. Gov. of the Passamaquoddy hopped onto the tailgate of my old truck and admired my kayak which is stencilled with Passamaquoddy basket and quill designs taken from a book his sister gave me for my birthday. I was deeply flattered by his interest, but more deeply struck by the poignancy and the irony of this descendant of hundreds of generations of sea-going people asking a white landlubber about this adaptation of a native craft. This was the second example in a day of the same deep yearning to recapture or reconstruct an ancient way of life nearly lost, to close the broken circle.

I left the reserve deeply excited about developments, moved by the profound friendliness and hospitality shown to me, and engulfed by the intense community feeling—that one could be embraced forever there on that windy point of rock with its tiny huddled houses and barking dogs on Passamaquoddy Bay.

Home again, I contacted the museum at Phillips Academy and told them about the dream and asked if we could come to Massachusetts to see the bones. The staff at the museum was receptive to this and we set a tentative date.

Two weeks later was the Annual Indian Days and First Annual Native Gathering at Pleasant Point. Older men had butch, flat-top hair-cuts, younger men had ponytails, and adolescents had elaborate "Mohawk" styles with scalp locks and roaches, not that different from adolescents anywhere in America, but more extreme. Who says there hasn't been a revolution in this country? There was evidence of a strong Plains Indian influence in the presence of tipis and headdresses, though the Governor wore traditional Passamaquoddy head-dress with feathers in a straight up crown. Here was a true melting pot with mixed racial, cultural and religious strains which will never be untangled, but could lead to a new vigorous hybrid. There was a young, blond cheerleader type with clearly Indian parents. One little African-American 3-year-old in a frilly dress was holding the hand of her clearly native mother. Booths displayed fine traditional crafts as well as souvenirs. I arrived in time for the public dancing, hoping to find others to tell about the bones, but saw no familiar faces, and after a couple of hours returned to our camp.

My long-time aquaintance, Deanna Francis, the sister of the Lt. Governor, is a spiritual person. She grew up at Pleasant Point and lived the miseries of that life of poverty and abuse nearly universal among broken people. But there is something in her that heals. She has done extensive university studies in botany and has completed her degree in osteopathy. She transplants native trees and plants and coaxes them to flourish in the hard soil of the Point. She also transplants ceremonies and songs from other tribes and coaxes them into life at the Point so that they can bear fruit and produce a new spiritual life there. She lives in a little house that she built herself off the road but close to others on all sides. At one time, many shook their heads when her name came up. Now more and more, her name is called upon with respect as one who is bringing new life from the roots of the nation. At this writing she is active in the struggle to prevent a liquid natural gas depot from being constructed at Sipayik, the Passamaquoddy reservation.

The morning following the annual Indian Days celebration, I set out to find this remarkable woman. When I got to her house there was much ceremonial activity going on, with drumming under a large, round lodge frame covered with boughs, and no white folks as there had been the day before. I asked if she was there. "Yes, but she's . . . occupied," was the answer. I left disappointed and returned to our camp to work in the woods the rest of the day.

The next morning I awoke feeling confused and panicky wondering if this business with the bones was just too crazy. Realizing I had to calm down, I took out the Bible to look for a psalm or something to soothe me, and opened it, looking at the first place it fell open. Now, I scorn those who put their finger in the Bible anytime they can't figure out what to do next. But, I'll tell you the Bible opened directly to the 37th chapter of the book of Ezekiel; the vision of the dry bones:

The hand of the Lord was upon me and he brought me out by the Spirit of the Lord, and set me down in the midst of the plain; it was full of bones . . . And he said to me, "Son of man, can these bones live?" And I answered, "O Lord God, thou knowest" . . . Then he said to me, "Prophesy to the wind, son of man, and say to the breath, 'Come from the four winds, O breath, and breathe upon these slain, that they may live . . .'" Then he said to me, "Son of man, these bones are the whole house of Israel. Behold they say, 'Our bones are dried up and our hope is lost; we are clean cut off.' Therefore, prophesy and say to them, 'Thus says the Lord God, 'Behold, I will . . . raise you from your graves, O my people, and bring you home into the land of Israel.'" [Ezekiel 37: selections, Revised Standard Version]

Quickly packing and closing up the camp, I hurried back to Pleasant Point and strode into the little house where Deanna sat at her kitchen table with friends. It was dark inside. We greeted each other warmly, having not seen each other for several years. They offered me food and drink. I settled for a cup of coffee. All the talk was about the calling of the whales which had transpired a couple of days before, when some of the Passamaquoddy went out to meet and call the whales and have conversation with them. A whale appeared immediately to tell them that they had been missed during the preceding years of silence and to give them instructions how to keep the communication open. Again I saw the recapturing of old tradition.

After a while I got up the courage to say why I was there. Everyone listened. I talked about the bones and passed around the blue book about Kollejedjwok. It was studied carefully. Deanna explained it to her friends, moving rapidly back and forth between Passamaquoddy and English. All nodded. "The bones need the right ceremony," she finally said. "We have it." She walked me back down to my car and I told her about Ezekiel 37. She listened and nodded, "Hmmm." Then with a great bear hug we said goodbye.

Arrangements were made with the staff of the museum for a visit. Deanna and two friends from the Maliseet reserve in Quebec arrived at our house in Blue Hill about midnight after an afternoon of ceremonial prayer and preparation at Sipayik. The next morning after breakfast, we set forth for the five-hour drive to the Robert S. Peabody Museum in Andover, Massachusetts. It was foggy and figured to be hot as we rolled into Belfast, then Augusta, then onto the Interstate. We listened to tapes of Micmac songs and speeches and studied the blue book.

Deanna brought out feathers—eagle and great blue heron—and while slowly and carefully telling the story of each one, she drew them into a fan with bright red yarn. I was afraid they would fly out her open window as we sped down the highway. By 1:00 p.m. we turned off I-495 into Andover and as we approached the museum, the Micmac lady from Big Cove said, "Pull into that gas station." I filled the car with gas while she disappeared into the restroom to reappear in a beautiful traditional dress decorated with ribbons and buttons. Meanwhile Deanna, also in traditional dress, took a large sea-shell from the trunk, filled it with dried sage and cedar and set it afire while the bewildered cashier craned his neck to see what was happening, and perhaps looking for the fire-extinguisher.

We all climbed back into the car, Deanna with the smoking shell on her lap, the smoke pouring out of the open windows with an odor like burning hemp as we proceeded down Main Street with me wondering how I would explain all this to the police officer I felt sure was about to pull us over. We arrived at the museum and parked just as—sure enough—a striped security car pulled in behind us. The two Native women blew purifying smoke over all of us before we approached the locked doors of the museum and knocked. A blue-uniformed security guard appeared quickly behind us.

"May I help you?" Assuming my best authoritative white male voice I intoned, "We have an appointment with the repatriation coordinator."

The guard bowed and backed away as the door opened from the inside and the entire staff of the museum came forward to greet us with nervous smiles and handshakes.

While we looked around curiously in every direction, the Museum Director, Ass't. Director, Repatriation Coordinator, and a curious technician led us up a broad, winding stairway lined with murals and maps of Native American cultures to the second-floor meeting room with a great conference table. On the table were carefully arranged some coffee and cake, cups, plates and napkins. The staff of the museum wanted to talk first. A long discourse about the museum and its policies and the highly complex process of repatriation ensued.

The two Native women listened patiently until they were given the opportunity to speak. Deanna began by telling them that seeing in the blue book a child buried with a porpoise convinced her that the Kollejedjwok Blue Hill Falls people were relatives of the Passamaquoddy because only they hunt the porpoise.

"The bones have to be put back so that we can rest," she said.

It was agreed that the repatriation process might take a year or more, that it was important that all Maine tribes join with the Passamaquoddy in claiming the remains, and that the staff of this museum would help in working with other museums so that each step of the repatriation process would not have to be duplicated. There was more talk but it was tedious.

It was time to bless the bones. All rose to go to the basement where the bones are kept. Deanna went outside to get certain ceremonial materials while we waited looking at the carefully arranged displays of objects taken from the Blue Hill Falls, so far away. Soon she walked in with a fiercely smoking bowl. The Director quietly ordered someone to turn off all the smoke alarms. We descended in a troop to the basement where a drawer with many compartments and covered with a white cloth rested on a table.

"This is all the Blue Hill bones we have," said a staff member, "All the rest were shipped off to Harvard years ago."

Deanna stepped up to the table holding the smoking bowl, waving the eagle feather fan over it, blowing the smoke over the paltry bones, talking softly and intimately in Passamaquoddy. A few of us stood in a semicircle behind her. Except for the low sound of her voice, it was deathly quiet.

Suddenly, she began to sing in a strong alto voice that echoed off the cold, gray-painted stone basement walls. How can I describe the voice? Pain, a wailing song of exile by the rivers of Babylon, the song of Wounded Knee and Sand Creek and mass graves, a song of memory extending far back beyond one lifetime, and yet a song of brave, even defiant denial of despair. Tears poured from my eyes and I began to pray silently a prayer of confession for the sins of our fathers and ourselves. The smoke was pungent, spicy, strong. Some museum staff members moved closer, some moved away.

The first song faded and the woman from Big Cove stepped forward to join Deanna in a second song with shaking deer hoof rattles. Voices in perfect harmony, the song rose and fell with the cold, gray smoke. Time collapsed in upon itself and we were transported through space as the remote past became the present and the sound of the distant Falls rushed upon our ears.

Then it was all finished. Deanna Francis walked out abruptly. One museum staff member wept copiously. Some awkward moments, some faint anti-climactic conversations about procedures, some artifacts half-heartedly viewed, and it was clearly time to leave. During the long drive home Deanna talked about the songs. The first was a song from the living to the dead promising to respectfully bury the dead in exchange for their spirits taking care of the living. The second was a blessing.

"How many of the old songs have you found?" I asked.

"Only a few," she said.

"Then how do you do your ceremonies?"

"We borrow songs from our relatives until we can dream new ones for ourselves."

Today Deanna is still deeply involved in restoring religious ceremonies. Trying to heal the broken circle. New shoots from the old stump. We arrived back in Blue Hill long after the late August dark had fallen, recounting the events of the day to the delight of my dear Becky, and fell into bed.

Western theology has tended to see Nature as distinct and separate from God; as God's handiwork or God's servant or God's creation, as though all that our eyes can see is a manufactured product. The result is an insoluble problem that has plagued Western thought for at least 2,000 years: the separation and alienation between spirit and flesh, mind and body, energy and matter. The separation has driven God out of Nature. The resulting alienation has led to the profaning, polluting, and exploitation of Nature that now threatens the life of the Holy Body and all bodies.

Seeing Nature as different from God and from us has also led to alienation from our own bodies as parts of the Whole—being born, living, dying, and being reborn, as was Christ and as is the whole Creation. We experience disunion with God and disunion with Nature in a very similar way: fear, disorientation, loss of values, anger, violence and loneliness. If you ask me, these maladies of modern civilization are an outgrowth of the idea of the supernatural God who stands apart from the Creation—the distant Father.

Now look at the conclusions of modern post-Newtonian physics. In the past century, in both the physics of the cosmos and the physics of the smallest sub-atomic particles, some startling developments have challenged the idea of the supernatural God. Modern physics finds that different laws apply in different conditions. The laws that seem to govern planets and stars do not work at all well with sub-atomic particles. What is more, there are large areas where physicists can discern no law and order, but rather chaos. There is random, unpredictable behavior in objects large and small. We see light behaving as both a wave and a particle. We are beginning to see that even our laws of physics seem to be metaphors, more like poetry than calculus. Or, if you will, we see that the behavior of the universe is less and less like a machine and more and more like a hugely complex, growing and changing organism: A living body—God's Body.

That's the almanack for this moon, but don't
take it from me,
I'm no expert. Go out and see for yourself.

This is the Awanadjo Almanack for the Full *Buck* Moon to the Full *Sturgeon* [or *Green Corn*] Moon, *Aqavirvik* or *Birds Molt* to the North Slope Eskimos, *Ab* on the Biblical calendar, *July/August* in Downeast Maine.

FULL TO LAST QUARTER *BUCK* MOON

If your neighbour's cattle have broke into your mowing, don't go to your lawyer, but see your neighbour, and both together see the fence: and if there be a dispute about this, then call on the fence-viewers, and they, if they know their duty, will so manage as to gain you both satisfaction.
From the Old Farmer's Almanac, July 1817

Oxen that rattle the yoke and chain or halt in the leafy shade, what is that you express in your eyes? It seems to me more than all the print I have read in my life.
From Walt Whitman.

July 22 is the feast day of St. Mary Magdalene, according to tradition the one person who was with Jesus when he was executed and who first saw him on Easter morning. She has her own apocryphal gospel, and legends abound about the true nature of their love for each other.

July 23 is the anniversary of Henry David Thoreau's arrest and incarceration for one night by Concord constable Sam Staples for not paying several year's poll tax in protest against the role of the state of Massachusetts in perpetuating slavery. The tax was paid that same evening by an anonymous person (probably Thoreau's aunt). The next morning, Thoreau was thrown *out* of jail when he refused to leave voluntarily.

July 26, 1875, Carl Jung was born.

NATURAL EVENTS: We are enjoying one of the finest summers in a long time here between the mountain and the sea, with adequate rainfall, little fog, just enough heat, and many bright "blue and green days", as our late friend Arlene Stover called them, with the fresh Canadian winds coming out of the Northwest. The word is out, too. We have lots of visitors from away and numerous pilgrims climbing the flanks of Awanadjo. In short, we have been going out to see for ourselves so much that we have hardly had time to record the events of this Almanack.

Meanwhile, we hear of record heat in different parts of the world: glaciers moving faster in Alaska, chunks of ice thousands of years old and as big as a county breaking off the Antarctic ice-cap. Perhaps these un-natural events are caused by human activity or natural events which occur on a much larger scale than we humans can easily comprehend, or both.

UN-NATURAL EVENTS: Conservative experts will objectively conclude from their data that these are perfectly natural events. Liberal experts will just as objectively conclude from their data that these are un-natural events caused by human activity.

RANK OPINION: If your house is on fire, you don't argue about how it started. The first thing you do is put the fire out. Then, you try to determine what caused it.

FIELD & FOREST REPORT: The "heliotrope," as most people call it around here, and which some incorrectly call "Queen Anne's Lace" (which is actually wild carrot), others call "Cow parsnip" which it is not, and others call "Valerian," which it just might be—but the so-called heliotrope which resembles no heliotrope in my guide book, not even the seaside heliotrope, (how am I going to get out of this sentence?); is going by with its ever fainter perfume, which some love and some hate, fading on the breeze. Its long, fluted hollow stalks four or five feet high and its tiny white flowers tinted with magenta in umbrels four inches wide are beginning to dry up. Can anyone tell us what this abundant plant really is—or how to reconstruct this sentence? [The plant is actually Valerian, and the sentence will remain unreconstructed.]

Recent rains have settled the dust and refreshed the fields and forests, doubtless providing the parched slug population with new hope of escape from oblivion. I feel for the slugs during dry times. They are shellfish out of water.

MOUNTAIN REPORT: Seeing the aphids nearly covering the seed stalks of the fields of lupine on the south slope of Awanadjo brings to mind Edwin Way Teale, the late naturalist of Concord, Massachusetts. "The plant lice [or aphids] are placidly drinking sap and giving birth to a seemingly endless succession of living young. Uncounted generations follow each other through the summer days. I look about me. Everywhere there are the new generations of another year—new apples, new robins, new flowers. I turn toward home with the feeling of having lived for a time the life of some ancient Methuselah watching the flow of generations passing by." The aphid, by the way, is parthenogenic, able to produce young without the benefit of male intervention. Among humans this attribute was considered Divine, and many ancient heroes were said to be born of virgins, including Sargon, Zoroaster, Jason, Alexander the Great, Jesus, and, more recently, Rev. Sun Myung Moon.

The other day on the summit of Awanadjo, I heard a man talking very loudly into a hand-held device. The disembodied voice of his friend on their boat at the yacht club several miles away soon came crackling back echoing from the trees. In former days one did hear disembodied voices on mountains now and then. Sometimes they were thunderous. Sometimes they were still, small voices. Now, more and more we hear small, whiny voices coming from the small, shiny amulets of cell phones.

SALTWATER REPORT: The Annual Gathering of the Fleet for this summer is now history. Many boats were blessed and so were many folks. The sound of bagpipes under a clear blue sky, the creaking of oars, the warm wind swelling in sails, and the murmur of water on rocks was as much a blessing as all the prayers.

CRITTERS OF THE WEEK: The chipmunk and the mourning dove who fed together peacefully under our birdfeeder for quite some time the other day. Every now and then they would raise their heads at the same time and startle each other momentarily, but then go back to their contented feeding.

SEED PODS TO CARRY AROUND WITH YOU: from Charles Dickens: *Nature gives to every time and season some beauties of its own; and from morning to night, as from the cradle to the grave, is but a succession of changes so gentle and easy that we can scarcely mark their progress.*

And from Basho, the Zen poet (1664–1694): *Clouds come from time to time—and bring a chance to rest from looking at the moon.*

I am struck by the fact that the more slowly trees grow at first, the sounder they are at the core, and I think the same is true of human beings. We do not wish to see children precocious, making great strides in their early years, like sprouts producing a soft and perishable timber, but better if they expand slowly at first, as if contending with difficulties, and so are solidified and perfected. Such trees continue to expand with nearly equal rapidity to an extreme old age.

From Henry David Thoreau

July 28, 1866, Beatrix Potter was born. In 1868, the fourteenth amendment to the constitution was ratified banning slavery; and in 1901, Rudy Vallee was born. He was the man that sang the Maine Stein song.

July 30, 1818, Emily Bronte was born. On this day in 1891, Casey Stengel was born.

July 31, 1944, Rebecca Haley McCall was born. And on this day in 1790, the U.S. patent office issued its first patent.

NATURAL EVENTS: Silently all around us, the trees are slowly adding their summer growth. Each tree in the forest swells imperceptibly as another seasonal ring is added to its girth. It might be as much as one/quarter to one/half an inch added to its diameter, or as little as one/hundredth, but on an acre the new wood might total as much one/quarter to one/half a cord or 32 to 64 cubic feet or even more. It is miraculous that this solid, versatile, strong material is composed chiefly of air, water, and carbon. The manufacture of this marvelous material is accomplished, not in a modern factory, but in the tiny plant cell.

The marvel of it reminds me of the man who shocked his

trendy vegetarian friends by expressing his disgust at their diet. He ate only meat, he said, because he considered plants a higher form of life. Before you laugh, consider that without plants, animals could not live. Plants are the foundation of the food chain. On the other hand, not many plants have to eat animals to survive.

Another marvel is this: One might even say that plants become animals at night and in Winter. When the sun shines and the weather is warm, a plant uses its green matter to produce and store sugars and carbohydrates. But when the sun does not shine or after the leaves fall off, the plant stays alive by metabolizing these stored foods, just as an animal does. This is why trees have two different types of rings each year, the wide light summer ring and the narrow dark winter ring—the plant ring and the animal ring.

When Jesus gave the blind man back his sight, at first the blind man said he "saw men as trees walking." He saw truly.

UN-NATURAL EVENTS: If you start seeing all plants in this marvelous light, pretty soon chain saws, lawn mowers, hedge clippers, brush chippers, and weed whackers become brutal instruments of torture.

RANK OPINION: How could anyone but the most heartless brute ever belly up to a salad bar again? It would be like enjoying a train wreck.

FIELD & FOREST REPORT: Black-eyed Susies, cheerful younger sisters of the Daisies and cousins to the Echinacea, shocking pink fireweed in bloom, along with the sweet-perfumed milkweed calling to the monarch butterflies. Coming into bloom is the Queen Anne's Lace, Meadow-sweet, and the first of the numerous kinds of Goldenrod.

MOUNTAIN REPORT: Great metallic blue-green dragonflies hanging in the up-rushing warm air along the slopes of Awanadjo. Blueberries are plumping up and turning blue. The pilgrim now has a good supply of refreshing fruit to enjoy while climbing. But note: This is the time of the blueberry maggot fly invasion and many fields will be sprayed with an insecticide. The blueberries on the mountain, however, are not sprayed, so if you eat them, you might get some protein along with your antioxidants.

SALTWATER REPORT: our encounter with orca

At the request of Audubon Society Schoodic Chapter, I am setting down this account. In the summer of 1979 we were camped on Leighton Neck on Cobscook Bay on the Greenlaw property. One morning Becky and I determined to go flounder fishing as the tide was beginning to go out. We had hand lines and clams we had dug for bait. We borrowed a 17' Old Town canoe from our neighbors and with our two children, Sarah and Daniel, aged 11 and 4 years at the time, set out for a couple of old posts left from Mahar's weir, now gone, which stood 100+ yards offshore at high tide. The weather was calm and foggy. We planned to paddle out to one of the weir posts and tie on to it and drop our lines.

As we paddled out, I saw a dark shape in the water perhaps 100 yards out beyond us, and figured it was a loon or a seal. It quickly disappeared beneath the water. We paddled farther and I saw the shape rise again, long enough to know that it wasn't a loon or a seal, but not long enough to determine what it was. In a few minutes we approached the weir post which rose two feet above the water. We paddled out beyond it and circled back around to head in toward it and to tie on to it.

At that moment, the same dark shape rose out of the water

within about four feet of the starboard side of our canoe. The flat curving shape was close enough to touch with a paddle, black and shiny. It rose about three feet from the water and was obviously a fin, curved gently back, with a rounded tip. The water was not noticeably disturbed by the huge creature rising next to our canoe.

We all looked down into the water. I saw an eye that seemed as big as a saucer [I suppose mine were that big by this time, too] but was probably about four or five inches in diameter, with white markings around it. I saw a huge mouth in a slight smile beneath the eye, and rough, light-gray patches like barnacles between the eye and the mouth. The body was very dark and hard to make out. The head of the creature was even with our bow or a foot or two behind, and the fin was at our midship. I had the impression at the time that at least a third to a half of the body was astern of us and that the head was about the size of the front of a VW Beetle [not a very scientific description, I know, but that was my first thought]. The immediate reaction of all of us was, "It's a whale."

After a moment of wonder and delight, we became alarmed at this huge shape so close to our little canoe. One nudge from the great beast and we would be into the cold water where no one survives for long. Our children were white-knuckled, holding onto the gunwales. We decided to return to shore without delay and I can remember looking forward at Becky and noticing that she appeared to be wielding several paddles at once. We landed the boat with exclamations of excitement and a little fear. After depositing the rest of the family onshore, I went back out immediately for another look, but there was no sign of the creature.

For the next couple of years, I took every opportunity to research the appearance of the creature as I recalled it. I checked out every book on whales I could find in the Blue Hill library. I am certainly no expert, but I eventually came to the conclusion that what we saw was a female Orca for the following reasons:

a) The large size and gently curved shape of the dorsal fin, unlike any other cetacean of like size.
b) The definite white markings near the eye and underneath.
c) The overall length which I estimated to be at least 25 feet and maybe 30 feet.
d) The calloused areas and general whale-like appearance.
e) The general intuitive conclusion we all shared that this was a whale.

This is a true account, and those who have heard us relate the story of our encounter over the years will tell you that our story has not changed substantially nor been embellished in any significant way in that time.

CRITTER OF THE WEEK: Great Orca, who swims, hunts, plays, makes love and gives birth in all of the vast uncharted expanses of both the Atlantic and the Pacific Oceans.

SEED PODS TO CARRY AROUND WITH YOU: from T.H. White, the English writer—*Nobody, living on the remotest, most barren crag in the ocean, could complain of a dull landscape so long as he would lift his eyes. In the sky there was a new landscape every minute, in every pool of the sea rocks, a new world.*

And from humorist Woody Allen—*I am at two with nature.*

I do not think it is important whether a man enters religion by the front door or the back door, as long as he enters. For only as he enters does he find peace. If to find God by the garden path is the back door, then by all means go down the garden path. We have no approach to heaven save by the lower senses, and so far the back door to religion seems the safest. If we can arrive at a position in which Jesus admired the lilies of the valley and St. Francis loved the birds as God's own creatures, we have stumbled upon the very source from which all religions took their rise.

From Lin Yutang (1895-1976)

August 1, 1779, Francis Scott Key, author of *The Starspangled Banner*, was born.

August 6, 1945, the atomic bombing of Hiroshima.

August 8, anniversary of the resignation of President Richard M. Nixon.

NATURAL EVENTS: We've been at the Awanadjo Almanack Cobscook Field Station, as we somewhat grandly call our one-room, log-frame camp "where the power never goes out." There, we labor when we wish and rest when we wish, and gradually, after a few days, find ourselves in a world dominated by Nature, not by man.

One day we sat on the beach watching the tide turn and back slowly down from the endless knotted and rolled rope of rockweed and eel grass, feathers, driftwood, and crab, clam, and mussel shells woven by the waves and left along the high tide line as far as the eye could see. After a while, we saw some movement in the long line of seaweed, and soon made out several sand-pipers strutting along and pecking at sand shrimp. Now and then they would stop and, standing on one leg, raise and stretch out a wing in a sweeping gesture like ballet. When folded down, the sand-piper's wing is a mottled and camouflaged brown which makes it nearly invisible against the seaweed, but when the wing is raised aloft and spread out, it shows a brilliant white fan of tiny delicate feathers, both achingly lovely and entirely useful.

The elegance of the sandpiper's quiet, mannered, and ancient dance and the artistry of its intricately colored feathers struck deep into the heart of this poor mortal. I've seen the best works of so many painters and bird-carvers from John James Audubon and Roger Tory Peterson to Blue Hill's Gad and Dennis Robertson, but as beautiful as their works may be, these artists would surely be first to admit that their labors always fall short of the beauty of their real and natural subjects.

RANK OPINION: We humans in our work can emulate and even create beauty, but we can never match, much less surpass, the beauty of the real. In the whole record of human endeavor, no architectural construction has come close to the beauty of a mountain or an island. No city can match the beauty or usefulness of a forest or a prairie. No human art or artifice can match the grace, dignity, or utility of Nature. No product of the Hollywood digital imagination is more elegant than the real creatures that live on the real earth. As proof, we see that Hollywood must resort to creating grotesque and ugly creatures, monsters, aliens, mutants. When we cannot surpass Nature, we degrade Her.

This announces the following truth: When we try to imitate Nature, we can come beautifully close; but when we try to surpass the real and natural, we cross the threshold into ugliness. When the end of our labors is to overcome or exceed the elegance of Nature, we fail. Only when we labor to enhance and increase the beauty and utility of Nature by Her own rules can we survive for long in this once achingly beautiful garden we have been given, a garden which can be beautiful again, when we have learned the lesson of our labors. The lesson is that no one creature can surpass the elegance of Nature, but that all creatures are simply creatures, formed in beauty to labor together.

UN-NATURAL EVENTS: A while back we received as a gift a beautiful potted plant with fleshy green leaves and orange flowers. The little white tag stuck into the soil said "Kalanchoe —propagation prohibited." Of course, you can imagine how the wheels started turning when I saw that. Propagation is reproduction: who's going to prohibit that? I called the Hancock County extension service to see what they could tell me. The common-sensible lady who answered the phone said, "I think it means the plant is copyrighted, but what are you going to do, sit and watch it to see that it doesn't propagate?"

WILD SPECULATION: What if we innocently put our Kalanchoe out in the garden and it starts (blush!) propagating itself? Will some uniformed minion of genetic engineering technology come and arrest it . . . or us?

ANOTHER RANK OPINION: You and I know that no greedy horticultural corporation, no stuffy puritanical commercial botanist is going to long prohibit any plant from propagating. Look around you. See all that green? Plants shamelessly propagating every where you turn!

FIELD & FOREST REPORT: Black-eyed Susan still in bloom, Shad berries and wild cherries ripe, blueberry harvest underway.

SACRED MOUNTAIN of the Week; Awanadjo, whose gentle slopes are climbed by hundreds of pilgrims each year to enjoy the beauty of old growth forest, and see the surrounding hills and mountains—Isle Au Haut to the South, Camden Hills to the West, Bald and Great Pond mountains to the North, Schoodic and Lead mountains to the East and of course, Cadillac and the mountains of Mount Desert Island to the Southeast in a great circle.

SALTWATER REPORT: Ospreys and terns are diving and feeding in the bays and coves while herring flash in the shallows or shatter the surface of the water. Mackerel are running and flashing in the bay and paddlers are waiting in line like Friday night shoppers to shoot the Blue Hill Falls.

CRITTERS OF THE WEEK: The beautiful shiny black crickets tucked away in the high grass and in the wood-pile singing their joyful song for no particular reason, just the way we whistle to add a lilt to our chores. The Japanese bring crickets into the house in little bamboo cages to bless the home with their joyful sound.

SEED PODS TO CARRY AROUND WITH YOU: from the 9th century Irish "Hermit's Song": *I wish, O Son of the living God, O ancient, eternal King, for a hidden little hut in the wilderness that it may be my dwelling. An all-gray little lake to be by its side. A clear pool to wash away sins through the grace of the Holy Spirit. Quite near, a beautiful wood around it on every side, to nurse many-voiced birds, hiding it with its shelter. A southern aspect for warmth, a little brook across its floor, a choice land with many gracious gifts such as be good for every plant . . . This is the husbandry I would take, I would choose, and will not hide it: Fragrant leek, hens, speckled salmon, trout, bees. Raiment and food enough for*

me from the King of fair fame, and I to be sitting for a while
praying God in every place. Translated from the Gaelic by
Kuno Meyer.

The great sea has set me adrift. It moves me. Like a weed in a
great river earth and the great weather move me, have carried
me away, and fill my inward parts with joy.

From Uvavnuk.

August 9, 1945, the atomic bombing of Nagasaki.

August 11, The Dog Days end, and Summer turns toward Fall
in Awanadjo Country.

August 15, Julia Child born, 1912. "Now where did I put that
cooking sherry?"

NATURAL EVENTS: There is a day in August when we wake
and feel that the Summer, though far from over, has turned
toward the Fall. The Dog Days end and there is a different
odor in the air, a yellow leaf, a cool night. We forget about
the heat and begin to fondly treasure each day, because we
know in our heart of hearts just how fast summer can drift
away, and just what the oncoming Fall and Winter will bring.

Paddling the salt water in modern kayaks, with their
design derived from the skin-covered craft and covered
canoes of Northern and sub-Arctic people, has become
increasingly popular in recent years. Kayaks are silent, clean,
and strictly human-powered. Though often made of plastic
or fiberglass, they are perhaps about as "natural" as a boat
can be. In a kayak, one sits not on, but in the water, creating
an intimacy with the sea that is unequalled. When the water

is calm, this can be a powerful meditative experience. I often repeat the words of Uvavnuk, the Eskimo woman shaman recorded by Nils Rasmussen (see above) as the water gently rises and falls, lifting then dropping me, and the whole sky spreads overhead with its vast distances and changing forms. Fish flash beneath. Red-eyed loons call and dive, coming up very close. Seals steal up behind and slap the water fiercely to alarm us. Harbor porpoises arch above the water just long enough to blow, then slide beneath the waves. Gulls, terns, and ospreys soar overhead, then fold their wings and plummet into the water to rise with a fish in beak or claws. There is no cathedral as vast and holy as this.

UN-NATURAL EVENTS: Kayaks can be un-natural too. A while back I paddled out to a beautiful island in the mouth of the Union River estuary. Offshore are some great bare ledges known by locals to have a large population of harbor seals that like to rest and bask in the sun much of the day, as we do. The accepted practice among local paddlers is to stay far enough away from the seals to preserve their tranquility: sort of like approaching a nude beach. This means staying at least 100 yards away. Yet on this day I sat on shore and watched a paddler approach closer and closer to a ledge occupied by perhaps 25 harbor seals until, in a frightened rush, they all slid into the water. With apparent glee, the kayaker continued paddling toward the seals now bobbing in the water and scattering from his approach. This man had no manners. In addition to the rude and needless disturbance of these peaceful creatures, imagine the cost in calories derived from diminishing fish supplies required to fuel these seals through such frantic activity. A nearby lobster boat plying its trade did not seem to disturb the seals. Kayaks most definitely do. Some say that kayaks remind the seals of killer whales. But, why would seals throw themselves into the sea at the approach of an Orca? My theory is that seals have been taught by their ancestors for ten thousand years to fear people in kayaks as seal hunters. It was a full thirty minutes before the seals returned to the ledge.

WILD SPECULATION: If harbor seals can learn from their ancestors to avoid harpooning hunters in skin kayaks, maybe they can learn and pass on to their descendants the knowledge of how to deftly overturn bumbling, ill-mannered tourists in gaudy plastic kayaks who disturb their tranquility.

RANK OPINION: We have our own knowledge and manners, but if we choose to go into the world of the seal and the sea, we would do well to learn from them—their manners, their knowledge. It is just not the same world as ours. We are guests when we go there. To ignore their animal wisdom may be our ruin, sooner or later.

FIELD & FOREST REPORT: Blueberry rakers are out on the barrens doing their back-breaking work. Many are migrants from the South. Many are Native Americans from farther North, particularly Micmacs or 'M'ikmaqs.' The culture of blueberries may have been in place when the Europeans landed. As mentioned before, the basic agricultural practice for this crop is the burning of the fields. This clears away competing vegetation and kills many of the insects that threaten the crop. The ancients saw how blueberries come in after a naturally occurring fire and took it from there. There is nothing quite like the sight from the summit of Awanadjo of the fields, barrens and mountain slopes burning in April.

MOUNTAIN REPORT: The rills which run down the mountain so briskly in other seasons are nearly dried up now as the whole body of the mountain breathes out its moisture to form the clouds overhead. The Blue Hill Heritage Trust, which holds in trust much of the mountain, has set up a register book. It is interesting to note the different places of origin and experiences recorded by climbers. The mountain is a lodestone for souls, with the power to draw them from a great distance.

SALTWATER REPORT: This year's fledgling ducklings and loons are nearly full-sized now, though they have not yet acquired their adult feathers. There still appears to be a parental bond between the adults and the young of both. For the loons, this will continue into next season. The loon family is strong. Even when they are fishing at great distances apart, they now and then hoot back and forth to keep track.

CRITTER OF THE WEEK: The curious, playful, intelligent, and story-telling harbor seal, with long memories inherited from their ancestors.

SEED POD TO CARRY AROUND WITH YOU: From the late oceanographer, Jacques Cousteau: *The sea, once it casts its spell, holds one in its net of wonder forever.*

PERICOPES

"Split wood and I am there. Lift up the stone and you will find me there . . . He who has known the world, has found the body . . ."
These words of Jesus from the 2nd century gnostic Gospel of Thomas have great power for those who find a holy presence in wood, stone, and world. They suggest that the world

is a sacred body, and recall to us the eucharist or holy communion. The fact that the church considers these words to be heresy should not daunt us. Let me say why.

For at least the past 500 years, the debate about the eucharist has centered largely upon the issue of whether the bread and wine are mysteriously changed into the real body and blood of Christ or whether they simply symbolize that body. The former is called "transubstantiation" and is the Catholic position. The latter is called "consubstantiation" and is the Protestant position. The Book of Common Prayer, Articles of Religion, 1801—stating the Protestant tradition— says, "Transubstantiation (or the change in substance of Bread and Wine) . . . is repugnant to the plain words of Scripture . . . and hath given occasion to many superstitions. The Body of Christ is given, taken, and eaten . . . only after an heavenly and spiritual manner."

Real wars between Catholics and Protestants were fought over this little nuance of theology, and blood has even recently been shed over it. It is a relief to those who believe in human progress that this issue means little or nothing to most of us today, beyond the horror of people fighting and dying over these obscure theological points.

People I meet are much more concerned with the mystery of our violence toward each other and the Earth than they are with the mystery of whether the elements of communion are literally or only symbolically the body of Christ. Can one mystery shed light on the other?

If we split the wood, if we turn over the stone, if we go back of the bread, past the flour, the mill, and the grain which sprouts and grows we know not how, past the soil, past the wind and rain; then where are we? We are into botany, plant physiology, molecular biology, genetics, soil science, and meteorology. If we go beyond that, we are caught up in geology and geophysics, astrophysics, and cosmology. If we choose to go beyond even that, then we have no place further to go. We reach the end of knowledge. We end in mystery.

Our church's Book of Worship says, "The wheat that is gathered to make one loaf and the grapes that are pressed to make one cup remind participants that they are one in the body of Christ, the church." That's good as far as it goes, but it does not go far enough. The Protestant view, that the communion is just spiritual and symbolic, not physical, ignores the reality that we actually are part of One Body, and It's a whole lot bigger than any church. The molecules of water in the bread and the cup have been traveling through the bodies of living creatures, evaporating into the sky, falling as rain, washing through all of the earth's rivers, filling her oceans, since the earth came into being.

Undoubtedly, some of the moisture in this cup literally *was* the blood of Christ, not to mention the blood of Gautama, and Gandhi. In the bread, a like course has been travelled by the carbon molecules, the building blocks of life. Undoubtedly, some of this bread literally *was* the body of Christ, as well as the body of Mary his mother, Saint Brigid, and Joan of Arc.

By eating this little meal, we are physically taking part not just in the body of Christ or the church. All creatures have shared this bread and cup. We are taking part in all creatures who came before us, and all who will come after us, and even more, we are taking part in the Great Holy Body which is the Creator, and the whole Creation.

Can this shed any light on the mystery of our violence to this Holy Creation? It reveals that we are not separated from the Creation, not its Master, not its pinnacle, not its reason for being, as we might think. That is our self-deceit, or our "sin," if I may use that word. It reveals that violence done to any part of the Holy Body is done to the whole Body. Violence done to the soil is *simultaneously* violence to those in the past whose dust the soil is and violence to those in the future who will derive their life from the soil. And so it is with the air, the water, and all other creatures.

In taking communion we act out with our own bodies the truth that back of all bread, beyond all our knowledge, is still a mystery. The mystery is that we are part of the Whole and the Holy. It is not for us as a part, to control or direct or even understand the Holy Mystery. It is for us to live peacefully and compassionately within that mystery.

When he says, "Consider the lilies, consider the birds," Jesus tells us that openly and non-anxiously pondering the birds and flowers, how they grow; and meditating on the ways of Nature, can be a way out of our anxiety—a healing.

Summer is a healing time. We take the advice of Jesus seriously around here these days. We are less anxious about what we shall eat and what we shall drink, so the food pantry gets fewer calls and we have big cook-outs and clam-bakes. And one need only go to the beach or the post office in summer to see how much less anxious we are about our bodies, what we shall put on. Just about anything goes.

Yet the deep anxieties may remain, just below the surface. The anxiety of being banished. That God is angry at us. That God will not provide. That we must work so hard, because we are not worthy of God's grace and providence. That we don't belong here, that we are strangers, aliens, sojourners in the land.

These anxieties lead to the hostilities that Paul describes, dividing us from our own true nature, our Christ nature, and separating us from Nature herself, just as Adam and Eve had to leave the Garden in the Genesis story. But, this story of our banishment from the Garden is not about our history, it is about our spirituality. Still, the Genesis account is true, I believe, as a cautionary tale. If—as we are free to do—we choose to transgress the boundaries that the Creator has placed around us—the ways of Nature, then we will leave the peace of Paradise behind, and we will suffer. But, if we can learn to leave our anxiety behind, and find our Christ-nature in Nature herself, we can break down the dividing wall of hostility and be at one again.

Why does Jesus ask us to consider the birds and flowers? Because they do not gather into barns, but are fed. They do not worry about tomorrow, but only live now. God cares for them, and they know it. So it can be for us in these days, at least for a time.

The ways of God and the laws of Nature are the same, as many who came before us knew, and as many who come after us will know. Science without religion is heartless. Religion without science is fantasy. Science is one eye, religion is the other. To see the whole shape of the world, we need both eyes. By considering the face of Nature, we can see the face of God.

That's the Almanack for this moon, but don't take it from me, I'm no expert. Go out and see for yourself.

Cod.

Haddock

This is the Awanadjo Almanack for the Full *Sturgeon* Moon to the Full *Harvest* Moon, called "Tingiivik" or "Birds Fly South" by the north slope Eskimos, *Elul* on the Biblical calendar, and *August/September* in Downeast Maine.

FULL TO LAST QUARTER *STURGEON* MOON

August. The opposing of peach and sugar, and the sun inside the afternoon like the stone in the fruit. The ear of corn keeps its laughter intact, yellow and firm. August. The little boys eat brown bread and delicious moon.

From Frederico Garcia Lorca

August 17 is Davy Crockett born in 1786. Crockett was one of this country's first national popular heroes. Few Americans have had more lies written about them. His motto was, "Be sure you're right, then go ahead." Post-modernists will ask, "How can you be sure you're right before you've gone ahead?"

August 19—Bill Clinton's birthday, 1946.

August 24—Printing of Gutenberg Bible completed, 1456. Liberation of Paris, 1944.

NATURAL EVENTS: The Dog Days are over and the hottest driest weather seems to be behind us. It's been a great summer and it's mighty busy in town with seasonal sounds of car alarms and drivers honking at each other. Right after the Labor Day Exodus, we have little reunions at the post office and the store, seeing people we haven't really talked to all summer. The town is quieter and we are relieved, knowing that some of the most beautiful days of the entire year are still ahead.

"Weather is here, wish you were beautiful," as they say. Tattered remnants of tropical storms bred in the far off Gulf of Mexico are beginning to bring some moisture to our parched gardens, and the nights seem cooler as Summer tips toward Fall. Leavings of Perseid meteor shower "falling stars" are still visible on a clear night. Interesting, how the Eyebright, which is a good herbal remedy for allergies, is coming into bloom right now, just as the ragweed with its fili-greed leaves and tiny green flowers, one of the most noxious sneezemongers of all, is also coming into bloom.

FIELD & FOREST REPORT: Summer weather has dried the stalks of timothy, red-top, orchard grass to a shiny buff color until some of the meadows look like wheat fields waving in the breeze. The flowers of late summer include milkweed, evening primrose, mullein, butter-and-eggs [like a tiny snap-dragon], orange jewelweed in damp shady places, and the numerous kinds of golden rod everywhere.

RANK OPINION: As mentioned previously, many fields around here are mowed or "bush-hogged" once a year to keep them from reverting to forest. A good time to do this is in mid to late August when most of the Summer's wildflowers have bloomed and plant growth has stopped, but woody plants have not yet stored sugars in their roots for the first flush of next year's growth.

MOUNTAIN REPORT: Blueberry raking drawing to an end. Having felt the footfalls of a thousand climbers, the trails over the mountain begin to look pounded and bare these days, like an old moose with the hair worn off.

SALTWATER REPORT: With the warmest water in many years and fisheries being depleted by over-fishing with high technology equipment, sonar, drift nets, it seems there is no stopping it. The rich life of the ocean may be going the way of the old growth forest. The lobster fishery seems stable, though. They are steaming away by the thousands in home-made outdoor brick stoves with smoke rising from crooked stove pipes, all along the tourist routes.

CRITTER OF THE WEEK: The trademark sea creature of Maine is *Homarus Americanus*, also known as the "Maine lobster." You see them in some of the airports where they can be flown to inland sites for exorbitant prices. They are fished all along the N. Atlantic seaboard from the Carolinas to the Maritimes, but Maine seems their true home. Ed Muskie used to demonstrate how to hypnotize a lobster before putting it in the boiling water. A good man.

SEED PODS TO CARRY AROUND WITH YOU: from the Book of Common Prayer: *O God, who . . . hast promised to all those who seek thy kingdom . . . all things necessary to their bodily sustenance: Send us, we beseech thee, in this our necessity, such moderate rain and showers, that we may receive the fruits of the earth to our comfort, and to thy honor . . .*

LAST QUARTER *STURGEON* TO NEW *HARVEST* MOON

For you shall go out in joy and be led forth in peace; the mountains and hills before you shall break into singing, and all the trees of the fields shall clap their hands, instead of the thorn shall come up the maple, and instead of the briar shall come up the blueberry, and it shall be to the Creator a memorial, an everlasting sign that shall not be cut off.

—adapted for Downeast Maine from Isaiah 55:12-13

August 26—Women get the vote by Constitutional amendment, 1920. Rebecca Haley & Rob McCall wed, 1967.

August 27—Mother Teresa born, 1910.

August 28—March on Washington led by Martin Luther King Jr., 1963.

NATURAL EVENTS: Rain, which finally drenched the ground hereabouts for the first time in many weeks. No words can describe the pleasant sound of rain after a long drought. *Gratitude to Water; clouds, lakes, rivers, glaciers; holding or releasing; streaming through all our bodies' salty seas, in our minds so be it,* writes poet Gary Snyder.

UN-NATURAL EVENTS: Extremes of weather are being reported from many quarters. Aside from the political aspects of global warming, the scientific evidence is getting increasingly clear. It is happening. Old-timers tell us that Blue Hill bay used to freeze every winter all the way to Long Island. It has only frozen over twice in the last 30 years. In Antarctica, the average annual air temperatures have risen 5 degrees Fahrenheit over the past 50 years, causing great chunks of the ice cap to break off in summer and an ever-diminishing area of sea ice in winter. Sea ice is the habitat for krill, which is a major food source for penguins and sea mammals, especially the great whales. Krill have declined 60 to 90% since the early 80s, according to government funded research. Great changes moving over the face of the Earth.

Are we witnessing changes beyond any in history, and will we become part of that history? *The old ones say, 'only the Earth remains.' You speak truly, you are right.*

FIELD & FOREST REPORT: Blackberries are ripe. Oh, what a delicious explosion of flavor and memory in one berry. The Queen Anne's Lace is in bloom in the fields and on the roadsides, its spicy aroma brings back so many childhood memories, a circle of lace with a tiny dark cross in the center. How can there be no Designer, ask the old naturalists, when there is such rich and repeating design everywhere we turn? Slice through an apple sideways and you will find a starfish. Look down upon the bloom of the Queen Anne's lace and find a compass rose. Even non-living matter tends to orderliness—crystals, snowflakes, waves.

MOUNTAIN REPORT: One Sunday before the full moon I climbed the mountain fairly early in the morning before church. It was beautiful and quiet as the whole town is on Sunday mornings. At the summit no one else was there, or I should say, I saw no one else. I often get caught up in a mystical rapture at times like this—and at other times too, as many a terrified passenger in a vehicle I am driving will testify. At least it's an earthbound rapture so far. This day I was standing on the very summit and reciting in my mind the words of the "heretical" Gospel of Thomas where Jesus says, "I am the All. Split the wood and I am there, lift the stone and you will find me there." At that precise moment, a deep whirring sound came to my right ear and an extremely large insect landed on my right shoulder. Utterly forgetting Who this visitor might be, I jumped out of my pantheisitic reverie and into the air, brushing frantically at the creature on my shoulder. I felt its hard, chitinous edges on the side of my hand as it flew off, scolding me with a piercing, ultrasonic

"E-e-e-e-e-eeeeeee!" Translated from the Cicadian, this means, "Yes, and I too am the All."

SALTWATER REPORT: On a clear day, the islands of Blue Hill Bay can be seen extending out to open ocean—Long Island, Tinker, Pond, Black, Opechee, Swan's, Placentia. Many are uninhabited. Some still have old granite quarries, abandoned around the turn of the century when reinforced concrete replaced granite for construction. See the silent piles of quarried stone ready for shipment, left right where they were, and now covered with lichen. Hardy Blue Hill men used to work these quarries and row home in their dories for weekends.

CRITTER OF THE WEEK: The earwig, a primitive proto-insect which likes to hide out in nooks and crannies during daylight to come pouring out in great numbers when disturbed. There are 18 species in North America, according to my guide book. The female protects the eggs after they are laid, as no other insect does, which is endearing. Earwigs do not invade your ears, thank heavens, but they can give you a sharp pinch with their tails, as I discovered on a summer day when one found its way into my shorts.

SEED PODS TO CARRY AROUND WITH YOU: from Gary Snyder, *Eating the living germs of grasses, eating the ova of large birds, the fleshy sweetness packed around the sperm of swaying trees, the muscles of the flanks and thighs of soft-voiced cows, the bounce in the lamb's leap, the swish in the ox's tail, eating roots grown swoll inside the soil, drawing on life of living, clustered points of light spun out of space, hidden in the grape. Eating each other's seed, eating, ah, each other. Kissing the lover in the mouth of bread lip to lip.*

From the gospel of John: *Who eats my flesh and drinks my blood abides in me and I in them.*

I thirst by day, I watch by night. I receive! I have been received! I hear the flowers drinking in their light. I have taken counsel of the crab and the sea-urchin, I recall the falling of small waters, the stream slipping beneath the mossy logs . . . I am most immoderately married. The Lord God has taken my heaviness away. I have merged, like the bird, with the bright air, and my thought flies to the place by the bo-tree. Being, not doing, is my first job.

From Theodore Roethke

September 3, Frederick Douglass began his flight to freedom, 1838.

September 5, Birthday of Jesse James, 1847.

September 6, Pilgrims set sail for the New World, 1620

NATURAL EVENTS: A hatch of pale green *Ephemerae* with clear lacy wings and copper-colored eyes swarmed in the September sunset light the other evening—living and dying by the thousands in a day or two, like mayflies in late summer. Adults' only function is to reproduce. They do not eat. Too busy, I guess. There are nearly 600 species of mayfly in North America. Many a trout fisherman spends the Winter trying to copy them at the fly-tying bench.

FIELD & FOREST REPORT: Leaves beginning to show hints of red and yellow in some places, particularly the red maples. Mornings are cooler, but as the day warms up the cicadas begin the late summer hum, the crickets chirp merrily, and the grasshoppers jump click-clack in the air.

MOUNTAIN REPORT: Thoreau wrote this about his climb up Katahdin in 1846: *Vast, Titanic, inhuman Nature has got [man] at disadvantage, caught him alone, and pilfers him of some of his divine faculty . . . She seems to say sternly, why came ye here before your time? This ground is not prepared for you . . . Shouldst thou freeze or starve or shudder thy life away, here is no shrine, nor altar, nor any access to my ear.*

SALTWATER REPORT: The Cobscook Falls is a tidal falls similar to the Blue Hill Falls but greater by several orders of magnitude. It is about two miles as the raven flies from our camp in West Pembroke, Washington County, Maine. At certain times of the tide, we can step out our cabin door and hear the Falls thundering two miles away. Twice a day the tide fills, then empties, two large bodies of water—Dennys Bay which is five miles long and two wide and Whiting Bay which is six miles long and one wide. Much of this water flows in and out between Mahar's Point and Falls Island. The channel is wide enough so that, when the Falls are still, one can shout across and wait to hear a brilliant echo reflected back from the wooded opposite shore, but narrow enough to create a spectacular cataract when the tide flows, and deep calls to deep. The charts show the Falls channel to be perhaps 300 feet wide and 63 feet deep at mean low tide, and remember that the tides there run 25 to 30 feet, so that at full flood the Cobscook Falls channel may be 90 or more feet deep.

Out in the channel is a pinnacle rising some 85 feet above the bottom like a mountain in the stream. Around, and finally over this ledge an unthinkable volume of water crashes, falls, and breaks for hours at a time, then gradually becomes still, until it begins to creep, then slide, then thunder, back in the other direction. Approaching the Falls when it is running full, one is first overwhelmed by the loud roar, then by the sight of the terrifying turmoil of swiftly rushing water with whitewater and standing waves extending a half-mile into the mouth of the bays. At first one sees only raw chaos, but if one watches long enough, a pattern of order begins to appear.

As the water rushes past the rocky peak in the strait, it is roughly divided into two torrents and between them a vast bowl or basin whose length could easily accommodate a large boat. The sides of the basin slant down toward the center several feet below the surface of the surrounding water which is itself marked by large eddies, upsurges and whirlpools. Downstream from the basin, the divided flood comes crashing together to form a series of wide and deep standing waves successively smaller as they diminish into the distance. From the shore, I cannot even see into the depths of the trough of that first great wave. It is so deep that flotsam disappears from view for some seconds before coming into view again, climbing the face to the peak of the first standing wave, then disappearing into the next trough.

One can't help but think of what the fury of that water could do to a human body. Boats do go through it, though. There is even a story about a man who dove in to save his parrot from drowning; both were rescued.

Words fail in describing this place. The vast, surging water perturbs the very air around it and fills it with sound, flavor, and moisture. There is a distinct smell as of a huge sea creature, a living thing whose awesome, overwhelming commotion is at once frightening and exhilarating, terrifying and ecstatic.

CRITTER OF THE WEEK: The Cobscook Falls.

SEED PODS TO CARRY AROUND WITH YOU: *As the hart longs for flowing streams, so longs my soul for thee, O God . . . Deep calls to deep at the thunder of thy cataracts, all thy*

waves and thy billows have gone over me. By day the Lord
commands steadfast love, and at night God's song is with me,
a prayer to the God of my life.   —Psalm 42

FIRST QUARTER TO FULL *HARVEST* MOON

Ice mountain melted ages ago and made this ridge, this place
of changes. Now we are rooted in it, we of the old ones, we
of the ones from afar; orchard grass meadow, balsam fir
thicket, we are rooted in the ridge of changes in the time of
changes. The winds carry strange smells; this is a day of
change.—adapted from the *Chinook Psalter*

September 11, Destruction of the World Trade Center in
2001 [See PERICOPES below]

September 13, Birthday of Jesse Owens, 1915.

September 14, Birthday of Margaret Sanger, 1883.

NATURAL EVENTS: Late summer humid air and storm remnants from the far Caribbean, started by the tiniest turbu-
lence in the air around a tropical butterfly's wing, grown to a
fierce storm and now diminished to a dying breath. Rained
pretty good, too.

At our Cobscook Bay cabin we observed a profusion of
caterpillars loping about energetically, hanging from trees,
and climbing window screens. Tiny green ones floated
through the air on long silk threads. Big, naked translucent
moon-colored ones with a glowing blue stripe down the back
and a blue dot on each segment shone in the path. Shaggy
black and yellow ones with long tufts of black and white
bristles on head and tail arched their backs and reared up like

tiny Chinese dragons. It was an astounding, three-ring Caterpillar Circus. Our little insect book, though it shows plenty of butterflies and moths, does not show any members of this menagerie. I am beginning to wonder if some mad lepidopteran doctor, like Dr. Seuss maybe, came by during the night and dropped them off just to amaze us.

UN-NATURAL EVENTS: Once good and useful farmland in our town and yours which took generations to clear, now growing up in aspen and wild cherry, while vegetables are shipped here from California and Chile.

WILD SPECULATION: Local agriculture will continue to become more feasible as climate warms and transportation costs rise.

RANK OPINION: There have been movements in statehouses across the country and even in the Congress of the United States to pass laws that would require the taxpayers of each town, state or of the nation to reimburse landowners who can prove in court that the land to which they hold title has been diminished in value by town, state or federal environmental regulations. This legislation is based on a reading of the fifth amendment which suggests that land cannot be taken by the government without due compensation, and is called "takings" legislation.

On the face of it, the debate seems to be about who has the right to say how land can be used—the individual who holds title to it, or the government. Should the individual have the right to use the land to which he holds title in any way he sees fit, or should the government have the right to limit or regulate such use? What looks at first like the little guy struggling against oppressive government is more a question of the rights of the individual versus the rights of the community as protected by the government. This raises some real questions in my mind.

First, I cannot fathom why the proponents of takings legislation are not mortally embarrassed in suggesting that the interests of the individual are not to be regulated or limited by the interests of the community, be it town, state, or nation. Are we to determine the value of everything we do only in terms of our own self-interest? Are we to feel justified in using up and depleting every resource for the benefit of our own generation with no thought to those who will come after us? Are we to suggest that this is the American way?

Suppose previous generations had done this? We would have no national parks, no public waterways, no public schools or highways or libraries or museums or monuments, no public works of any kind funded by the community and designed to last for more than one generation. I see in this type of legislation a raw, unbridled greed and selfishness thinly veiled by a false appeal to imaginary traditional American values.

Second, is the question really one of who owns the land; the individual or the government? If so, then the answer is, "neither one." The land is owned by its Creator. "The earth is the Lord's and the fulness thereof," reads the scripture. We cannot own what we do not create. The most ancient scriptures affirm that the land is not ours to do with as we wish. The use of the land is only provisionally ours.

The Old Testament, upon which many call in defense of absolutely free use of land, clearly declares that we are limited in our uses of the land by divine commandment. "When you reap the harvest of the land, you shall not strip your vineyards bare, neither shall you pick up the fallen grapes after the harvest. You shall leave them for the poor and the sojourner. I am the Lord your God." (Leviticus 22) "The land shall not be sold forever, for the land is mine; for ye are strangers and sojourners with me." (Leviticus 25:23) The land is God's. We use it at God's pleasure only as long as we use it for the benefit of all others as well as ourselves, for the short time we occupy it.

If you don't like the scripture, then consider what might happen if each person were to use "his" land without thought to others. If a brook runs over my land and then into yours, am I to be considered within my rights to poison that brook so that you may not take fish or drinking water from it? Am I to be allowed to build a huge brush fire on a windy day that allows smoke and ashes to blow over your land and house? Shall the government stop protecting the life, liberty, and pursuit of happiness of my neighbors, my descendants, other living creatures because it inconveniences me? Hoo boy! That's the road to ruin.

FIELD & FOREST REPORT: Purple asters, shining red bunch-berries, A few late lupine spires, goldenrod and (a-choo!) ragweed, as well as bob-o-links in the bayberry bushes, katy-dids in the Queen Anne's lace, butterflies in the goldenrod, grasshoppers in the gravel, and goldfinches in the garden.

MOUNTAIN REPORT: Awanadjo raises her silent mass above the bay, clean and heavy against the sky with colors of cop-per, rust and yellow on her flanks. She is our symbol, she is the natural head and face of our town. We live on her body. In winter she is robed in white, in summer rich green. In spring and fall she is often covered with cloud. Much of the mountain is privately-owned, yet we hold it in common.

It is often said that, "a man can do whatever he chooses with his own land." Yet our predecessors for countless gener-ations have chosen to do those things with the mountain which for the most part have little harmed its beauty, its ecology, its utility, and its accessibility to the prudent villager or pilgrim of their own generation and the ones succeeding. Our ancestors did this for us and for generations they would never know. They could have destroyed the beauty of the mountain because it was "their land." They did not. For them, some things were sacred. And for us?

SALTWATER REPORT: The water of the bay is at its warmest right now. Sometimes over 60 degrees F. Still, no one swims voluntarily for very long.

CRITTER OF THE WEEK: Migrating monarch butterflies heading for Mexico, flutter over the open water of Blue Hill bay far from land. How can something so fragile be at once so strong?

SEED PODS TO CARRY AROUND WITH YOU: from Robert Frost: *The mountain held the town as in a shadow. I saw so much before I slept there once: I noticed that I missed stars in the west, where its black body cut into the sky . . . There ought to be a view around the world from such a mountain.*

PILGRIM'S JOURNAL: [from the week of September 11, 2001]. Tuesday night while the dust was still settling over the island the Dutch bought from the Indians for $26.00, over the bodies of the quick and the dead, the good and the bad, we stepped outside to look at the sky above our little house in Eastport—the great sky which rises over Moose Island and Manhattan Island alike. It was so very quiet.

The stars were clearly bright, but the lights in the sky did not move and flash as they usually do. There was no high and distant roar. For the first time since the commencement of air traffic 75 or more years ago, people stopped flying hither and yon for a time, in a quiet tribute to those who died by means of exploding aircraft. This silence in the immeasurable dome of the heavens was something our generation has never known. It was the silence of the evening of the second day of Creation, the silence pierced 2000 years ago by the melody of angels singing Peace on Earth, Good News to All People. Silent Night, Holy Night.

Thousands of people going to work in tall buildings, going about their business, doing what they thought was right, trying to be good, were in an instant thrown from Time into Eternity, from the Moment into the Mystery. Tens of thousands of hearts were broken. Some, perhaps, will never mend. Millions of tears are still being shed over a horrendous event, an unspeakable crime which is being called an act of war. It is a strange war, though, in which all the soldiers died instantly. Still, as in most modern wars, many more innocent civilians than soldiers lost their lives.

Rising above the towering flames, the smoke and dust, we can almost see this as a shifting and colliding of tectonic plates, an eruption of molten lava once hidden deep in the human soul, now released in a furious cataclysm. To single out any person, group, or nation for retaliation can only prolong the agony that the world has suffered for hundreds of generations, the weak and innocent suffering most of all, and the powerful the least.

How can we Americans, who think of ourselves as the most powerful nation the world has ever seen, be so vulnerable? How can so few bring such destruction upon so many? The temptation is, as it has always been, to strike back blindly; thrash about in wounded rage, to kill the killers and murder the murderers. But, the killers have already killed themselves.

If there are others who bear responsibility, let them be judged in an international court of justice. Let the whole story be told. If there is a judgment of God here, what, and upon whom, might it be? Is it not upon the whole earth? The Bible is quite clear on these matters: "Vengeance is mine, says the Lord, I will repay . . . Lay not up for yourselves treasures on earth . . . The leader among you will be the servant of all . . . Those who live by the sword will die by the sword." The Koran, too, tells us that no one is a believer until he loves for his brother what he loves for himself. These sound like weak platitudes, but isn't this our faith? If we do not exercise this ancient wisdom now, then when?

The coming days will be a real test of faith for all of us. We are told that our nation will never be the same after last Tuesday, and that is surely true. But, how will we be different? What will change in this country we dearly love? Will we arm our nation even more, spend billions on our security, raise our perimeters, take to ourselves still more of the world's resources, guarding them ever more zealously from the rest of the world, maintaining our standard of living at the expense of millions of others? Will we pull up the drawbridge of our country and prepare ourselves to strike back angrily and fearfully at every demon, real or imagined?

Or will we do an entirely new thing? Open our hearts to the cries of the world; open our hands to the weak and needy of every nation; and pray for the peace of Jerusalem. Weep with those who weep. Be faithful to the unfaithful, and peaceful toward the unpeaceful. Give to the Red Cross and the United Nations; and act in our own lives the way we want the whole world to act. Call for a multilateral international tribunal on terrorism and economic justice, while vocally opposing the vengeful calls for more innocent blood to be shed.

We *can* be patriots for peace. We can declare henceforth every September 11th a World Sabbath. Ever after on this day, let the heavens be silent. Let the airplanes be grounded. Let the trains and tanks and traffic stand still. Let the banks and the stock exchanges cease their getting and spending. Let no money change hands. Let us all walk on the streets and paths and ways of the world and see each other face to face as God-created human beings.

On the site of the former World Trade Center build a shrine, a basilica of world religions, a cemetery, a hospital, an orphanage, a home for the aged, a college of peace, and a garden of food and flowers.

For generations to come we *can* make the leap of faith from the towering inferno of fear, hate, vengeance and war into the arms of the one God who weeps with us today; and who speaks ever and again the words "Peace, Peace," until at long last there is peace.

**That's the Almanack for this moon, but don't
take it from me.
Go out and see for yourself.**

This is the Awanadjo Almanack for the Full *Harvest* Moon to the Full *Hunter's* Moon, called *Tishri* or *Ethanim* on the Biblical calendar, and *September/October* in Downeast Maine.

FULL TO LAST QUARTER *HARVEST* MOON

All through my life I never did believe in human measurement. Numbers, time, inches, feet. All are just ploys for cutting nature down to size. I know the grand scheme of the world is beyond our brains to fathom, so I don't try, just let it in. I don't believe in numbering God's creatures.

—From Louise Erdrich

September 20, Birthday of Jelly Roll Morton, 1885.

September 21, birthday of H.G. Wells, 1866.

September 22, Autumnal Equinox

September 26, George Gershwin born 1898, T.S. Eliot born, 1888. The House Bank declares congressional representatives may no longer make overdrafts, thus restoring the system of checks and bounces, 1991.

NATURAL EVENTS: The occasional monarch butterfly still paints its solitary bobbing streak of orange and black across land and water to its winter place in the far Southwest, California, Mexico. Smaller white and yellow sulphur butterflies, fritillaries and tiny coppers are active in the little white asters. Now and then the long, high wavering V of migrating geese can be seen in the sky and their haunting call seems rusty red, like the leaves of the maples; like the backs of the migrating red-shouldered hawks now circling below the cliffs of Awanadjo in silent concentration on the ground below. Overhead the ravens are circling about 1000 feet above the summit, then diving and dancing in pairs like Fred and Ginger, but more erotic. Next moment, the ravens are screaming *Hawk!* and plunging out of the clouds to attack the floating hawks. At certain moments in the shadow of our mountain, we can perceive that all creatures are engaged in a subliminal, wordless conversation with each other—cloud, water, raven, hawk, gull, wind, sun, stone, and tree communicating without a glance their consensus with the Creator who saw everything that had been made and it was good.

UN-NATURAL EVENTS: California potatoes and Washington State apples in the produce section of the local market hauled all the way across the country by gas-guzzling trucks to the state of Maine where we already grow perfectly good potatoes and apples.

WILD SPECULATION: Getting back to the hawks and ravens; the ravens have an antipathy for the hawks. Perhaps it is because the ravens tend to stay in one area and the hawks are great travellers in their Fall and Spring migrations. Perhaps the ravens view the hawks with suspicion and harass them as though they were gypsies moving through town. By the way, the word "hawk" is borrowed from the vocabulary of the birds. The ravens were yelling *"Hawk!"* with great excitement in between muttering under their breath during the hawk migrations long before any humans developed the power of speech, or even walked on their hind legs. Your backyard hens know the same word. When any large bird flies over, even a seagull, the hens scream *"Hawk!"* and run for cover.

FIELD & FOREST REPORT: The fields are full of goldenrod of several kinds (Peterson's Field Guide lists more than 25 varieties, others list more than 60) and a few tattered Black-eyed Susans. Purple asters are coming into bloom, a sure sign of the coming Fall. The milkweed pods are drying and beginning to crack to reveal seed and silk. The apple trees are loaded this year. Early varieties have already dropped, but fall apples are turning sweet and red.

MOUNTAIN REPORT: On the mountain's south slope, the blueberry bushes are beginning to flash scarlet to brassy orange. In a few places the rare Pearly Everlasting raises its tall stalks and small, dry white flowers whose demeanor will change little throughout the frosty Fall and into the bitter Winter. The large erosion control project in which tons of soil were spread, graded, seeded and lined with staked hay bales on the Morse piece during the summer is sprouting with green grass. We even found some turnips growing there. The town has reason to be pleased and proud at this effort to reclaim the Southeast flank of Blue Hill.

SALTWATER REPORT: There never seems to be a low tide in the Salt Pond into and out of which pour the Blue Hill Falls. Even when it is low tide in Blue Hill Bay, the Salt Pond still seems to be at least half full.

CRITTER OF THE WEEK: The large black and yellow spiders in the meadow and garden which spread their large webs with the distinctive white zig-zag line and hung with the shrouded bodies of their prey. I saw three of them in the meadow on the South side of the mountain. Jonathan Fisher observed the very same kind, recording it in his journal on August 20, 1825, and August 12, 1826. He calls it a "wheel-net" spider. "I was amused," he writes, "with seeing a wheel-net spider, within the space of about an hour demolish his old net, and construct a new one."

SEED PODS TO CARRY AROUND WITH YOU: from John Muir, *Nature's object in making animals and plants might possibly be first of all the happiness of each one of them, not the creation of all for the happiness of one. Why should man value himself as more than a small part of the one great unit of creation? And what creature of all that the Lord has taken the pains to make is not essential to the completeness of all that unit—the cosmos? The universe would be incomplete without man; but it would also be incomplete without the smallest transmicroscopic creature that dwells beyond our conceitful eyes and knowledge.*

And from John Steinbeck, *Can you live without a willow tree? Well, no you can't. The willow tree is you.*

LAST QUARTER *HARVEST* TO NEW *HUNTER'S* MOON

Birds nest in my arms, on my shoulders, behind my knees, between my breasts there are partridges, they must think I am a tree. The Canada geese think I am a fountain, they all come down and drink when I talk. When deer pass, they pass over me, and perched on my fingers, the sparrows eat, the ants think I am the earth, and men think I am nothing.

Adapted from Gloria Fuentes

NATURAL EVENTS: The Monarch is probably as close to a celebrity butterfly as you are going to find. Their bright orange and black wings are recognized immediately by beginning lepidopterists and young children. Their long fall migration to Winter quarters in the highlands of California and Mexico is reported on the evening news, and their gatherings in those southeastern forests are visited by eco-pilgrims from all over the world. When it was announced that the Monarchs might be threatened by the pollen of genetically-altered pest resistant corn, the story made the front page of newspapers and may have indirectly contributed to the destruction of experimental corn fields by eco-activists.

I want to call attention to another, far less well-known butterfly that may be equally deserving of our admiration: the Mourning Cloak, *Nymphalis antiopa*. Though less numerous than the Monarch, the Mourning Cloak is fairly common around here. Though slightly smaller and darker in color, the Mourning Cloak is exquisitely beautiful with wings of a deep, velvety brown or purple bordered in yellow and lined with rows of iridescent blue spots. Most endearing is the Mourning Cloaks' way of staying through the tough Maine winter with the rest of us instead of flying away to warmer climes like the Monarch, or just laying its eggs and dying like other butterflies. In doing this, it becomes the first butterfly to appear in these parts to cheer our hearts in late March or early April, fluttering about on winter-worn wings during the first warm days of Spring. I love them for that. Where are they today, getting ready for the long winter? I don't know. Maybe some of you do. I suspect that they have loaded up on nectar, filling their veins with a natural glucose-based anti-freeze, and have found a quiet sheltered place to wait out the coming cold so that they can be the first ones out in Spring, a monumental natural event, a resurrection waiting to happen.

FIELD & FOREST REPORT: Flocks of Fall warblers swooping and dipping in the winterberry and bayberry bushes and calling, "Tip . . . Tip".

MOUNTAIN REPORT: In the Wisdom Woods just to the Northeast of the summit there are several big dead spruces with broken stubs of branches sticking out of them. These make different pleasing tones when struck, like a natural marimba. I often stop and play a little tune on them with my hiking stick. One day I did this and heard a scratching sound rising up from inside the hollow trunk until a little red squirrel popped out of a hole overhead scolding me angrily. Sleeping late, I guess.

Some marvelous mountain-climbing days this past week with many pilgrims going up for a little healing. Cool nights and warm days bring brown garter snakes and green snakes out in the path.

SALTWATER REPORT: We found the body of a five-inch flounder on the beach at our camp the other day. It was changing from the upright-swimming juvenile to the flat, bottom-dwelling adult form. It seemed precious and monstrous at the same time.

CRITTER OF THE WEEK: That little flounder.

SEED PODS TO CARRY AROUND WITH YOU: from Robert Frost: *When a friend calls to me from the road and slows his horse to a meaning walk, I don't stand still and look around on all the hills I haven't hoed, and shout from where I am, "What is it?" I thrust my hoe in the mellow ground, blade-end up and five feet tall, and plod: I go up to the stone wall for a friendly visit.*

Sunshine is delicious, rain is refreshing, wind braces us up, snow is exhilarating; there is really no such thing as bad weather, only different kinds of good weather.
—From English writer John Ruskin

September 30, James Meredith becomes first black student at the Univ. of Mississippi, 1962.

October 1, founding of the People's Republic of China, 1949.

October 8, the anniversary of Chief Joseph's surrender at Bear's Paw in 1877. Forced by the U.S. Army to leave their traditional home in the Wallowa Valley, now Idaho, Chief Joseph and a small band of Nez Perce set out to travel to the federally prescribed reservation, but were constantly attacked by settlers. They tried to defend themselves, but were severely beaten. They were finally forced to surrender to the army under Generals O.O. Howard and Nelson Miles, who acknowledged Chief Joseph to be one of the greatest leaders and warriors in history. Strange how we honor such nobility after we have nearly ruined it. Here are Joseph's words of surrender:

"Tell General Howard I know his heart... My people, some of them have run away to the hills and have no blankets, no food; no one knows where they are—perhaps freezing to death. I want to have time to look for my children and see how many I can find. Maybe I shall find them among the dead. Hear me my chiefs. I am tired; my heart is sick and sad. From where the sun now stands, I will fight no more forever."

NATURAL EVENTS: The invasion of lady-bird beetles or lady-bugs as we call them. Hundreds on the warm side of buildings, dozens in the house, single ones bumping into your nose and riding on your hat. People from miles around reported seeing them. What's up? They bring good luck, that's what. Imagine how we would feel if it were any other insect. But with the benign lady-bug, we are amused and feel somehow blessed. I've heard that the "lady" in the name is derived from "Our Lady"—that is the Blessed Virgin, Mother of God, the female aspect of the deity, or, if you will, the Goddess in Christian tradition.

Also notice the woolly apple aphids which look like small flies floating through the air on a tuft of white wool. Sometimes there are so many that they look like a little snow flurry. And see the clarity and whiteness of "October Light" as it illuminates the colored leaves and reflects off our white clapboard houses.

UN-NATURAL EVENTS: Obsessive lawn-mowing. Now that the season is over, we can look back to see that mowing a lawn weekly or more is a dubious undertaking. This past summer provides a good example. If we mowed regularly through July and August, chances are that, because of the drought, we developed some large brown, dead patches of lawn. We also diminished the diversity of plant, small animal, and insect species in our immediate environment; and we added a load of carbon dioxide and other pollutants to the over-burdened atmosphere. Lawn mowers, having no pollution control devices, are major offenders in the summer smog crisis experienced in Hancock County and many other places.

One of the greatest obstacles to slacking off on obsessive mowing is the social pressure. If we let our lawn grow beyond the approved height of about three inches, there may be little remarks from the neighbors. "So, is your lawn-mower broken?" Or, "You gonna sell hay?" In some parts of the country, there have even been lawsuits brought by neighbors against people who choose not to mow. If everyone around us is mowing the lawn down to a butch flat-top every week, it is hard to not keep up with the Joneses. This reminds me of the great country singer George Jones. According to Nicholas Dawidoff in his excellent book *In the Country of Country*, George Jones mows his lawn every day, then goes into the fully-appointed barbershop in his own home and gets his hair cut. Every day. On the other hand, Bob Dylan is reported to have said, "If you don't let your hair grow out, it will grow in."

Lawn-mowing presents a yawning cultural chasm (like hair-cutting), but with pluck and goodwill we can bridge the chasm. To the social pressure a first response might be the revered "It's-my-land-and-I-can-do-whatever-I-want-with-it" dictum. This appeals to strict constructionists and property rights advocates. No one is materially harmed by another's shaggy, natural lawn, as near as I can tell. It's really a matter of esthetics.

A second response is the "creeping suburbanism" argument. We live here because we like the country life, and country people are independent and take care of their micro-environment, or "lawn", as they darn well please. In the suburbs people may peer out of their windows day and night to see what their neighbors are doing, then rise in the morning and try to outdo them. We country people still don't (I hope). Obsessive ritual lawn-cropping is a clear symptom of creeping suburbanism.

A third response is the most powerful "natural wildlife refuge" argument. On longer, more langourous lawns, watch the finches gorging on dandelion seeds, listen to the crickets in the long grass, see the proliferation of small creatures from slugs to chipmunks to mourning doves, see the richness of a longer lawn, and you may soon acknowledge the enormous value of a natural yard.

Here are some suggestions for improving the health, vitality and diversity of our micro-agricultural and ecological system next summer:

Cut the mowing schedule in half. If it was every week this summer, cut it to every two weeks next summer. This will halve the labor *and* the pollution.

When mowing, raise the blade to the highest position to allow the grass to remain longer, thus holding moisture in the ground, which helps trees and other plantings and creeping creatures.

Set aside certain areas in the yard for natural preserves to be mowed only once during the season. This will allow native plants and wildflowers to get established attracting bees, butterflies, exotic sphinx moths and nectar- and seed-eating birds like hummingbirds and finches. Longer grass also attracts chirping crickets, grasshoppers, katydids, and numerous others. One annual mowing will keep woody plants out.

Leave some wild margins that are not mowed at all. These areas provide habitat and encourage the presence of larger birds and animals. Wild margins also screen and muffle noise from traffic and other sources and hold much more moisture in the soil during times of drought.

RANK OPINION: Mowed areas around buildings are fine for preventing moisture damage to structures, for discouraging wildlife from moving into the attic or cellar, and for sitting out in the sun, but obsessive lawn-mowing is not healthy for our micro-environments or for the larger environment. As far as hair-cutting is concerned . . . Hey, it's your head.

MOUNTAIN REPORT: Awanadjo lives up to her name, "small, misty mountain," wreathed in cloud and mist and exerting her powerful and benevolent influence on those who take the trouble to climb her rocky sides—soothing the mind, healing the heart.

CRITTER OF THE WEEK: The blue jays diligently planting acorns. Studies show that the jays can remember the location of hundreds of hidden acorns. The ones they forget are the forests of the future.

SEED PODS TO CARRY AROUND WITH YOU, from French philosopher Blaise Pascal: *Nature is an infinite sphere of which the centre is everywhere and the circumference nowhere.*

And from poet Donald Jeffrey Hayes: *May hills lean toward you, hills and windswept mountains, and trees be happy that have seen you pass.*

FIRST QUARTER TO FULL *HUNTER'S* MOON

This grand show is eternal. It is always sunrise somewhere; the dew is never all dried at once; a shower is forever falling; vapor is ever rising. Eternal sunrise, eternal sunset . . . on seas and continents and islands, each in its turn, as the round earth rolls.   From John Muir

October 9, Benjamin Banneker, planner of the District of Columbia dies, 1806.

October 11, Eleanor Roosevelt born, 1884.

October 12, Luciano Pavarotti born, 1935.

NATURAL EVENTS: The Lady-bug convention continues. They are apparently an Asian variety that was introduced in the Gulf states in the 70s for the control of aphids. The larval stages are sometimes called "aphid lions" because of their voracious appetite for aphids. Actually, through a hand lens the little critters look like tiny ferocious Chinese dragons.

UN-NATURAL EVENTS: Tracks of four-wheeler ATVs are visible where they have repeatedly gone around the rocks placed across the foot of the old road over the town land on Blue Hill mountain. Farther up the mountain, I can see where the knobby tires of these vehicles have torn up the fragile soil. Now, this is common land, it belongs to all of us. The rocks were put there by our elected road commissioner to keep out unauthorized vehicles. Probably 99 out of 100 of us who go up the mountain go on foot, hoping to minimize intrusion upon the life of the mountain and damage to the soil.

There might be good reasons for an ATV to go up the mountain. One would be to take up a person who, due to age or infirmity, could not enjoy the heights in any other way, though we've helped carry an occupied wheelchair up, as well as many little children. Another would be to rescue a sick or injured hiker, though this could also be done on foot as it always was. Another would be to do necessary services on the radio tower, though there have been times when I've seen two people ride up on an ATV with only a small tool-box which either could have easily carried up on foot. My big gripe is with people who do it purely for recreation, thinking they have a right to ignore rocks and signs placed to stop vehicular traffic and to protect the common land. It is the blindness of a few to think that they have a God-given right to violate the common good of the many.

Now that we're getting warmed up to the subject, have you

noticed the advertisements for "sport utility vehicles" in national news magazines? The Mitsubishi Montero Sport ad says, "It came to comfort the earth. The planet wasn't exactly designed for your comfort." Hmm. The Creator must have goofed. The Jeep ads suggest that their vehicles can satisfy the human desire to return to Nature. This is not about Jeeps. I owned a Jeep that had been returning to Nature for 27 years and threatening to make the return final at any moment. This is about the suggestion that we need a motor vehicle to help us return to Nature.

One Jeep is called "Renegade." A renegade is someone who will not submit to a human authority trying to define his or her life: hardly a description of a person who tries to express independence by buying the latest heavy metal toy/tool of the Unholy Petroleum Empire. Probably the best-known renegade was the Apache guerilla leader Geronimo who, with a small band, evaded the US Cavalry for many years. In the 1880s an elite corps of men who had all won athletic honors at West Point, knew the terrain, and had the very finest horses were unable in a search lasting months to locate a single member of Geronimo's band, many of whom were on foot. Now and then, a renegade was captured. *The American Indian*, edited by Raymond Friday Locke, contains an account of a journalist's visit with a wounded member of Geronimo's band in an Army hospital. Before he would talk, the Apache motioned that he wanted a cigarette. Given the fixings, he skillfully rolled one and asked for a match. Given the match, he kicked one leg out from under the bedsheets and striking the match on the sole of his bare foot, lit his smoke. This man had not been eluding the US Army for years in the toughest terrain by driving around in a Jeep.

Another Jeep is the "Cherokee Chief." Probably the best-known Cherokee chief was Sequoyah who invented the

Cherokee alphabet by means of which his people within 20 years went from being illiterate to being 90% literate in their own language—an unparalleled accomplishment. Though he was crippled, Sequoyah also walked the Trail of Tears when thousands of Cherokees were forcibly marched from their homelands in Georgia to concentration camps in Oklahoma 2,000 miles away. Thousands died on the march. Needless to say, Sequoyah was not driving a Jeep.

Some say that the manufacturing of these vehicles is good for the economy. The truth is that there is man's economy and God's economy. If man's economy is not in accord with the Creator's, then when push comes to shove, which it rapidly is, the Creator's economy will remain and man's will fall and be forgotten.

So, anyway . . . If you want to get off the road, get off your tail and walk; or may Geronimo do more than let the air out of your wide-guy tires.

RANK OPINION: My little wish for those who use off-road vehicles destructively: "May their breath smell like exhaust, may their blood turn to motor oil, may their hindquarters grow to resemble their knobby tires, and may all their parts be back-ordered 'til the end of time."

FIELD & FOREST REPORT: The colors are fading a little. But, just wait. There will be one last show in a couple of weeks, when all the other leaves have fallen and then the hackamatacks suddenly turn a pale burnt gold against the dark spruce, fir and pine—one last breath of the dying season.

HUNTING REPORT: Moose and duck season are underway. Have you heard the apocryphal reports from the North country about blaze orange ducks? Apparently a Canadian farmer was fed up with having his domestic ducks shot by hunters and came up with a plan to feed his breeding ducks blaze orange surveyors tape and other cheap plastic blaze orange items which he shredded and fed to them along with their regular feed. The result was that his domestic ducks began laying blaze orange eggs. When these eggs hatched, the emerging ducklings were also blaze orange. Since hunters are understandably reluctant to shoot at anything blaze orange since it might be another hunter, this first generation of blaze orange domestic ducks reached breeding age. Due to flooding from heavy rains in the Fall of 1999, many of these blaze orange domestic ducks escaped to the wild and began breeding with wild ducks resulting in an increasing number of blaze orange wild ducks. Over the past several years, it seems that natural selection is producing large numbers of wild ducks of this same blaze orange color which are beginning in some Northern areas to out-number the traditional brown, and buff-colored creatures. In many areas, according to reports, more and more duck hunters are coming home empty-handed while at the same time duck numbers are growing. Many experts agree that there is good science behind this phenomenon, as any chicken farmer will tell you who regularly feeds marigolds to his hens to make the yolks more orange.

And in this case, if you have swallowed this report so far, the yolk is on you.

MOUNTAIN REPORT: On the wooded slope of Awanadjo near the Osgood Trail, we saw a spritely weasel nonchalantly bounding along fallen tree trunks and stopping long enough to observe us very curiously. I thought immediately of Annie Dillard's words on weasels. *Weasel! I'd never seen one wild before. . . . The weasel was stunned into stillness as he was emerging from beneath an enormous shaggy rose bush four feet away. I was stunned into stillness . . . Our eyes locked, and someone threw away the key . . . Our look was as if two lovers, or deadly enemies, met unexpectedly on an overgrown path when each had been thinking of something else . . . It emptied our lungs. It felled the forest, moved the fields, drained the pond; the world dismantled and tumbled into that black hole of eyes.*

I would like to learn, or remember, how to live . . . The weasel lives in necessity and we live in choice, hating necessity and dying at the last ignobly alone in its talons. I would like to live as I should, as the weasel lives as he should. And I suspect that for me the way is like the weasel's: open to time and death painlessly, noticing everything, remembering nothing, choosing the given with a fierce and pointed will.

PILGRIM'S JOURNAL: On the old maps of the area, what is now called Billings Pond was First Pond, Douglass Pond was Second Pond, and Woods Pond was Third Pond. We were only vaguely aware until recently that there is another, and were fortunate to be guided by the late Conrad Rupert on a visit to Fourth Pond, a hidden, pristine area of pond, marsh, wetland and old growth woodland way out in what is called "The Kingdom" in West Blue Hill. All four ponds are strung together like jewels along Carleton Stream which empties into the Salt Pond. The First Pond is Agate, the Second is Copper, the Third is Jasper, but the Fourth Pond is the wildest gem, Tourmaline.

CRITTER OF THE WEEK: The long-tailed weasel in the woods on Awanadjo.

SEED PODS TO CARRY AROUND WITH YOU: from Edwin Way Teale: *On such October days as this, we look about us as though in some new and magic land. The mystical draws close behind the luminous veil. We see the things about us and sense larger meanings just beyond our grasp. Looking back on such a time, we add—as Thoreau did one autumn day—"And something more I saw which cannot easily be described."*

And from Elizabeth Lawrence: *Even if something is left undone, everyone must take time to sit still and watch the leaves turn.*

PERICOPES

It is easy to see how central oil is to Western religion. Oil is the fat of the land, and of the lamb. When Sarah, the Mother of Israel, and her descendants lit a lamp in their tents, it was a wick set in tallow, the fat of the lamb. When King David was anointed, it was with olive oil. One of the great miracles in the Jewish tradition came during the Maccabean revolt when the lamp in the Holy of Holies kept burning after it rightfully should have run out of oil. This event is celebrated to this day as Hanukkah. The very name "Messiah", which in Greek is "Christ," means literally "The One Anointed with Oil."

When Christian Europeans came to this country, they still got their oil from sheep and pigs—tallow and lard. They made candles from these, adding the natural oil of the bayberry, to light their homes. But it was not enough. More people wanted more oil; so the wild whale became the prey of so many Ahabs; and whale oil lighted this country through the 19th century. All of this oil was taken from the bodies of other living things—olives, bayberries, sheep, pigs, whales.

Then, when the whales were nearly gone, a man named Drake found a way to take petroleum, "rock oil," from the body of the greatest living thing—the Earth. Soon we were harpooning Earth's enormous body for more and more oil to light our lamps and keep us warm, just as those before us had taken oil, grease, fat, tallow, and lard from other living bodies.

Before we started killing the whales, we produced our own oil by raising sheep, pigs, olives, corn and the like. When we started killing the whales, we crossed. We stopped making and started taking our oil; and we have been taking, not making it ever since. This is unholy. The Lakota [Sioux] word for white man is "Wasichu" or "fat-taker"—the one who takes the fat he did not make.

The world political climate is now dominated by those who have the oil or can take it by force. Our leaders are again anointed by oil. We are, as Becky says, "The Petroleum People." We are entirely dependent on the unholy oil extracted from the body of the Earth. We have forgotten how to make it, and like a helpless retrograde infant, can now only take it.

The final irony is this: The Jewish people gave divine status to the lamb which gave the oil they needed. Early Christians adapted this language and called Jesus "the Lamb of God" because he gave them the oil of life. In our own time, many have begun to view the whale and the Earth, from which we have taken our oil, as also holy and worthy of reverence; just as those who came before us revered the lamb and called it "holy."

This is good. Surely the lamb gave its life that we might live. But there are always more lambs. So also did the whale die for us, and more whales may yet survive. But there is only one Earth and if we sacrifice the Earth, cooked in the heat and suffocated in the smoke of her own burning oil, then we have made an unholy sacrifice. If we continue to take what we did not make, then, we shall also be sacrificed . . . by all that is good and holy.

And by our own hand.

That's the Almanack for this moon, but don't take it from me.
Go out and see for yourself.

This is the Awanadjo Almanack for the Full *Hunter's* to the Full *Beaver* Moon, called "Nippivik" or "Setting Sun" to the north slope Eskimos, *Marchesvan* or *Bul* in the Bible, and October/November in Maine.

FULL TO LAST QUARTER *HUNTER'S* MOON

I walk in your world, a mercy, a healing. Like a cooper of barrels you bind the mountains with ribbing. Your hand rests on the rambunctious seas, they grow peaceful, the brow of a sleeping child. Autumn is a king's progress, largesse lies ripe on the land. Up, down the furrow your midas touch rains gold, rainbows are from your glance. Fall of rain, evenfall, all all is blessing   —Daniel Berrigan

October 18 is St. Luke's day, on the Christian calendar, also the anniversary of the beginning of the German War Crimes trials at Nurnberg in 1945.

October 20 is the anniversary of MacArthur's return to the Philippines in 1944.

October 21 is the anniversary of the "Armies of the Night" storming of the Pentagon in 1967 by opponents of the Vietnam War, including yours truly. Aye, those were the days.

NATURAL EVENTS: We're busy enough here, letting the long, langorous Summer and Fall fall away behind us, and doing those things that upright, nearly hairless primates can do to prepare for Winter. That means gathering ourselves in and buttoning up the house, putting up the wood, cleaning the woodstoves, and beginning to live a little more in remembering than in anticipation. Nicely enough just at the same time, as all Northern peoples do, we begin remembering and retelling our holy stories. They will give us great joy, comfort, sorrow and triumph over the next half year, until the Earth wakes up again and the holy stories move out of our houses and hearts into the wide Creation where they will be re-enacted again on the grandest scale. As within, so without.

Of course we know the scientific explanation that the turning of the leaves is caused by the dying of chlorophyll cells due to the shorter days and cooler weather making visible other pigments that have been present in the leaves all along, like xanthophyll which is yellow-orange. But somehow this explanation cannot do justice to the breath-stopping crimson of a swamp maple, or the flaming orange-red of a sugar maple, its leaves illuminated from behind by the thick, white October light against an utterly blue sky, or the neon-fuschia of the humble huckleberry bushes which make even the red to rust leaves of the blueberry bushes look pale. The thought came to us the other day coming down the mountain that the leaves, like us, begin to show their true colors as they come to the end of their lives.

Every few years the colors are so bright that the more enthusiastic among us begin to declare that it is the "most beautiful Fall in ages." Others are more cautious in their pronouncements, like the neighbor I met on the mountain the other day. "Aren't these the most beautiful colors you've ever seen, Doug?" I effervesced. He cocked his head a little and said with a straight face, "Maybe. At least since last year."

UN-NATURAL EVENTS: Look. Here's an advertisement for a treadmill. Yes, a treadmill that you set up in your spare room. It can go at different speeds up to 10 mph and can even simulate walking up-hill. Has a digital display to let you know how far you've walked without going anywhere. It's all yours for list price of $699.99. Now, those who had to submit to the old treadmill at work all day can go home and walk on their own new one.

RANK OPINION: The Passamaquoddy at Sipayik have dramatically raised the issue of native fishing rights by publishing photographs of the taking of harbor porpoises in violation of the federal marine mammal protection act, and maybe some state regulations, too. They assert that they have aboriginal rights to take porpoise as their ancestors did, regardless of government regulations. Native people in other parts of the country have made similar claims. They have a point. There is ample evidence that the porpoise and the maritime Abnaki people have had a sacred relationship for a very long time. The Passamaquoddy spiritual leader Deanna Frances pointed out to me in archaeological records the presence of porpoise bones buried with human bones at the Blue Hill Falls archaic site dating back some 4,000 years. These records can be found in "The Nevin Shellheap: Burials and Observations" by Douglas Byers published by the Peabody Museum Foundation of Phillips Academy, 1979.

It is probably none of my business: I am not a Passamaquoddy nor a fisherman nor a native Mainer— though I have been paddling on Passamaquoddy waters for more than 30 years—but I do believe that some ancient sacred ways should take precedence over more recent laws of the land.

This has been supported by court decisions in the West regarding Native American religious practices. The relationship between the Passamaquoddy and the porpoise is probably one of these. If it is this traditional sacred relationship that motivates the Passamaquoddy to take porpoises in contradiction of the laws of the state and nation, and not simply the chance to exploit an undeveloped fishery resource or the chance to assert their sovereignty in other matters, then they could easily prove their sincerity by taking porpoises in a traditional and sacred manner.

That would mean using spears and harpoons from human-powered traditional sea-going craft such as kayaks and canoes. I do not suggest this lightly, but with the utmost sincerity. Countless times over the last 30 years, I have been in striking distance of porpoise, seal, and even orca, in these waters. Adrift on the great sea, these are religious experiences. These days, no one needs to kill threatened species simply to eat. Food for the body is readily obtained. But spiritual experiences that feed the soul are much harder to come by. They strengthen both young and old, men and women, and renew the family bond between humans and other creatures.

If the Passamaquoddy, or other tribes claiming aboriginal fishing rights, are serious about the traditional sacred relationship with marine creatures, they could prove it by hunting them in a traditional sacred manner. If, on the other hand, they are only interested in economic exploitation of marine resources and political leverage, that will become clear to everyone soon enough.

FIELD & FOREST REPORT: Hunters are out for ducks and other migratory waterfowl. Overwhelming colors of brown, orange, red fill our vision. Seeing the bright foliage I thought of how family and friends gather from far and wide for the death-watch around the bed of a person who is dying. I remember a chat I had with the man at the town dump. I remarked how the leaf-peepers were out in force from as far away as Florida. He said, "I hate this time. I love the spring when everything is budding green, but now everything is dying. I hate it."

MOUNTAIN REPORT: Thousands of tiny crickets and grasshoppers still dance underfoot in the unmowed meadow below the blueberry fields. I can never recall so many before [at least since last year]. Milkweed seeds float in the air. A few late lupine blossoms raise their purple or pink spires shyly against the wind, surrounded by the dry, gray, rattling pods of their earlier-blooming brothers and sisters. The opaque red of blueberry leaves and the more translucent larger leaves of huckleberry are the background for the fluffy spires and tassels of goldenrod. Here and there the ghostly white stalks of pearly everlasting rise above the stony fields.

SALTWATER REPORT: The other day I paddled Northeast in the inner bay in high winds, heading towards the steamboat landing a half mile across the bay but soon got tired of bucking wind and waves and headed upwind towards the two little islands off of town beach. I nestled in between them out of the fierce wind and saw five lesser yellow-legs, like tall sandpipers as they strutted about, then fleeing with alarmed whistles at sight of me. Many arctic waterfowl are now migrating over our bays and inlets on their way south, stopping now and then and giving us a brief glimpse of their fantastic forms.

I paddled to the milldam where the mill brook runs out into the bay. Looking under the great granite bridge, seeing the brook sparkling down, I was thinking that one could simply scurry down from Main Street and even walk on the granite ledge all the way under the bridge. Just at that moment two youths did just that. I waved. They waved. I paddled away marveling at how inner and outer nature and events correspond. An old friend used to say, "A coincidence means you weren't noticing the other part of what's going on."

CRITTER OF THE WEEK: Flights of a small fly with a tiny tuft of white fluff on its abdomen. They look like tiny snowflakes as they float by your face. What are these snow-bugs, these flurry-flies? They are the woolly apple aphids moving from their summer place, the apple tree, to their winter place, the elm.

SEED PODS TO CARRY AROUND WITH YOU from the Chinese poet Wei Ying Wu: *The moon is full, the autumn nights grow longer, in the north forests startled crows cry out. Still high overhead, the star river stretches, the Dipper's handle set to southwest. The cold cricket grieves deep in the chambers, of the notes of sweet birds, none remain. Then one evening gusts of autumn come. One who sleeps alone thinks fondly on thick quilts. Past loves are a thousand miles farther each day, blocked from my drifting and my sinking. Man's life is not as the grass and trees, still the season's changes can stir the heart.*

And from another Chinese poet, Hsiao Kang: *Green leaves that dawn after dawn grow yellow, red cheeks that fade with passing days. If our world is made up of such changes as these, is it strange that my heart is so sad?*

O lovely raw red wild autumn turning, it's time to think of the blood, the red searing. Who's there? What's that? O, to survive what must we do to believe? In the trees, my grandson. In these roots. In these leaves.   From Dorothy Livesay.

October 25 is St. Crispin's Day. Crispin and Crispinian were shoemakers who made shoes for the poor for free with leather provided by angels. They were martyred for their faith in 290 AD, and according to tradition their beheaded bodies floated across the English Channel to Faversham where they are still revered.

October 30 is the anniversary of Orson Welles' *War of the Worlds* broadcast in 1938, and also the birthday of Charles Atlas who, as powerful as he was, has long since gone to where no one kicks sand into anyone else's face and he can rest easy at last.

October 31 is All Hallow's Eve on the Christian calendar, Samhain on the Celtic.

November 1 is All Hallow's or All Saint's Day.

November 2 is All Souls Day, for those of us who aren't saints.

NATURAL EVENTS: Winds and rains of the past week have stripped many of the trees of their leaves, but the oaks still are fully-clothed, though their leaves are turning toward a dull yellow, then brown. The tough, leathery oak leaf holds on fiercely for much of the winter making a sharp whispering when the bitter winds blow. On the mountain, oak saplings in late winter are tufted with the shredded stems of leaves which never let go, but were finally twisted off by the relentless wind, leaving a tenacious bunch of fiber behind.

As the leaves fall from the trees and the frosts progressively injure, then kill, the weeds and grasses; a world of skeletons, and the skeleton of the world are revealed. Now we see the shapely anatomy of the trees which will support their living organs again next year, but now rattle like bones in the wind. Now, with the fur gone, we see the bones of the earth under her skin, the curved spine of the mountains, the rocky ribs protruding in fields and blueberry barrens. The knobs, the ridges, the edges, the hard angles of the bones of Earth which have been hidden by summer's softness are gradually revealed, stolid and unmoving, the way the bones of a huge decomposing whale emerge on the beach, while time and tide do their ancient work to expose them.

Un-natural events: Bill McKibben, former Sunday School teacher and now renowned Nature writer, describes the difficulty of teaching children about the outdoors when their prior knowledge of Nature comes from watching nature programs on television. Children get used to nature TV where some creature mates, or gives birth or dies or jumps high or calls loudly or chases and kills another creature every 60 seconds or so. After a while, the slow pace and subtle changes of real Nature take too much time and patience for many youngsters to apprehend. Exciting events do happen in real Nature, but there is a lot of inactivity and patient watching in between. Video games are more exciting than actual hunting. Real things take time. When we are in a hurry and impatient, the truth is never seen. It takes too long to reveal itself.

Also un-natural are machine-made Halloween decorations. For thousands of years, the symbols of this season have been hand made from natural materials in particular abundance at this time of the year—pumpkins, cornstalks and Indian corn, apples, nuts, and the like—as a sign of gratitude and craft. The old pagan druidic spirits must be disgruntled to see plastic jack o' lanterns, skeletons, ghosts.

Then, there are the hunters in their big trucks loaded with equipment and an ATV in the back to absolutely guarantee they won't have to walk. The thought of people going hunting and fishing in these things reminds us how the once-mighty human hunter has fallen to a state of utter helplessness and total dependency on the internal combustion engine. Compare to young Fannie Hardy's account of how she, barely out of her teens, with her father and one other man made a six week journey up the Passadumkeag to Nicatous, Gasabais, Fourth Machias, and West Grand Lakes and back again, bringing no meat and only a minimum of gear. They portaged between lakes sometimes two miles or more and fished or hunted for their food. Fannie did all the cooking [not to mention portaging, and probably a lot of butchering and keeping the camp.] She brought two dresses and a pair of boots. She didn't believe a woman should wear pants. Fannie also considered Thoreau "not a true woodsman."

A rank opinion is what Fannie Hardy would offer about anyone who would need to take a 3 1/2 ton steel and plastic machine into the woods to go hunting or fishing. Not a true woodsman.

FIELD & FOREST REPORT: A few purple asters still peek out from sheltered places, but most of last summer's weeds and flowers are dry brown stalks and tufts, just skeletons rattling in the wind.

MOUNTAIN REPORT: On the summit of Awanadjo one day this past week, a weak low pressure was being pushed Southeastward by a great windy Canadian high. Mare's tails and other high clouds flagged the sky. Ravens continued to circle high over the summit dancing, swooping, chasing, playing tag, gurgling, lightly croaking in conversation.

Coming down from Awanadjo, for some unexplainable reason, but perhaps because of the dying of the summer season, I had the thought again that our soul is our sole possession. Neither a great body nor a great mind can make a great soul. Our body and the bodies of all living things belong to the earth—come from it and like leaves return to it. Our intelligence and the intelligence of all living things belong to the Great Mind—come from it and like morning mist return to it. But our soul is our own to do with it as we will. Even if our body is lying in a hospital bed and our mind is confused, our soul is ours. We make it or we don't. It cannot be taken from us against our will. We nurture our soul and love it and keep it, or we neglect it or just give it away to someone we think might care for it better. John Keats wrote, *Call the world if you Please "The vale of Soul-making."* What would you give in return for your soul? Jesus tells the story of the successful farmer who had such a huge harvest that he tore down his barns to build bigger barns, rather than share the harvest. At the end of the day the Lord said to him, "tonight your soul will be required of you." But he had given it away.

SALTWATER REPORT: Urchin and scallop dragging is underway. It seems incredible to an ignorant landlubber like me that the tiny bits of shellfish flesh can be worth the plowing up of the bottoms of our bays leaving them muddy and nearly lifeless. I can remember when we used to watch small schools of squid trying to corral large schools of herring in Cobscook Bay. We even remember one night when hundreds of squid were marooned by the receding tide to lie on the beach making sucking sounds trying to breathe out of the water. We spent hours picking them up and throwing them back into the water. We haven't seen a squid there in years. We also wonder about the recent appearance, for the first time along the high-tide seaweed line, of dead seals and cormorants, the imagined enemies of salmon acquaculture.

CRITTER OF THE WEEK: The squid. According to *The Ocean Almanac*, the squid, also called "cuttlefish" has ten arms compared to the eight of the octopus and specimens as much as 175 feet long have been recorded. They occasionally attack the sperm whale, one of the largest of the whales.

SEED PODS TO CARRY AROUND WITH YOU: from poet Rainer Maria Rilke: *Lord, it is time. The summer was very big. Lay thy shadow on the sundials, and on the meadows let the winds go loose. Command the last fruits that they shall be full, give them another two more southerly days, press them on to fulfillment and drive the last sweetness into the heavy wine. Who has no house now, will build him one no more. Who is alone now, long will so remain, will wake, read, write long letters and will in the roads to and fro restlessly wander, when the leaves are blowing.*

And from Maine songwriter David Mallett: *The cold that comes to saints and thieves, the hollow sun, the naked trees, the paling field, the crumbling leaves, they do their dance of death. I wait for love, I wait for wind. I cannot let the winter in. I count the places that I've been, and the friends that I have left.*

NEW TO FIRST QUARTER *BEAVER* MOON

For you shall go out in joy and be led forth in peace; the mountains and hills before you shall break into singing, and all of the trees of the field shall clap their hands, instead of

the thorn shall come up the maple, and instead of the briar
shall come up the blueberry, and it shall be to the Creator a
memorial, an everlasting sign that shall not be cut off.
                              —adapted from the prophet Isaiah.

NATURAL EVENTS: The yellow-shafted flicker is a surprisingly large bird, larger than the bluejays who are also busy now. Flickers often hammer away on dead trees and branches like woodpeckers (which they are). Their call is a shrill "flicka, flicka, flicka," thus another example of a word from bird language being added to human vocabulary. "Chickadee," "phoebe," and "hawk" are others.

UN-NATURAL EVENTS: More cursed dragging. I am no expert, just a Midwestern landlubber, but the big changes in Cobscook Bay over the last 25 years as seen from our rocky beach may be attributed to ruthless dragging. Few fish washing up on the beach anymore. No more schools of herring being corralled by squid. No more flounder fishing. According to sonar scanning, the bottom of the bay looks like a desert of mud with little tufts of kelp here and there. We see the draggers plow relentlessly back and forth from dawn to dusk every day; more than seventy were in sight at one time. What is the effect on the remaining fish and other sea life of being raked up in a huge iron chain drag, hauled into the air, dumped on the deck, picked over, and thrown back into the water? What is the effect on small and large creatures with clouds of billowing mud day after day? What is the effect on the coastal air of scores of diesel engines, many poorly-tuned, straining to pull heavy drags for a few pieces of meat the size of a quarter?

RANK OPINION: It's a crime against Nature. This is not my opinion alone. A prominent marine field biologist has told me that people would be shocked if they knew what the bottom of Blue Hill Bay looked like, that is, an empty mud-flat. Divers of my acquaintance have said the same. It's underwater clear-cutting and strip-mining.

FIELD & FOREST REPORT: Walking through the grass on a raw, wet and windy day this past week, I saw lying on the ground a tattered piece of rough-textured paper, colored with several different swirling shades of grey like some very expensive, handmade art paper. Looking up high into the tree above me, I found the source of this finely-crafted page torn from Nature's book. There hung the remnants of a hornet's nest with a few torn shreds from the comb moving in the wind. A hornet's nest high in a tree would be a sign of a hard winter to come to some folks, but I've encountered some very close to the ground as well near our camp at Cobscook Bay this year. There, on a sunny day it is sometimes quiet enough to hear the hornet's mandibles scraping as they chew off tiny bundles of wood fiber from the bare cedar shingles of our cabin leaving behind tight little zig-zags of lighter gray. From there they fly to the nest and add this bit of pulp to the growing edge of the irregular globe. Day by day, trip by trip the hanging paper house grows as layer is added over layer. The hornets are artists in paper, creating a spherical book with no straight lines, no flat surfaces, no corners, and no black and white—only a thousand shades of gray. To the one who will read it, this book is full of knowledge about the evolution of hornets and their cousins the wasps, bees, termites, and ants. It tells volumes about the designs and patterns of Nature including the sphere, the cone, and the hexagon and the breath-taking ability of collective intelligence to build beautiful useful structures.

We humans have great individual intelligence, but rather limited collective intelligence while the social insects have the opposite. I can explain. Our large collective enterprises [think Manhattan] seem to run counter to Nature, while those of the insects work in accord with Her. I have a paperback copy of E.O. Wilson's *The Insect Societies* which I found rather remarkably on a rainy fall day years ago in the middle of the street in West Concord, Massachusetts. This is a fascinating book—500 pages of texts, notes, charts and tables—by one of the greatest minds of our time, but it falls far short of the beauty and clarity of the natural paperback book which hangs high in that tree as its pages blow away one by one.

MOUNTAIN REPORT: There may be some areas of so-called "old-growth" forest around the summit of Awanadjo. I have counted 140 rings on a downed tree no more than 10 inches in diameter near the summit, where nearby trees may be as much as 24+ inches in diameter, suggesting that they may have been standing longer than the 245 years that Europeans have been here. What is more, the Fitz Hugh Lane painting of Blue Hill dated c. 1855, shows the lower slopes bare, but the summit heavily forested as today. It seems reasonable that loggers may have left some of the heights untouched due to the difficulty of bringing the logs down.

There are several places near the summit that have the "forest primeval" feeling to them. Huge, moss-hung trees, lichen-covered ground undisturbed by human feet, the smell of ancient humus built up so slowly ever since the last Ice Age. To stand in those Wisdom Woods is to be in the presence of a Great Creature which is 12,000 years old—the boreal forest.

CRITTER OF THE WEEK: The Old Forest, older every day.

SEED PODS TO CARRY AROUND WITH YOU, from Annie Dillard— *All day long I feel created. I can see the blown dust on the skin of the back of my hand, the tiny trapezoids of chipped clay, moistened and breathed alive. There are some created sheep in the pasture below me, sheep set down here precisely, just touching their blue shadows hoof to hoof on the grass. Created gulls pock the air, rip great curved seams in the settled air; I greet my created meal amazed.*

FIRST QUARTER TO FULL *BEAVER* MOON

Look you out northeastwards over mighty ocean teeming with sea life; home of seals, sporting and splendid, its tide has reached fullness.

From the ancient Gaelic, translated by James Carney

November 5, Susan B. Anthony cast her ballot, earning a fine, 1872

November 7, Eleanor Roosevelt died, 1962. Mary Robinson elected first woman president of Ireland, 1990.

NATURAL EVENTS: October light gives way to November gray, though the *Old Farmer's* calls for a warm month. Trees mostly bare, deer hunters in the woods, flashes of blaze orange in town. Blaze orange becomes a part of the uniform around here for those who like to tramp around outside. Even the dogs wear it. I buy a cheap orange knit hat and cut the top off it, then roll it over my dog's head so no one will mistake him for a white-tailed deer.

FIELD & FOREST REPORTS: The Eastern Larch, tamarack, or "hackamatack," as it's called around here, is having its moment of glory, dominating the scene for a brief moment now that the more showy hardwoods have mostly lost their leaves. The hackamatack is our only deciduous conifer. Unlike the more numerous ramrod straight spruce and fir, the hackamatack often curves sinuously like a dancer. Its needles are now falling and dusting the ground with a beautiful burnt gold. For all of its grace, it is the hardest of soft-woods and makes decent firewood.

You may remember a report last month about our axe handle being mysteriously gnawed by some unknown creature as the axe stood with its blade in the block and its handle pointing up and away. I later caught the culprit red-handed, or rather, "red-coated," being as how it was a red squirrel. By this time the axe handle was chewed to the point that it was closer to a hatchet handle, and since it was cracked anyway, I decided to replace it.

Accordingly, I sawed the old handle off and put the axe head in the firebox of the wood-stove to burn out the stub of the handle. In the morning I retrieved the axe head and wedges from the stove and fitted a new handle. This reminds me of the fellow who said, "That's a great old axe. I've had it for 25 years and it has needed only two new heads and four new handles." When I got the new handle fitted, I struck the axe into the chopping block again. Next day when I went to the wood-pile, I saw that Little Red had begun chewing on my new axe handle and made quite an excavation in it, casting in doubt the theory that they chew these things for the salt left by perspiring hands, since the new handle had yet to be used. This new carving didn't please me, so I brought the new axe into the house and laid the old axe handle on top of the chopping block, where each day Little Red took a little more wood out of it. His most magnificent effort was an attempt, unsuccessful so far, to drag what's left of that old axe handle into his home under the wood-pile.

WILD SPECULATION: What's happening here? Maybe Little Red chewed the axe handle initially because it had some salt on it. Then, maybe he kept chewing on it because he thought of it as his, like the old shoe that becomes the puppy's toy. Then, maybe he chewed the new axe handle because it looked like the old one he liked so much. Or, maybe he's just squirrelly and wants to drive me nuts.

MOUNTAIN REPORT: At the summit the low angle of the sun emphasizes the deep scoring and gouging of the solid stone of the mountain by the ancient glaciers dragging loads of gravel and stone ever so slowly over the summit of the mountain from North-northwest to South-southeast. That low sun angle also reveals letters and numbers carved into the stone at the summit long ago—the date 1856, initials "CSW," "AW," "GAO," and is that "J.F."? It is not permitted to deface the rocks these days.

SALTWATER REPORT: Most of the pleasure boats are now gone from their moorings in the bay. Lobster traps are hauled out now as the dragging season continues. The loons have left the ponds and are out in the bays in their winter plumage of dark gray to black above and light below, the same coloring as so many aquatic creatures. Their hoots, howls and wails can be heard across the bays sounding like the spirit of the North Wind breathing through the sharp chasm between Fall and Winter.

CRITTER OF THE WEEK: The busy, noisy blue jays. They are the sentinels of the woods and fields, and the sentries for other creatures. Jays are so attentive that you cannot enter their territory, even with all the stealth you can muster without them sounding the alarm: "Hey! hey! hey!" On the other hand, we heard one on the mountain the other day making the sweetest, gentlest sound—so unlike a jay, almost a gentle cooing—that we couldn't imagine what it was until we saw it.

SEED PODS TO CARRY AROUND WITH YOU: From Henry David Thoreau: *The jay is one of the most useful agents in the economy of nature, for disseminating forest trees . . . Their chief employment during the autumnal season is foraging to supply their winter stores. In performing this necessary duty they drop abundance of seed in their flight over fields, hedges, and by fences where they alight to deposit them in the postholes . . . It is remarkable what numbers of young trees rise up in fields and pastures after a wet winter and spring. These birds alone are capable , in a few years time, to replant all the cleared lands.*

PILGRIM'S JOURNAL: It's a marvel how our lives often follow a course that we did not plot. A song written over 40 years ago by yours truly, to the tune of Roddy MacCorley, has proved truer than I could ever have imagined:

*I'm leaving now for the mountainside, where the pine
     grows bent and small,
And the wind that bites the pine tree branch has a lonely
     gray wolf call,
And the hard rock face of the mountainside shattered by
     the ice and snow,
And nobody goes to the mountainside, but that's where I
     will go.*

*The world will steal back all it gives, each potlatch hides a
     thief,
We lose our joy in seeking joy, our peace in seeking peace.
The mountain has a granite heart, it cannot take or give,*

215

And nobody lives on the mountainside, but that's where I
will live.

The world chokes out the vine of hope as the mountain
kills the pine,
The world will starve a good, young thought, why should
it nourish mine?
The mountain cripples every tree, in the teeth of time and
snow,
And nothing will grow on the mountainside, but that's
where I will grow.

The mountain never speaks in years, its rocks don't think
in time,
And I must die, I cannot add the mountain's years to
mine,
My good wool shirt will fall apart; my leather boots will
mold,
And nothing is old on the mountainside, but that's where
I'll grow old.

PERICOPES

Fear and anxiety, lack of faith in the world around us are not
our natural condition. It is faith itself which is the natural
condition. That is why Jesus said, "Be not anxious about
tomorrow. Consider the lilies of the field. Have faith like
a grain of mustard seed." That is why the Letter to the
Hebrews says, "Faith is the assurance of things hoped for, the
conviction of things not seen. By faith we understand that
the world was created by the word of God, so that what we
see was made out of what we do not see." The blind man

knows that what we see is not all there is. Much more is what we do not see.

More recently, around the time the Millerites were predicting the end of the world, Henry David Thoreau wrote about the floating milkweed seed, "Thus, from generation to generation it goes bounding over lakes and woods and mountains . . . And for this end these silken streamers have been perfecting themselves all summer, snugly packed in this light chest, a perfect adaptation to this end—a prophecy not only of the fall, but of future springs. Who could believe in prophecies that the world would end this summer, while one milkweed with faith matured its seeds?"

In perfect faith, the lilies of the field bloom in bright array, the mustard seed sprouts and grows we know not how, the milkweed seeds float over the mountain, and the eagle rises up and spreads its wings to the South; all with no anxiety for tomorrow. Faithfulness is the true condition of Nature, the natural condition. It is the absence of faith that is un-natural. It is faith that makes us well, whole and healthy, as Nature in her steadfast, innate faith in the coming season stays well, whole and healthy.

That's the Almanack for this moon, but don't
take my word for it.
Go out and see for yourself.

This is the Awanadjo Almanack for the Full *Beaver* Moon to the Full *Cold* Moon, called *Siqinrilyaq* or *No Sun* by the north slope Eskimos, *Marchesvan* or *Bul* in the Bible, and November/December in Downeast Maine.

FULL TO LAST QUARTER *BEAVER* MOON

There is always something to hunt. The world teems with creatures, processes and events that are trying to elude you. Every ground is a hunting ground, whether it lies between you and the curbstone, or in those illimitable woods where rolls the Oregon River. The final test of the hunter is whether he is keen to go hunting in a vacant lot.

From Aldo Leopold

November 14, Birthday of Mamie Eisenhower, 1896.

November 16, Birthday of W.C. Handy of ragtime and honkytonk, 1873.

November 21, Mayflower Compact signed 1620.

November 22, John F. Kennedy assassinated, 1963.

NATURAL EVENTS: The deer season is underway around here. It seems the tensions between hunters and anti-hunters are ever greater. Humans have always hunted. Hunters, along with fishermen, formed the first wave of European migration, and the first contact with Native Americans. The result was an exchange of knowledge, technology and culture. Uncounted Europeans preferred the Native way of life to European culture and adopted it readily, disappearing from white society except for trading purposes. The man in orange far below me on the mountain is doing what we have always done. Hunters preserve today the largest body of ancient wisdom about the animals and forests, much of it handed down for many generations.

Anthropologist Dorothy Lee writes, *"The great care with which so many of the Indians utilized every portion of the carcass of hunted animal was an expression, not [just] of economic thrift, but of courtesy and respect . . . the religious relationship to the slain."* Good hunters today—and there are many—maintain that religious relationship. Unfortunately, there are too many bad hunters lacking wisdom, sensitivity and respect for the Creation. These are the ones who feel that it is their right to kill and destroy, rather than a sacred privilege fraught with great responsibility. These are the ones who feel that the land and the animals belong to them, rather than belonging to the Creator.

UN-NATURAL EVENTS: Bad hunters. They are easy enough to track. Just follow the trail of beer cans, blasted trees, litter, trespassing, lies, and wounded animals.

RANK OPINION: Bad hunters give good hunters a bad name.

WILD SPECULATION: What if the good hunters were to set up large loop snares baited with six-packs of cheap beer in the areas where bad hunters travel; that is, near roads and houses. Zoop! Tend your trap-line daily. Catch and release.

FIELD & FOREST REPORT: The last apples are picked in most orchards and the drops are now food for birds and deer. If you have apple trees, picking up the drops and composting or feeding them to pigs or sheep will help curtail the spread of diseases such as scab.

MOUNTAIN REPORT: Climbing up over the blueberry fields before the first heavy lasting snows, we see "ice tusks" two to three inches long where water has frozen and been pushed, extruded up through the soil to form long striated crystals. These are a late Fall phenomenon occurring before the ground is thoroughly frozen. The brown of the oak leaves and golden yellow of the hackamatack can be seen for miles in every direction as they stand out in contrast to the deep greens of the spruce, fir, and pine. In the Wisdom Woods, the ice is an inch thick in the old mining holes, and icicles hang from the bare cliffs.

SALTWATER REPORT: The water of the bay is sometimes warmer than the air these days. A skim of ice moves out over the saltwater in places where fresh water pours in from the land.

CRITTER OF THE WEEK: The white-tail deer, our Maine woods variety, recognized by its buff to reddish back, turning to gray in the winter, and white underneath with a surprisingly long tail or flag seen best when it is fleeing. Antlers occur only in the male. Ernest Thompson Seton says the Algonquin name is *Wa-bai-ush* and records a very large specimen buck at 350 pounds in weight, but more commonly 150 to 200 and rarely more than about four feet high at the shoulder. Their senses are especially acute as demonstrated by their huge eyes and ears. Their main defense is flight. Farmers have told me that whitetails can leap a 10 foot fence to get at the apples in an orchard.

PILGRIM'S JOURNAL: I have been a gun-owner all of my adult life, and as a young man, I hunted some. The turning point for me came on a summer night in Northern Wisconsin lake country when I was called from my dinner to deal with a white-tail doe which had been hit on the road near the camp where I worked as the maintenance man. Her hind legs were both broken, but she was wide-eyed and very much alive there in the darkness by the road. I was required to dispatch her with a small caliber rifle that was inadequate for a merciful kill. I did it, but it was too much for me. I never again shot a deer. I continued for a while shooting "varmints," that is, porcupines, raccoons and squirrels. Then one summer day in Colorado, practicing to improve my marksmanship, I dropped a Kaibab squirrel at about 100 yards, a remarkable shot, I thought. When I picked her up, I found that she was a nursing mother. My heart broke. I have never shot another animal, though I've been sorely tempted more than once by woodchucks in the garden and porcupines under the cabin. The best cure for such things, I've discovered, is urinating around the garden patch or cabin.

Like Aldo Leopold, I am still a hunter, though. A spiritual hunter. [see *Snow* Moon]

SEED PODS TO CARRY AROUND WITH YOU: From Walt Whitman:

I think I could turn and live with animals, they're so placid and self-contain'd. I stand and look at them long and long. They do not sweat and whine about their condition, they do not lie awake in the dark and weep for

*their sins, they do not make me sick discussing their
duty to God. Not one is dissatisfied, not one is de-
mented with the mania of owning things, not one kneels
to another, nor to his kind that lived thousands of years
ago, not one is respectable or unhappy over the whole
earth.*

LAST QUARTER *BEAVER* MOON TO NEW *COLD* MOON

*When you arise in the morning, give thanks for the morning
light, for you life and strength. Give thanks for your food and
the joy of living. If you see no reason for giving thanks, the
fault lies within yourself.*

Tecumuseh, Shawnee and pan-Indian leader, died 1814.

November 25, Pope John XXIII born, 1881. Joe DiMaggio
born, 1914. Third Thursday of November becomes national
Thanksgiving day by order of President Lincoln in 1863.

November 29, C.S. Lewis born, 1898.

November 30, Winston Churchill born, 1874. [We were delighted when our new grandbaby looked like Winston Churchill until someone told us that all babies look like Winston
Churchill.]

NATURAL EVENTS: Giving thanks is a natural event, per-
formed by virtually all cultures and peoples since the Beginning. Giving thanks can be seen as a revolutionary act,
because it ritually expresses our universal dependence on
Grace and Providence. No man, no matter how wealthy, privileged, powerful, or intelligent can cause a seed to grow or
fashion an ear of corn or a wild turkey. God provides. No
one has a right to more than his share. Giving thanks leads to

justice. Giving thanks can also be seen as an act of deep ecology, because it expresses our dependence on the web of life. We do not give thanks for that which we ourselves have made, but we give thanks for gifts. Life is a gift, as are earth, air, and water. We did not make them, but without them we are dead.

I usually go to the schools around Thanksgiving to thank them for their food offerings before I truck them up to the food pantry. Sometimes the principal will ask the assembled children what they are thankful for. I'll never forget young Scott Grindle, blind since birth, saying, "I'm thankful we live in such a beautiful, beautiful, beautiful place."

RANK OPINION: This brings me, for some reason, to a minor excursion into the subject of the most fitting bird for thanksgiving. What bird was it that Noah first released and which did not come back, indicating to the thankful aboard the ark that there was dry land not far away? Was it the turkey? No. What birds showed God's providence to a thankful prophet Elijah by bringing him bread in the morning and meat in the evening during the great famine? Turkeys? No. What bird awakens us at dawn with its raucous thanks for the morning light and its life and strength? Is it the turkey? Hardly. And what bird is it that poet Mary Oliver described this way: "Nor have they delicate palates; without hesitation they will eat anything you can think of—corn, mice, old hamburgers—swallowing with such hollering and gusto no one can tell whether it's a brag or a prayer of deepest thanks . . ."? Is she describing a turkey? Not at all.

Do flocks of turkeys gather daily through all kinds of weather in tall treetops world-wide laughing boisterously at each other's jokes? Do turkeys dive off the top of the world's mountains into exhilarating loops and barrel rolls and dancing duets and games of tag in celebration of the joy of living? No, indeed.

No, as all of these examples so amply show, the true universal birds of thanksgiving are the crows and ravens. Yet, in spite of all of this overwhelming evidence we Americans have characteristically chosen the turkey as the symbol of thanksgiving. Why? Because it is good to eat.

But, you see . . . maybe if we ate crow now and then we would remember like Tecumseh to be thankful for what we have—the morning light, our life and strength, our food, and the joy of living.

CRITTER OF THE WEEK: The turkey, of course. A common flocking ground bird at the time of the arrival of Europeans here, it played a large part in the diet of Native Americans, and its fine tail feathers were used for decoration and adornment. The wild turkey was largely hunted out of New England in the last century, but they have returned in ever increasing numbers, are now a significant game bird, and are wily enough to elude many a hunter. Now, the domesticated turkey has lost the ability to live in the wild and fend for itself and is mostly known for its excessive consumption of food and its overweening vanity, not unlike other domesticated creatures including the American Human. Domestic turkeys are known to drown in heavy rain. To their credit, however, they never lock their keys in the car, or shoot each other while hunting humans.

SEED PODS TO CARRY AROUND WITH YOU: From poet e.e.cummings:

i thank You God for most this amazing day: for the leaping greenly spirits of trees and a blue true dream of sky; and for everything which is natural which is infinite which is yes. (Now the ears of my ears awake and now the eyes of my eyes are opened.)

NEW TO FIRST QUARTER *COLD* MOON

In the beginning God created the heaven and the earth. And the earth was without form, and void; and darkness was upon the face of the deep . . . And God said, Let there be light: and there was light.   From Genesis 1

December 6, Feast of Saint Nicholas, Great Halifax Explosion, 1917.

December 7, Pearl Harbor destroyed by Japanese air force, 1941.

December 8, James Thurber born, 1894

NATURAL EVENTS: This time of the year we are likely to feel that we are being plunged into darkness. On a cloudy day here, nearly half-way to the North Pole, streetlights start blinking on around mid-afternoon and the days are still getting shorter. The gathering cloak of darkness and the low angle of the sun create this mood of late fall. Darkness seeks to dominate the light. But the light, as limited as it is, has great power too.

Around the time of the New *Cold* Moon, while I was going about my business in town an hour before sunset, I caught sight of a bright light in the western sky that was not the sun. Finding a place where I could see the horizon, I was suddenly overwhelmed by the greatest display of solar reflections and refractions that I have seen in my short half-century of life. Glancing back, hoping that it wouldn't fade, I rushed into the church and then home to find witnesses to this amazing natural event. Lest you think I was dreaming, I will tell you that five other people saw the same as I did—multiple wheels and circles of white and rainbow light tinting the dome of the sky from horizon to apex. Here is what we saw.

In the western sky we saw the muffled glowing disk of the sun like a luminous sphere of cotton hanging an hour above the horizon line of spruce and fir. Then as our gaze expanded far outward, we saw the storied "circle 'round the sun" with the diameter of a score of suns and tinted with faint rainbow colors. The bottom quarter of the circle was cut off by the horizon but at the right and left, north and south, were two brilliant "sun-dogs" or parhelions, mock suns suspended on the great circle like jewels on a bracelet and reflecting the brilliance of their original in the center. The sun-dogs were anointed at top and bottom with flame of bright rainbow colors.

Next our eyes moved to the top of the great circle where we saw part of another circle just resting on the first, its arc rising into the sky like horns or the points of a glowing crown. What a marvel. But that was not all. Tilting our heads back in jubilation, we saw a circular rainbow at the very apex of the sky directly overhead, not just an arc, but a full, entire circle of the whole spectrum of all colors floating high in the blue heavens.

I've seen the circle 'round the sun before and a sun-dog now and then, but never have I witnessed such a breathtaking display of circles upon circles in the sky. Yes, I know that this phenomenon can be explained by ice crystals in the high atmosphere, but that paltry explanation will never satisfy those who hunger and thirst for wonder.

RANK OPINION: When I say that Blue Hill mountain and the Falls are sacred places, I do not mean this in a metaphorical sense. I mean it in an actual sense. In the United States of America, we recognize, for the most part, two kinds of sacred places: cemeteries where the dead are put to rest, and churches where we are told that the dead are not dead but only sleeping. Churches and cemeteries are designated as sacred by us human beings. These are places where we feel that we must speak softly, tread reverently. I think that we Americans may be alone in all the world in recognizing only man-made rather than natural sacred places.

We have no sacred wells and springs of water as do so many other cultures from the Arabs to the Irish. We have no sacred rocks as do the Australian aborigines, the Buddhists, the Hindus, again the Irish, and others. We have no sacred pools and waterfalls, as do the Japanese, the Jews, the Native Americans and others. We have no sacred caves and grottos as do the French, the Spanish, the Irish, and on and on. We have no sacred mountains as do other peoples from the Jews to the Tibetans to the Chinese to tribal peoples. Virtually all cultures, save our own, have their sacred mountains. In short, our sacred places are of our own making. We simply do not recognize those made by the Creator of heaven and earth.

Perhaps as a result of this, we tend to see the whole Creation as ours rather than God's to use in whatever way serves us. We have used it and abused it because we do not see it as sacred. This has not served us well, and we are beginning to see the results. I will not elaborate at length on the beleaguered state of the Creation. I will only mention as examples the many days each year that the air in our peninsula is unfit to breathe due to high ozone levels, and the collapse of salmon and ground-fishing—facts which virtually no one questions.

A natural sacred place is a place not man-made, where people have traditionally gone to gain strength, comfort, peace of mind and vision for the future. These places are most often unique geological formations, often at the meeting of land and water or land and sky, which have been visited over generations for refreshment, renewal and inspiration.

We can define sacred places by the effect they universally have upon human beings. In such places we feel one or more of the following effects:

- reduction of stress, enhanced sense of well-being, peace of mind.
- ecstatic experience, the spirit leaving the body, moving through space and/or time.
- increased creativity, intuitive problem-solving, new answers to troubling questions.
- new hope and inspiration, a renewal of faith, a personality change, or *metanoia*.
- ego-reduction, selflessness, a sense of immersion or belonging in the universe.

It is my opinion that we are only now beginning to become aware of our sacred places, yet we are in danger of losing them. If we can acknowledge that there are such sacred places in our midst that are not made by us, it will help us and our descendants to view the whole Creation with reverence and respect.

FIELD & FOREST REPORT: Sacred groves from coast to coast.

MOUNTAIN REPORT: The mountain is very quiet these days. Little human traffic. The woods are as though at prayer. They are waiting for the great Ceremony of Death and Resurrection with the trees, rocks, the ravens and the skies, and the few lucky humans as celebrants. The passion and death is beginning. The resurrection will come in the Spring. All religion is a pale copy of the living Scripture that is Nature.

SEED PODS TO CARRY AROUND WITH YOU: From Black Elk, *The first peace is that which comes when we realize our oneness with the universe and all its powers, and when we realize that at the center of the universe dwells the Great Spirit and that this center is really everywhere and within each one of us.*

And from Alexander Pope: *All the world is one stupendous whole, whose body Nature is, and God the soul.*

FIRST QUARTER TO FULL *COLD* MOON

Winter in the old house, breezes flying across the floor. I was content in the warmth of people around me, until their madness chilled my heart . . . He came one winter stealthily to my door and made me love again, leaving me just footprints in the snow. —From Red Hawk, Abnaki woman poet.

December 12, Francis Chichester completes solo voyage from England to Australia, 1966.

December 13, St. Lucia's Day, traditional solstice celebrations begin in Scandinavia with Lucia's crown of candles.

December 14, Apotheosis of George Washington, 1799.

NATURAL EVENTS: The Millbrook has its source somewhere up north of Awanadjo and runs along below its west shoulder and receives run-off from the mountain. The brook is slow-moving for most of its length which includes some beaver flowage, but when it gets about a quarter mile from the bay, it starts a 400-ft. drop that in former times provided enough head for seven mills within that last quarter mile. Finally the brook runs under Main Street into a small fire pond, then over a dam into the harbor. The brook is a delight, providing amusement for children, some trout if you know where to catch them, an upstream highway for eels, and the music of falling water in several places. My grandchildren love to visit these falls.

Coming back from the post office, I looked over the bridge into the little fire pond and saw what at first seemed to be a seal, but soon revealed itself to be an otter diving, rolling, and cavorting playfully in the water, with the typical sleek coat, the long, vertically-flattened tail, and the broad, weasel-like head with tiny ears. Mr. Otter [Or is it 'Ms.'; who can tell but another otter?] would dive deep and soon a stream of bubbles would rise and move around the surface of the pond, until the otter would rise upright in the water with mouth slightly open and head back to chew and swallow its catch. The neighborhood ducks kept their distance. We watched this rare appearance for a long time, and felt exceedingly fortunate not being chained to a desk or housebound on this marvelous day.

Ernest Thompson Seton describes otters as around 40 inches in length, and 20 pounds in weight with a diet of fish, frogs, shell-fish. Our neighbor Rufus Candage suggests they eat eels as well.

RANK OPINION: With the Christmas season approaching, religious symbols abound. Some are convinced that there is only one way to the Spirit: the one they have chosen or the one into which they were born. In our culture, that way is predominantly Christian. Christian language and practice, and even architecture have been laid over older practices which are considered inferior and often labelled "pagan" or "heathen." It is interesting that "pagan" comes from the Latin "pagus" which means "village," or "rural." "Heathen" is derived from the Old Germanic "heath" which is open land with no people. These words refer to spiritual practices scorned by the civilized centers of religious and political power, the cities with their cathedrals and universities, the establishment, if you will.

But established religion has never succeeded in erasing that faith which is indigenous to the country heart, only in driving it into temporary hiding. Now all around our peninsula this "country spirituality" springs ever new like grass through the pavement because it is an irrepressible expression of birth and life, death and rebirth, fertility, the seasons, hope and joy, and living close to Nature and Creator as we do in the country.

See the green balsam wreathes of Christmas: feminine symbols of the cycles of life. See the masculine fir tree decorated with lights: symbols of the unconquered sun rising again in the sky after the Winter solstice. See the holly and mistletoe: symbols of the mystery of life in death left over from the pre-christian religion of the Celts. For every person who practices solely the established, church-going spirituality, there are dozens—maybe hundreds—who are inspired by the ancient so-called "pagan" symbols and cycles of life. Our little towns, our houses and streets are fairly bursting with the symbols of the old religions at this season. The veneer of the established religion is very thin.

Does this mean that all spiritual practices are equally good? By no means. The ways of death are to be shunned. Sacrifices or destruction of life on any altar are evil, regardless of whether the altar is religious, economic, political, or military. Love must overcome hate and fear, nor can love ever be used as an instrument of hate or fear, for then it is no longer love. Injustice to the weak and powerless is evil. Wasting is evil. The use of spiritual, political, or economic power for personal gain at the expense of others, is evil. Ingratitude is evil. Worshipping the work of our own hands or minds and ignoring the Creator is evil. There are good spiritual practices and evil spiritual practices, regardless of the religion. To paraphrase Alexander Solzhenitzyn, the line between good and evil passes, not between religions or political parties or countries or races, but through every human heart.

FIELD & FOREST REPORT: Only the feisty red squirrel remains busy on warmer days. The red clusters of winterberry and wild viburnum or highbush cranberry and the fluffy maroon seed clusters of the sumac flash brightly against the snow.

MOUNTAIN REPORT: This week we were swept by a snow squall as we stood on the summit of Awanadjo sharing hot tea and chocolate kisses. A flock of chirping finches of more than one kind wheeled and careened through the air like a school of feathered fish, then landed in a tall dead spruce spreading themselves out over the branches as though they were decorating the tree for the season in muted browns, reds, and even gray-greens. I am told that it has been a practice among the Chinese to predict the future by the patterns of flocks of birds. Prediction? Exuberance and tranquility in the midst of life and death.

SEED PODS TO CARRY AROUND WITH YOU: from Henry Wadsworth Longfellow, *Then pealed the bells more loud and deep, / "God is not dead, nor doth God sleep! / The Wrong shall fail, the Right prevail, / with peace on Earth, good will to all."*

The Blue Hill peninsula has been an international crossroads for an exceedingly long time. The "Red Paint" people brought a pre-Columbian culture that likely extended North along the Atlantic seaboard, through the present maritime provinces of Canada, to Iceland and Greenland, and perhaps as far South as Brittany on the coast of France. Furthermore, archaeologists have unearthed an ancient Norse coin at Naskeag suggesting either the presence of Europeans or trade with the Continent since long before the time of Columbus.

After the European settlement, men born on this peninsula sailed to countries at the far corners of the earth, and returned. Beginning in 1792, according to research by Dr. Otis Littlefield and Rebecca Herrick available at the Blue Hill library, many ships, built here and manned by local people, travelled widely and brought back the knowledge of far-flung cultures. The *Cirginia*, built and launched here in 1833, travelled as far as Cuba. The *D. Randolph Martin*, 170 tons, built here in 1842, sailed to the Netherlands and France. The *Tahmaroo*, built here in 1844, sailed to Panama, Chile, and San Francisco. The *Equator*, built here in 1850, travelled around the horn and into the Pacific. There were many others, sailing to far places and returning, with Blue Hill peninsula men who had seen the wonders of the world.

With the exception of one foray to St. Andrews in what is now New Brunswick, Jonathan Fisher was not an international traveler. Like Thoreau who liked to say he had "traveled extensively . . . in Concord," Fisher traveled extensively in Maine, but he traveled most extensively in his study, where he visited many lands and cultures of the world, reading Pascal's *Pensees* in French, the works of English and German scholars in their languages, studying geography and natural history, and reading the Bible and commentaries in Hebrew and Greek.

It is clear that from the beginning, the people of this peninsula were learned, and maintained a thirst for more learning. As a demonstration, consider for a moment the remarkable number of schools built in this town. The 1762 settlement at Mill Island built a school-house almost immediately. In 1803, Fisher and others founded the Blue Hill Academy, which drew from surrounding towns. Then, the neighborhood schools appeared; then George Stevens Academy; then the summer music school at Kneisel Hall; then the Consolidated School. Recently, we have seen the founding of the Bay School, and the Liberty School. For a town of this size, this is a truly admirable record of effort expended in the cause of education.

The atmosphere of openness which provided a suitable environment for the earliest summer visitors 120 years ago, and a home for the internationally-regarded Kneisel Hall since the 1920s, as well as later cultural developments like the Bagaduce Chorale, the Concert Association and galleries, was always the atmosphere of Blue Hill. The habit of learning, curiosity, open-ness to new people and new ideas did not come with the first rusticators, but was here from the beginning.

Are there threats to the life of this pleasant land? There are. The values of small towns and villages are under siege world-wide. Anonymity threatens the fabric of local society. The pressure of the larger society, the increasing velocity of money, the pathological compulsion of the powerful to exploit the meek as though it were their God-given right to do so, the merchandising of Nature as though it were a manufactured product to be bought and sold; all are destroying many once-pleasant places. Must we build more enormous houses for use only during the short summer season or by only two or three people year 'round? Must we have more and bigger cars, boats, and markets? How are we to be exempt from such pressures and changes?

In our case there are two prominent dangers. The first danger is that we will feel that we are here because we are better and more deserving than others, that we are entitled. The second danger is that pressures from outside will divide us and draw us into fruitless battles among ourselves: the working class versus the leisure class, the native versus the newcomer, the comfortable versus the struggling, the old versus the young. If we lose our commitment, even our devotion, to our churches, towns, schools, our children, our neighbors, and our sacred places, then what has befallen so many communities will befall us. If we allow ourselves to be divided against each other, then we are lost.

The scriptures as well as history make it abundantly clear that when the people turn their backs on each other and on God, the Creator of the heavens and the earth; when the people give their allegiance to those things that are false, then both the people and the land will surely suffer. Remember Jeremiah:

I thought how I would set you among my children, and give you a pleasant land, a heritage most beauteous of all peoples. And I thought you would call me My Creator and would not turn from following me. As a faithless husband leaves his wife, you have been faithless to me, O Israel.

The powerful forces that have destroyed small communities around the world will not miraculously be deflected from us by divine intervention. As our towns grow and change, we face the choice of being moved from the values long held here, or growing and changing. Shall we be moved from our faithfulness to our communities, each other, and the gospel? Or shall we not be moved?

Jesus was born of powerless parents into a world that was hostile to hope and compassion, yet he carried a power greater than any economy, or totalitarian government, or man-made system—a power of hope that overcomes fear and despair, a power that is not the folly of a few misguided human hearts, but that is embodied in the Creation itself, and will come to pass.

Loren Eiseley was an essayist and naturalist who was born in the bleak Nebraska plains country and raised as the only child of a deaf and mentally unstable mother, yet who found defiant hope and rejoicing in the heart of the Creation. Resting during a long hike, he fell asleep.

When I awoke, dimly aware of some commotion and outcry in the clearing, the light was slanting down through the pines . . . like some vast cathedral . . . There on [a] branch sat an enormous raven with a red and squirming nestling in his beak. The sound . . . was the outraged cries of the nestling's parents who flew helplessly in circles . . . The sleek black monster was indifferent to them. He gulped, whetted his beak on the branch and sat still. Up to that point, the little tragedy had followed the usual pattern. But suddenly out of that woodland, a soft sound of complaint began to arise [from] small birds of a half dozen varieties drawn by the anguished outcries of the tiny parents. No one dared to attack the raven. But they cried there in instinctive common misery. They fluttered as if to point their wings at the murderer . . . And he, the black bird at the heart of life, sat on glistening in the light, unmoving.

The sighing died. It was then I saw the judgment of life against death. I will never see it again so forcefully presented. For in the midst of protest, they forgot the violence. There, in that clearing, the crystal note of a song sparrow lifted hesitantly in the hush. Another took the song, then another, from one bird to another, doubtfully at first, 'til suddenly they took heart and sang from many hearts joyously together, under the brooding shadow of the raven. In simple truth, they had forgotten the raven, for they were the singers of life, and not of death.

Hope and joy are not mere human qualities. They are hard-wired into the universe. Like the song sparrows, the angels over Bethlehem had the power to sing defiant songs of joy and wonder in the shadow of a world obsessed with death. That power is ours too, regardless of our culture or condition. That is why we gather to sing in the darkest days of the year.

We, too live in the shadow of a world obsessed with death. Shall we be disintegrated by the cold eye of meaninglessness, or shall we defiantly tell the stories and sing the songs of joy and wonder? Shall we turn our backs on each other and wander off one by one to be consumed in the darkness, or shall we gather around the light that overcomes darkness? Shall we close our hearts to the poor and the powerless, or shall Mary and Joseph still find a place with us?

That's the Almanack for this moon, but don't
take it from me.
Go out and see for yourself.

This is the Awanadjo Almanack for the Full *Cold* Moon to the Full *Wolf* Moon, called *Siqinyasaq* or *Returning Sun* by the north slope Eskimos, *Tebeth* in the Bible, and December/January in Downeast Maine.

FULL TO LAST QUARTER *COLD* MOON

The thin snow now driving from the North lodges on my coat. How full of the creative genius is the air in which these flakes are generated. I could hardly more admire if real stars fell and lodged on my coat . . . wheels of the storm chariots. As surely as the petals of a flower are fixed (in number) each of these snow stars comes whirling to the earth pronouncing thus with emphasis the number Six.

H. D. Thoreau's journal, Winter 1856

December 15 is the anniversary of the Boston Tea Party 1773 when a gang of men dressed as Indians boarded the HMS Beaver in Boston harbor and heaved the cargo of tea into the salt water to demonstrate their disgust with onerous taxes supporting the government and business, a sort of welfare for the elite and powerful. Time for another tea party.

December 21, the Winter solstice, a festival as old as civilization and perhaps older. Various religions have adorned this primal season with their own trimmings, but the return of the Sun goes far deeper than organized religion. Religions come and go, and so does the Sun, but the Sun comes and goes forever.

NATURAL EVENTS: The days are now the shortest and the nights the longest of the year. It's fascinating and deeply endearing the way we humans celebrate the light during the time of its longest absence. We feast and visit and exchange gifts and sing hymns to the light, in a fine testimony to the human spirit.

WILD SPECULATION: Maybe we are biologically inclined to tell our holy stories in Winter, passing on the information necessary for spiritual survival. Christian, Jewish, Celtic, and Native American holy seasons with their cycles of storytelling begin in late Fall and extend until Spring.

RANK OPINION: It's easy to decry the commercialism of Christmas, but very hard to fight that urge to buy gifts so as to see the delight in the eyes of the receiver. Yet, can nothing other than a product manufactured far away by people we don't know truly delight us? Is no handmade gift of love enough?

FIELD & FOREST REPORT: With the disappearance of warm weather plant life, the hardy species gain more attention. Various kinds of mosses and lichens add color to the rocks and forest floor. The lichens have a powerful acid that eats away at the surface of the rocks so that they can hold fast with their tiny filament roots. Lichens grow very slowly. A gravestone that's 20 years old may not have any lichen on its surface, but a gravestone 100 years old will be spangled with circles of bright orange 2 to 3 inches in diameter or more. Some of the larger patches of lichen that we see on rocks have been growing before the white man came.

MOUNTAIN REPORT: Coming down from the mountain the other day, I peeled some "rock tripe" off a big glacial boulder. Its flat, gray, brittle, fan-like structure seemed as dead as a fallen leaf. But arriving home I put it in water and it turned green and soft immediately, proving itself very much alive. Rock tripe is supposed to be good survival food, too. I hope I never have to eat it.

CRITTER OF THE WEEK: Winter ducks including Bufflehead and Old Squaw still paddling around barefoot in their down coats. The Old Squaws seem to talk to each other quietly, then they all laugh uproariously as though someone had told a good joke. Their laughing echoes over the cold gray water.

SEED PODS TO CARRY AROUND WITH YOU: from naturalist Edwin Way Teale: . . . *Had lunch in the city with two scientists, a botanist and an ichthyologist. The botanist said he never kept a garden and the ichthyologist said he never went fishing.*

And from Old Coyote: *Beneath the winter's chilling snow, the heart of summer beats below. Beneath the old world you can see, there breathes a new world that will be.*

LAST QUARTER *COLD* MOON TO NEW *WOLF* MOON

Winter is a dreary season, heavy waters in confusion beat the wide world's strand. Birds of every place are mournful, but

the hot and savage ravens, at rough winter's shriek. Crude
and black and dank and smoky; dogs about their bones are
snarling, on the fire the cauldron bubbles all the long dark
day.
Anonymous Gaelic poet, translated by Frank O'Connor.

December 25, Christmas Day. This celebration has gained in
significance over the last 150 years largely due to its obvious
commercial possibilities. As recently as 1850, however, Christmas was a minor holiday and the Boston public schools
remained in session on this day.

December 29, Feast of the Holy Innocents, on the Christian
calendar, marking the day on which Herod ordered the
killing of all Jewish boys under the age of 2, hoping to kill
the new-born King of the Jews, of whom he had heard. Ironically, this day is also the anniversary of the massacre of the
innocents at Wounded Knee, South Dakota, in which some
200 old men, women and children of the Sioux nation were
cut down by the Gatling guns of the Seventh Cavalry in 1890.
Never forget.

NATURAL EVENTS: The heavy snows before Christmas are
welcome as an insulating blanket to keep the frost from going
too deep and provide many of the pleasures of living in the
North—beauty, quiet, and good skiing and sliding.

The celebration of this season is a natural event, and a delicate thing. I remember walking on the path in the dark down
to our camp with no light but the pale moon. If I tried to see
everything with my eyes, I was blinded by the darkness, and
thought that I had lost the path. But when I waited until the
moon light was enough, and felt the path beneath my feet, I
felt the roughness on either side when I wandered off, which

guided me back to the smoothness where my feet were on the well-worn way. I could have found my way with my eyes closed in darkness.

Each of us brings our own share of darkness to the season: the grieving for those who have gone on into the light and whom we miss desperately, or for those who are dying or abused or in prison; our fears of the powers of darkness out there in the world or within each one of us; the incomprehensible cruelty of war, the subtle cruelty of aggression, domination and greed, the darkness that lurks in our own hearts, the hearts of our children, the hearts of our leaders, and the hearts of the poor and neglected.

This season is a delicate thing because we run the risk of denying or painting over the truth with glitter and false joy, gifts and songs, chatter and chimes. But the truth is both darkness and light. The darkness is real and tangible and cold and will never go away. We do both these days: we walk in darkness *and* we see a great light. The darkness is not just within us, it is in the world too. Likewise, the light is not just outside of us, it is inside us too. It is in our children, our leaders, and the prisoners, the oppressed and neglected and suffering.

We bring all of the darkness of the old world to this fire. "For all the boots of the tramping warriors," said the great Jewish poet and prophet Isaiah 2500 years ago, "and all the garments rolled in blood shall be burned as fuel for the fire . . ." We bring the rough, dense, cruel and dark fuel of the material world to this fire. We turn ourselves inside out and put the hard and bitter, painful and shadowed stuff of ourselves and the world to the flame, so that it may catch, burn and give us light and warmth. We nurture and husband this light and warmth that shines in the darkness and hold it, breathing on it to keep it glowing. Then we pass it to the little child in the cold stable, to our children, our leaders, the creatures, to feed the light that glows within them. It is a very small thing that we do, but no darkness is great enough to extinguish even the smallest light.

The darkness will always come, but within it the light. The light will shine in the darkness, always and forever, and enough to light our way. And the darkness will never overcome it.

MOUNTAIN REPORT: Climbing after a recent snow, billions of snow fleas, perhaps the most numerous animal on the face of the Earth according to some authorities, hopped about on the white snow. While the sun was warming the woods, tiny bits of ice fell from the trees and swelling drops of water hung from spruce branches winking bright rainbow colors before falling with millions of others into the bright mist rising from the forest floor. Small events can be described, but combined, they multiply the wonder geometrically creating major events of indescribable power.

SALTWATER REPORT: The sacred Blue Hill Falls continue their back and forth rhythm each day like the slow swinging of the pendulum on a giant Earth-clock, keeping moon time.

CRITTER OF THE WEEK: The beautiful, shapely and fragrant balsam fir, the quintessential Christmas tree, loved by pagans and Christians alike since the time of the Druids. Legend has it that Martin Luther first brought a fir tree into the house to mark this season. Do not feel that you are wasting a tree if you buy or cut a fir for the season. After Christmas, it can be placed outside and hung with treats for the birds. Later, the boughs can be cut off and laid over the garden or across icy walkways for traction, or piled in the backyard for small animal shelter. The trunk can be used as a bean pole.

SEED PODS TO CARRY AROUND WITH YOU: from Charles Wesley, *Hail the heaven-born Prince of Peace! Hail the Sun of righteousness! Light and life to all he brings, risen with healing in his wings.*

NEW TO FIRST QUARTER *WOLF* MOON

You have noticed that every thing the Indian does is in a circle, and that is because the power of the world moves in circles and everything tries to be round . . . Every thing the power of the World does is done in a circle. The sky is round and I have heard that the earth is round . . . Birds make their nests in circles for theirs is the same religion as ours . . . Even the seasons form a great circle in their changing, and always come back to where they were. From Black Elk

December 30 is New Year's Eve and

January 1 is New Year's Day, also called the Feast of the Circumcision, whichever you prefer.

January 5, Beginning of Great Ice Storm of '98. Also Twelfth Night. Today is also the feast day of Saint Simeon Stylites. Born in 390, he was one of the Desert Fathers and sort of the Shipwreck Kelly of his age. He lived on a six-foot-square platform atop a 60 foot pillar.

January 6 is Epiphany, the traditional Twelfth Day of Christmas on which my true love gave to me twelve drummers drumming, and in Christian tradition, the day that the three wise men finally reached the stable. It is theologically correct to take down your Christmas tree today. On this day in 1878 poet Carl Sandburg was born.

NATURAL EVENTS: For the past several wintry weeks I have been puzzled to see and hear flocks of robins in the woods and brush low on the mountain near the road. The robins number in the dozens and sing the familiar songs of summer. At first I found this alarming as though it were a sign that things are out of balance and disaster is on the horizon. It has not been unusual to see an occasional robin during the cold winter months in past years hereabouts, but flocks of them in winter seemed ominous. Though we have experienced this year a November with cold weather and the most snow on record, the global warming threat still lurks in the back of the mind, and with it, apocalyptic fears. Casting about for an explanation, I remembered that this year has been remarkable for the abundance of fruit, both wild and cultivated. The apple trees were overloaded in the fall, and the winterberry bushes came in heavy with carmine red berries. What is called winterberry around here is a middling high shrub, *Ilex laevigata*, a member of the holly family with smooth deciduous leaves and clusters of berries which remain after the leaves fall. These clusters of berries are often gathered in early winter and put into window-boxes, wreathes, and evergreen indoor arrangements with balsam and white pine.

Our local winterberry bore extremely heavily this year and many glades were bright with thick berry clusters. I had always thought of robins as worm- and bug-eaters, not fruit-eaters like the grosbeaks and cedar waxwings, but I had noticed previously that some bushes which were heavy with berries two weeks ago were now stripped clean in areas where the robins had been reveling. So, today as I came down the mountain and arrived near the end of the trail near the road and was showered with robin song from every direction, I became determined to investigate. First, I looked under the low alder, bayberry and laurel bushes and found the snow heavily spattered far and wide with brown bird droppings speckled with yellow seeds. No other bird was present in the abundance that the robins were as they flocked and landed, fluttered and chirped, leading me to think that these must be robin droppings.

Furthermore, says I to myself, this is a great out-pouring of exuberance and energy among the robins, a wild party which must be fueled by something. A lot of calories are being burned up here. There are many anecdotal accounts of birds being inebriated by feeding on fermented fruit. Are these berries really edible or are they some deadly poison? Curious, I reached up and pulled a red winterberry off a low branch and squeezed it between my fingers to see a barely-moist, mustard-colored pulp pushing out bearing a load of dusky yellow seeds. It sure looks like fruit, I thought, entertaining some vague idea that even though this peninsula has been populated by hungry people for thousands of years, I was about to discover some new miracle food source. Then, looking around to make sure no one was watching and feeling like the first brave soul to eat an oyster, I popped the winterberry into my mouth like some illicit and forbidden fruit that could drop me in my tracks or, by its intoxicating nectar, cause me to tear off my clothes and go rolling around in the snow howling like a coyote. I chewed. I even swallowed. But nothing happened. It tasted vile. I waited. Then tried another. Still nothing. I checked my pulse, then sauntered on down the road. Though a little disappointed at the complete absence of revelation, still, I was renewed by my climb over the mountain and by the reckless abandon [for a Northern Protestant] I had exercised in eating that awful berry, like the world's first person in the quest for wisdom, or belonging, or joy like the robins'. Finally, I was mightily encouraged by all of this because what I desire more than explanations of Nature, is intimacy; as should any poor man who wants to live a lifetime with Her. I found that intimacy on the tip of my tongue.

MOUNTAIN REPORT: Deep snows cover Awanadjo with a narrow path about 18 inches wide pressed down by the boots of pilgrims winding all the way up and down her sides. Once the trail is broken, later climbers follow it religiously. (I think that's the right word.) Here and there are the tracks of snowshoes ranging off the beaten path under spruce branches still bending with the weight of the pre-Christmas snows, sparkling like diamonds on a sunny day.

Climbing in deep new blue snow a couple of days ago the tracks of snowshoe hare, red squirrel, partridge and other active winter creatures provided the choreography for a fascinating visual re-enactment of each ones' activity over the previous two days. Here a snowshoe hare entered a small clearing and hopped nonchalantly across into the woods, then hopped out again a little farther along. I could see him/her hopping as though it had just happened. Over there a partridge landed, then took off, leaving a true and original snow-angel pattern of wings and head in the soft powder. I was a witness to the daily lives of the woods creatures. And over here the tracks of a bobcat or Canada lynx, carefully, daintily following the snowshoe hare. What was the outcome of that encounter, if there ever was one? To a careful observer, a cover of soft snow gives secret insight into the private lives of other creatures not available during other seasons.

SALTWATER REPORT: Ice extends over most of the harbor, though there is open water from Twin Oaks Island on out. The old-timers say that the bay used to freeze all the way out to Long Island. I have seen photos of horse races on that ice.

CRITTER OF THE WEEK: The bobcat or Canadian lynx. Ernest Thompson Seton says, "Of all the Northern creatures, none are more dependent on the Rabbits than is the Canada Lynx. It lives on Rabbits, follows Rabbits, thinks Rabbits, tastes like Rabbits, increases with them, and on their failure, dies of starvation in the unrabbited woods."

PILGRIM'S JOURNAL: It's been the way of Western culture to view time and history as a straight line moving from beginning to end. Christianity, Judaism, even Marxism have this straight line view. Black Elk's is different. "The power of the world moves in circles . . ."

I tend to go with Black Elk. I believe that our lives go in circles and that this is ordained by a Power far greater than ourselves. You'll notice I didn't say a Benevolent Power, and here's why:

The other day I had a day off and decided to split some wood into stove size. I strode briskly to the woodpile to begin. Wait a minute, I need my gloves. They're in the house. I returned to the house to find the gloves in the pocket of my coat. Taking the coat off the hook, I rummaged through the pockets to find the gloves and returned the coat to the over-loaded hook, which pulled out of the wall dropping coats, hats, and hook to the floor.

I headed for the kitchen tool drawer to get a screwdriver to fix the hook. When I opened the drawer I noticed that for the 100th time, someone had borrowed the hammer and screwdriver and not returned them to their proper place. I steamed off looking for the vile offender. I found the beloved criminal struggling to hang a large picture, but not having the right picture hanger. I headed for the back hall to find my carpenter's bag wherein I knew there was the right picture hook. My carpenter's bag was covered with Christmas boxes and wrappings to go to the dump. I stacked the boxes and lugged them out to my truck for the next trip to the dump. In the back of the truck was a rug that I had gotten from a neighbor. I couldn't throw the boxes on top of the rug, so I set them down and wrestled the rug out of the back of the truck and into the house, and down the hall to where it was to be spread out. I started to unroll the rug, but noticed that the floor needed to be swept first.

In a slight daze now, I went to the pantry to fetch the broom. I heard a voice calling something about a picture hanger. I turned and headed for the back hall just as the phone began to ring. I snatched it deftly off its cradle. "Hello? No. He's not. Can I take a message?" I tried to listen for the message and root around in the drawer for a pencil to write it down. "OK. Bye." I found a pencil. The point broke. As the telephone message faded in my memory, I rushed to the pencil sharpener. It wouldn't turn. I grabbed my knife to whittle a new point on the pencil, but the knife was too dull, so I whipped the steel across it. I started to whittle, then thought "Not on the floor, you callous oaf!" I decided to whittle it into the stove, you know, energy conservation. I lifted the stove lid and noticed that the fire was nearly out and needed to be fed immediately if not sooner. Back I went to the woodpile again, I found the right piece of dry oak and decided to split it up a little so that it wouldn't put out the fire.

Suddenly, light dawned on Marblehead. I was bathed in a sense of the mythical oneness, the rightness, the roundness of things. Like dust to dust, I am back to the woodpile. Like the turning of the seasons, I am back to where I began. The power of the world moves in circles. Now where did I put my gloves?

SEED PODS TO CARRY AROUND WITH YOU: from the Book of Ecclesiastes: *The sun rises and goes down and hastens to the place where it rises. The wind blows to the south and goes round to the north—round and round goes the wind, and on its circuits, the wind returns.*

And from the Book of Genesis: *While the earth remains, day and night, summer and winter, cold and heat shall not cease.*

FIRST QUARTER TO FULL *WOLF* MOON

January 8 is the anniversary of the Battle of New Orleans, 1814. In this battle, Andrew Jackson and the French pirate, Jean LaFitte, joined forces to defeat the British. As far as the history books tell us, this was the only time in our entire history when our government has ever collaborated with known criminals. Ever. Though an important battle, it was not decisive because the war had ended two weeks before with the signing of the Treaty of Paris. There is a lively Cajun fiddle tune called *The Eighth of January* that Johnny Horton borrowed back in the '50's for his big hit *The Battle of New Orleans.*

January 11, End of the Great Ice Storm of '98.

January 13, National Geographic Society founded, 1888.

NATURAL EVENTS: Warm, wet upper air from the South being held back by a thin horizontal wedge of cold air from the North which kept the ground below freezing, caused rain to freeze upon contact with the earth during this week in 1998. Millions of trees loaded with the burden of an ice coating from one to three inches thick could not stand the weight and were broken down. It is hard to describe the damage over the entire northern New England and Southeastern Canadian forests. The sound of trees breaking under the load was constant for three days and nights. Many places were without electrical power for a week or more.

FIELD & FOREST REPORT: Visiting friends whose house is on a high ridge and surrounded by wind-swept blueberry barrens, we watched the snow buntings rising and turning in a small flock over the ice-covered flats. Coming as they do from the tundra, they rarely perch in trees even when trees are available, but fly from place to place and land on the ground. These beautiful sparrow-sized, brown, buff and white creatures spend the summer North of the Arctic Circle. We are on the Southern edge of their winter range. While we labor under the onslaught of the storm, they come here on vacation.

SALTWATER REPORT: Beyond the outflow of the Blue Hill Falls flocks of old squaw and scoters gather in a gaggle or floating raft. Duck's down coats keep them warm, but why don't their skinny legs freeze? Water temperature below 40 degrees, but little ice in the bays and coves as yet, except where fresh water pours in over the saltwater and freezes.

CRITTERS OF THE WEEK: The old squaw and the snow bunting.

SEED PODS TO CARRY AROUND WITH YOU: from Edwin Way Teale—*This midwintertime represents a pause in the turning wheel of life . . . All the events of spring and summer and autumn, of sprouting and growth and seed time, the beginning and the end, lie ahead. The whole circle of the seasons stretches away before as we view the year from the cold plateau of January.*

PILGRIM'S JOURNAL: Around mid-day on the sixth day of the ice storm, feeling stir-crazy and cabin feverish, I went to the Post Office and to the hospital and the church to see what was what. At Merrill & Hinckley's store there were many shoppers in a jolly holiday mood while the generator roared and the cash registers rang up batteries and bottled water as well as regular food items, with much talk about the weather and when would the power come back on. I saw Ed Schneider out walking, grinning from ear to ear with his ice creepers on. "The last pair Ellen Walker had left when she closed the store," he said. This got me to thinking. I went home and found the pair I had carefully made out of light chain, stove bolts, and T-braces a couple of years ago, then never used. I tinkered with them for a while until they seemed serviceable, fastened them to my boots, then walked around the yard a couple of times and up to the church to test them. They did the job fine.

Then it was time to gather some snacks and a little salt cod and head up the mountain to see if I could satisfy my perpetual hunger to look El Shaddai, the mountain god, in the face. With prayers and trepidation, I started up over the blueberry fields on thick ice. I had hoped to be the first one to make the climb, but I noticed the faint, fresh footprint of a medium hiking boot, apparently without studs or crampons. Every blade of grass and blueberry twig was encased in crystal an inch or more in diameter. The ice acted like a lens magnifying the twigs and weeds so that each ice sheath was filled with color.

Looking up, the top of the mountain rose still clothed in mist. I could hear ice crashing off the trees in every direction. As I walked by, a large limb tore off a tree behind the mouldering foundation of the house where Eliot Sweet was born 90 some years before. As the trail got steep I walked gingerly and marveled at the cruel beauty.

When I got past the top of the blueberry fields, the wind was picking up. The trail through the scrub oak was a tunnel of arched icy saplings and here the ice was even thicker; as much as two inches in diameter around every branch and twig. Climbing up through this glittering tunnel, I came out just below the East cliffs as trees swayed and groaned in the wind and ice fell in showers. The vast number of bent and broken trees reminded me of old photos of Belleau Wood in France during World War I with the trees utterly shattered by artillery fire. This is a war of sorts between the trees and the ice. The larger trees still standing looked threatening to me, weighted as they were with untold hundreds of pounds of ice and swaying in the wind. The sound of falling ice and breaking branches continued steadily. Holding my breath, I scooted under some of the taller spruces, anticipating the crash of an icy treetop on my back at any moment. An oak limb as large in diameter as my head had recently fallen in the path. It made a good handhold, and in due time I made it safely to the radio-tower covered so thick with ice near the top that none of its mechanical features was distinguishable. It stood, a gnarly white column of ice whipped by mist and fog.

As I walked into the Wisdom Woods, the top of a huge spruce, burdened beyond its strength by ice and the freshening wind, came crashing down just a few feet behind me. I turned to see the end of its broken shaft a foot or more in diameter bouncing on the cushion of its branches, as the ice showered down around it. This was sobering as I thought of all the big spruces I would have to pass below before I reached the mountain road again. Scrambling up the slope toward the summit, I repeated Psalm 121, "He shall not let your foot be moved . . ." My biggest fear was slipping on the ice and twisting an ankle or worse, and being left there.

At the summit the wind was a little less. The fire tower was muffled in white, daubed with frost to a depth of 2-4 inches and draped with icicles. The view below was faint and obscured by flying mist, but I could barely make out the shape of Woods Pond several miles away. The explosive reports of breaking trees and the clattering of falling ice came from all directions.

I said my mountain-top prayers, then decided to go down by the state trail, stopping at the hiker's register first to inscribe my name and the date there for the first time ever. I became aware of the real danger I was in at about this time, and also my own foolhardiness at attempting this climb under such conditions. I waited for a tree to fall on me, or for my homemade ice-creepers to come apart, leaving me to slide all the way down the mountain and end up a broken, bloody mess in the parking lot at the Post Office in town to cries of derision from my neighbors. But I also felt led through the ice in the same way that the Hebrew children were led through the Red Sea. Disaster and chaos on my right and left, behind and before, but foolish me slipping along down the slope, unscathed.

It was then that I began to think of the process of grace that had brought me safe this far. Not that I deserved no punishment for my foolishness, but that I was like the salmon that is driven to make it all the way up-river. Not better, stronger or smarter than any other, just here by grace—and still a sinner. Not survival of the fittest, but survival by grace. I was reminded of the week's scriptures from Isaiah 43 which talks about God leading the children through fire and water, but in Maine at this time of the year, it is not water so much as ice. God loves fools and children, and led me through as one or the other.

The rest of the climb down was intricate and frightening as the sound of crashing trees and ice heightened the tension and threatened my essential concentration. I spooked a partridge—the only other animal I saw in my lonely two hour climb—and it boomed across the trail in front of me to find refuge in an ice-encrusted tree growing on the steep side of the stream that follows the trail down. Soon, the end of the steep trail and the beginning of the flat appeared ahead, while the wind increased and breaking trees fell behind.

I finally arrived down on the mountain road feeling as though I had been to a higher world, and feeling blessed to be alive. Like Coyote or Prometheus stealing fire from the gods, I had foolishly stolen across the face of El Shaddai who could have destroyed me with one breath. Like the hike around West Quoddy Head in a hurricane, like the encounter with Orca, like the crow dance in the orchard and countless other adventures, a fierce hunger and thirst for one more pilgrimage in the wild world had overwhelmed my reason and common sense. Maybe I was just one more death-wish madman trying to jump the Grand Canyon.

Or maybe this was another careful rehearsal for the final meeting with the Numinous from which no one returns. Maybe it was a quest for one more face-to-face encounter with the Great Mystery to gain one more blessing to bring back and heal the world a little, a treasure that "moth and rust cannot consume and thieves cannot break in and steal."

Walking back along the road to my truck, I looked up at the summit and saw the hoary head of Awanadjo wreathed in heaven. Right before I reached the truck, the tacky little homemade ice-creeper on my left foot fell completely apart.

PERICOPES

It would be safe to say that in most situations, you are going to find that people are more interested in talking about the weather than they are in talking about the Godhead or Holy Communion. Annie Dillard wrote: *There are seven or eight categories of phenomena in the world that are worth talking about, and one of them is the weather. Any time you care to get in your car and drive across the country and over the mountains, come into our valley, cross Tinker Creek, drive up the road to the house, walk across the yard, knock on the door and ask to come in and talk about the weather, you'd be welcome.*

T.M. Longstreth in his classic *Knowing the Weather*, wrote:

> *There have always been those who loved [the weather] for its own sake, as born anglers love fishing regardless of the catch. These weather-lovers are part scientist, part poet. They rejoice in the forms and colors that glorify the weather. They delight in extremes. They are gratefully aware that nobody can regulate the weather, nor charge admission to it, and are happy that it is forever out of the reach of politicians.*

There was a time when I disdained discussions of the weather as trite and frivolous small talk, unconcerned with the Deeper Questions of Life. That has changed as I have gotten older. Talk of the weather is now very important to me. Why? Because I have come to the conclusion that weather talk is talk about ultimate things, or God talk. We stand in the same condition of helplessness before the unpredictability of the weather and the powers of climate and season as we stand before the mercies of God. Weather is one of the most visible expressions of God. So, when we talk about the weather, oftentimes we are really talking about God.

Any parson will tell you that God and the weather are very

closely connected in the minds of many. How many times have I heard the father of the bride say only half jokingly at the wedding rehearsal, "We're hoping for good weather for the wedding tomorrow. Put in a good word for us with the Man Upstairs, would you, Reverend?" The reasoning goes like this: God has control of natural events like weather, and the parson talks to God, so, the parson can have some effect on the weather. Theological niceties aside, this is a widely held view.

Jesus talked about the weather as it relates to ultimate things. At one point some fundamentalists asked him to produce a sign from heaven. He answered them, "When it is evening, you say, 'It will be fair weather, for the sky is red." And in the morning, 'It will be stormy today, for the sky is red and threatening.' You know how to interpret the appearance of the sky, but you cannot interpret the signs of the times."

The scriptures also tell of his power over natural events, like the story when Jesus got into the Big Fisherman's boat to get away from the crush of the crowd along the shore. He taught the crowds for a time from the boat. When he was finished, he told Simon to go out to deep water and let down his nets for fish. Simon replied, "Teacher, we have worked all night and didn't catch a thing. But if you say so, I'll try again." They let down their nets and caught so many fish that the nets began to come apart, and they had to call to other fishermen for help.

When Simon saw the power of his Master in this, he fell down before Jesus saying, "Go from me, Lord, for I am a sinful man." Jesus answered him, "Do not be afraid, follow me and I will make you fishers of men. From now on you will be catching people." The Greek word is *zogreo*, meaning "to take alive, ensnare, capture." By their Teacher's natural power, Simon, Andrew, James and John took a huge haul of fish alive. At the same time, Jesus took them alive. And by the same power, others were taken alive by them.

Jesus was a force of Nature. He *was* El Nino, after all. Such forces of Nature make us feel powerless, humble, and grateful, as Simon did, but they also *bestow* power. The Great Ice Storm of 1998 humbled us quite severely, but it also excited us and brought us together. This is good; we need this. In an age when we are waging wars in the name of God, crowing about conquering space, overcoming aging, and creating life by cloning, it is good to admit how powerless we really are to stop a single cloud in its motion or a single snow flake from falling. The power of the skies, the tides, the winds, the big weather are the powers of God outside us and beyond our control. If we will let them, they have the power to take us alive forever.

As God said to Elijah:

"Go forth and stand upon the mountain before the Lord." And, behold, the Lord passed by, and a great and strong wind rent the mountains, and brake in pieces the rocks before the Lord; but the Lord was not in the wind: and after the wind an earthquake; but the Lord was not in the earthquake: and after the earthquake a fire; but the Lord was not in the fire: and after the fire a still small voice.

That is all. If anything you have read in this book helps you tear down the wall between you and the rest of Creation and feel more at home in Nature, I will be more than gratified.

**That's the Almanack for now, but don't take it from me.
Go out and see for yourself.**

Selected Bibliography

Aiba & Katsuhira: *AKITA ALMANAC, Living and Nature*, Soensha Publ., Akita City, Japan, 1966

Basler, Roy, ed.: *Collected Works of Abraham Lincoln*, Rutgers Univ. Press, 1953

Berton, Pierre: *Niagara, A History of the Falls*, Kodansha, New York, 1997

Booth, William: *Sparkles and Other Poems*, Horizon, N.E. Harbor, Maine, 1993

Borland Hal: *Book of Days*, Alfred A. Knopf, Inc., New York, 1976

Dillard, Annie: *Holy the Firm*, Harper & Row, New York, 1977

————: *Pilgrim at Tinker Creek*, Harper & Row, New York, 1974

————: *Teaching A Stone To Talk*, Harper & Row, New York, 1982

Holy Bible, King James Version. Some biblical quotes have been adapted to reflect Maine flora and fauna.

Keats, John: in a letter to George and Georgianna Keats, April 21, 1819

Kelly, Sean & Rosemary Rogers: *Saints Preserve Us!*, Random House, New York, 1993

Lame Deer, John Fire & Richard Erdoes: *Lame Deer Seeker of Visions*, Touchstone, New York, 1972

Locke, Raymond Friday, ed.: *The American Indian*, Hawthorn Books, New York, 1970

Long, William J.: *The Spirit of the Wild*, Doubleday, New York, 1956

Mallett, David: *Autumn*, 1993, Cherry Lane Music

Mooney, James: *The Ghost Dance Religion*, Smithsonian Institution, Washington, D.C., 1982

Niehardt, John: *Black Elk Speaks*, University of Nebraska Press, Lincoln, NE

Old Farmer's Almanac, Yankee Publ., Dublin, New Hampshire

Red Hawk 'pipikwass', *When No One Was Looking*, Little Letterpress, Knox, Gulf of Maine, Turtle Island, USA 1990

Seton, Ernest Thompson: *Lives of the Game Animals*, Charles Branford & Co., Boston, 1905, 1928, 1953

Teale, Edwin Way: *Circle of the Seasons*, Dodd Mead & Co., New York, 1953

Thoreau, Henry David: *Autumn*, Houghton Mifflin, New York, 1984

————: "Cape Cod," in *Backwoods & along the Seashore*, Shambhala, Boston & London 1995

————: *Faith of Seed*, Island Press Washington, D.C., 1993

————: *Journals* (any edition)

————: *The Maine Woods* (any edition)

Wesley, Charles: *Hark! The Herald Angels Sing*, Music by Felix Mendelssohn

Whitman, Walt: *Leaves of Grass* (any edition)

Yu-tang, Lin: *On the Wisdom of America*, John Day Co., Philadelphia, 1950

ANTHOLOGIES

A number of quotes in this book come from the following anthologies:

Astrov, Margot, ed: *American Indian Prose and Poetry, The Winged Serpent*, Capricorn, NY. 1962

Marsh, William and Banford, Christopher, eds.: *Celtic Christianity*, Lindisfarne Press, Hudson, NY 1982

McLuhan, T.C., ed.: *Touch the Earth*, Outerbridge & Lazard, New York, 1971

NATURE, An Illustrated Book of Quotations, Running Press, Philadelphia, 1992

Old Farmer's Almanac Sampler, Robb Sagendorph, ed., Ives Washburn, Inc., New York, 1957

Elizabeth Roberts & Elias Amidon, eds.: *Earth Prayers From Around the World*, Harper & Row, New York, 1991

Terres, John, ed.: *Things Precious and Wild*, Fulcrum, New York, 1991